# Shop Cabinets
# & Tool Stands

## OTHER PUBLICATIONS

**COOKING**
Weight Watchers® Smart Choice Recipe Collection
Great Taste-Low Fat
Williams-Sonoma Kitchen Library

**DO IT YOURSELF**
Golf Digest Total Golf
How to Fix It
The Time-Life Complete Gardener
Home Repair and Improvement
The Art of Woodworking

**HISTORY**
Our American Century
What Life Was Like
The American Story
Voices of the Civil War
The American Indians
Lost Civilizations
Mysteries of the Unknown
Time Frame
The Civil War
Cultural Atlas

**TIME - LIFE KIDS**
Student Library
Library of First Questions and Answers
A Child's First Library of Learning
I Love Math
Nature Company Discoveries
Understanding Science & Nature

For information on and a full description of any of
the Time-Life Books series listed above,
please call 1-800-621-7026 or write:

Reader Information
Time-Life Customer Service
P.O. Box C-32068
Richmond, Virginia 23261-2068

## SHOP SAFETY IS YOUR RESPONSIBILITY

CUSTOM WOODWORKING

# Shop Cabinets & Tool Stands

By the editors of Time-Life Books
and *Woodsmith* magazine

Time-Life Books, Alexandria, Virginia

# Shop Cabinets & Tool Stands

Classic Workbench

# TOOL STANDS

74

Drill Bit Cabinet

Radial Arm Saw Stand

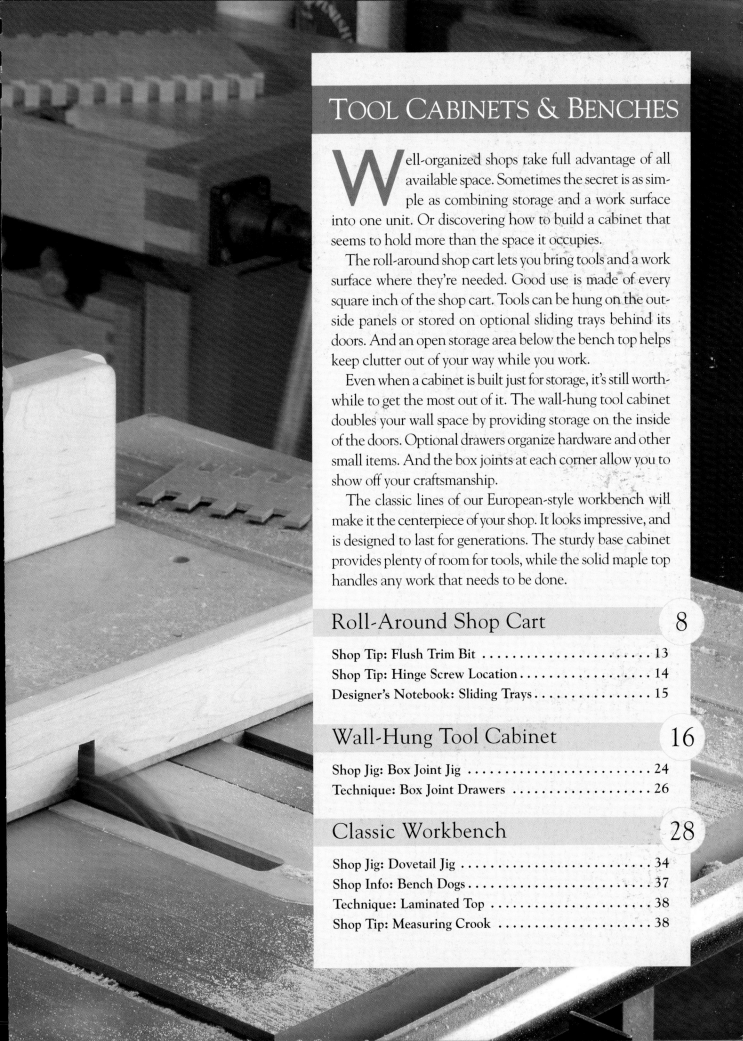

# TOOL CABINETS & BENCHES

**W**ell-organized shops take full advantage of all available space. Sometimes the secret is as simple as combining storage and a work surface into one unit. Or discovering how to build a cabinet that seems to hold more than the space it occupies.

The roll-around shop cart lets you bring tools and a work surface where they're needed. Good use is made of every square inch of the shop cart. Tools can be hung on the outside panels or stored on optional sliding trays behind its doors. And an open storage area below the bench top helps keep clutter out of your way while you work.

Even when a cabinet is built just for storage, it's still worthwhile to get the most out of it. The wall-hung tool cabinet doubles your wall space by providing storage on the inside of the doors. Optional drawers organize hardware and other small items. And the box joints at each corner allow you to show off your craftsmanship.

The classic lines of our European-style workbench will make it the centerpiece of your shop. It looks impressive, and is designed to last for generations. The sturdy base cabinet provides plenty of room for tools, while the solid maple top handles any work that needs to be done.

# Roll-Around Shop Cart

*With plenty of storage space you can customize to your needs, a durable work surface, and wheels that let you roll it to where you need it, this versatile cart is likely to become an essential part of your shop.*

Storage and bench space. There never seems to be enough in the shop. Power tools and accessories out in the open end up buried under sawdust. And when a project gets started, the bench gets hidden under a pile of lumber. What I needed was storage space that could double as a bench or work surface. And it had to be mobile. This way I could move it easily around the shop where it was needed. The solution to these problems is the shop cart shown above.

**STORAGE SPACE.** First of all, there's plenty of storage space, both inside and out. A divided section inside the cart

holds power tools and supplies. And an open area under the top is the perfect place to keep clamps handy.

**OPTIONAL TRAYS.** The large storage spaces behind the doors can be divided into smaller areas by adding a few sliding trays. These trays pull out on full-extension slides. This makes it easy to find those tools and parts that always seem to hide way in the back. All the details for adding this option to your shop cart are covered in the Designer's Notebook on page 15.

**PEGBOARD PANELS.** I chose pegboard for the side and back panels. They make it simple to hang often-used items on

the outside of the cart. That way, the tools and accessories I reach for most stay with my work surface so they're right at hand.

**LOCKING CASTERS.** One thing I really like about this cart is being able to roll it where it's needed. Or out of the way when the job is finished. And once you've got it where you want it, the locking casters keep it in place.

**JOINERY.** Another feature of this cart is that it's easy to build. Since the doors and outside panels are all frame and panel construction, I used a simple stub tenon and groove joint throughout. All the joints can be cut on the table saw.

# EXPLODED VIEW

**OVERALL DIMENSIONS:**
43½W x 21D x 32⅞H

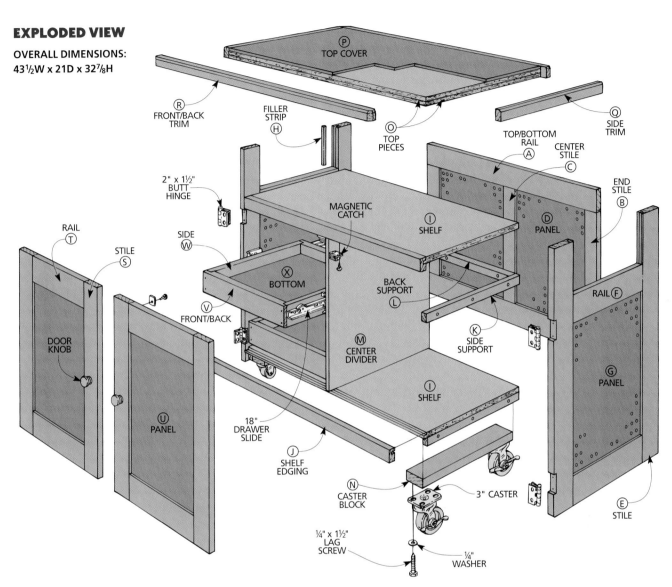

## MATERIALS LIST

**BACK**

| | | |
|---|---|---|
| A | Top/Bottom Rails (2) | ¾ x 3 - 34½ |
| B | End Stiles (2) | ¾ x 2¼ - 17 |
| C | Center Stile (1) | ¾ x 3 - 17 |
| D | Panels (2) | ¼ pgbd. - 14 x 17 |

**SIDES**

| | | |
|---|---|---|
| E | Stiles (4) | ¾ x 3 - 28½ |
| F | Rails (4) | ¾ x 3 - 14 |
| G | Panels (2) | ¼ pgbd. - 14 x 17 |
| H | Filler Strips (4) | ¼ x ¼ - 6 |

**SHELVES**

| | | |
|---|---|---|
| I | Shelves (2) | ½ ply - 18¼ x 34½ |
| J | Shelf Edging (2) | ¾ x 1½ - 34½ |
| K | Side Supports (4) | ¾ x 1 - 18 |
| L | Back Supports (2) | ¾ x 1 - 33 |
| M | Center Divider (1) | ½ ply - 18¾ x 20 |
| N | Caster Blocks (2) | 1 x 3 - 17¼ |

**TOP**

| | | |
|---|---|---|
| O | Top Pieces (2) | ½ ply - 19½ x 42 |
| P | Top Cover (1) | ¼ hdbd. - 19½ x 42 |
| Q | Side Trim (2) | ¾ x 1¼ - 19½ |
| R | Front/Back Trim (2) | ¾ x 1¼ - 43½ |

**DOORS**

| | | |
|---|---|---|
| S | Stiles (4) | ¾ x 3 - 22 |
| T | Rails (4) | ¾ x 3 - 12½ |
| U | Panels (2) | ¼ hdbd. - 12½ x 16½ |

**HARDWARE SUPPLIES**

(36) No. 8 x 1¼" Fh woodscrews
(4) 3" casters
(16) ¼" x 1½" lag screws
(16) ¼" washers
(2) 1¼" door knobs w/ screws
(4) 2" x 1½" butt hinges w/ screws
(2) Magnetic door catches

## CUTTING DIAGRAM

1 x 3½ - 36  (1 Bd. Ft.)

| N | N | |

**ALSO NEED:**
½" FIR PLYWOOD - 48 x 96
¼" HARDBOARD - 48 x 48
¼" PEGBOARD - 48 x 48

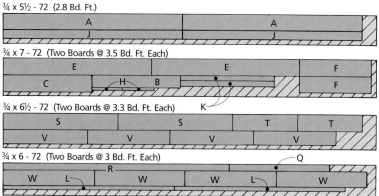

¾ x 5½ - 72  (2.8 Bd. Ft.)

¾ x 7 - 72  (Two Boards @ 3.5 Bd. Ft. Each)

¾ x 6½ - 72  (Two Boards @ 3.3 Bd. Ft. Each)

¾ x 6 - 72  (Two Boards @ 3 Bd. Ft. Each)

## BACK & SIDES

The roll-around shop cart is really just a simple cabinet. It's made up of a back, two sides, and two hinged doors (refer to the Exploded View on page 9).

**BACK.** I started work on the cart by making the back. The back is just a frame and two pegboard panels.

The frame consists of a top and bottom rail (A), two end stiles (B), and a center stile (C) *(Fig. 1)*. The stiles fit between the rails and support the two pegboard panels (D).

**JOINERY.** After I cut the frame and panel pieces to size, I used a stub tenon and groove joint to join the frame and the panels together (Details in *Fig. 1*). I use a two-step process to cut this joint — first I cut the grooves, then I cut the stub tenons to match.

**CUTTING THE GROOVES.** The grooves are cut in the rails and stiles for two purposes. First, they hold the panels in the frame. And second, they serve as open "mortises" for the stub tenons.

The important thing is to cut the groove so it's centered on the edge of the frame piece. To do this, start by setting the blade height to the desired depth for the groove (¼").

The trick to getting the groove perfectly centered is to start with the blade roughly centered on the workpiece, and make a first pass *(Fig. 2)*.

Then without moving the rip fence, flip the piece end-for-end and take another pass *(Fig. 3)*. By placing the opposite face of the workpiece against the fence, the groove is automatically centered on the edge.

**TEST THE FIT.** Now check the fit on the panel. If the groove isn't wide enough for the panel, move the fence and repeat the process. Make the fence adjust-

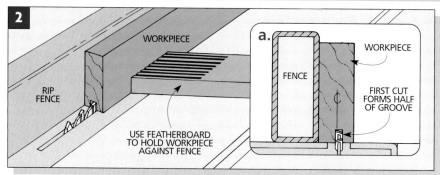

**BACK ASSEMBLY**

TOP RAIL (3" x 34½")

PANEL (14" x 17" - ¼" PEGBOARD)

CENTER STILE (3" x 17")

END STILE (2¼" x 17")

BOTTOM RAIL (3" x 34½")

**NOTE:** ALL FRAME STOCK IS ¾" THICK

a. RAIL

b. END STILE

c. CENTER STILE

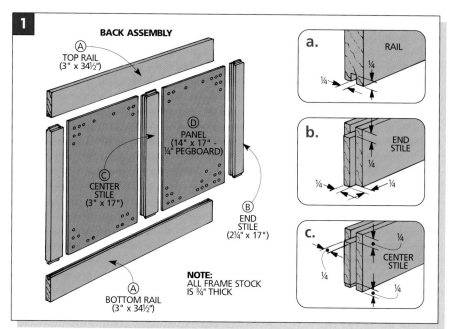

WORKPIECE

RIP FENCE

USE FEATHERBOARD TO HOLD WORKPIECE AGAINST FENCE

a. FENCE — WORKPIECE — FIRST CUT FORMS HALF OF GROOVE

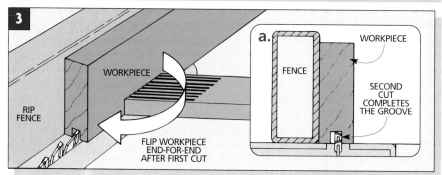

WORKPIECE

RIP FENCE

FLIP WORKPIECE END-FOR-END AFTER FIRST CUT

a. FENCE — WORKPIECE — SECOND CUT COMPLETES THE GROOVE

ments small. Since you make two passes on the workpiece, any adjustment will be doubled (moving the fence $\frac{1}{32}$" results in a groove that's $\frac{1}{16}$" wider.) When you get a snug fit, cut a groove in each of your frame pieces.

**Note:** The center stile (C) has a groove on each long edge.

**CUTTING THE STUB TENONS.** After the grooves are cut, the next step is to cut stub tenons to fit the grooves. To do this, I use the same type of procedure as above, flipping the piece, and "sneaking up" on the final cut.

**SETTING UP THE SAW.** Start by setting the height of the blade, using one of the grooved pieces as a gauge *(Fig. 4)*.

Next, set the rip fence so the distance between it and the *outside* of the blade is just slightly less than the depth of the groove *(Fig. 5)*.

**CUT THE TENONS.** The secret to getting a tenon with a good fit is to cut it slightly oversize. Then "sneak up" on the final thickness until the tenon just slips into the groove with a friction fit.

To cut the tenon, make the first pass at the shoulder of the tenon *(Fig. 6a)*. Then slide the workpiece over to complete the tenon at the end.

Now flip the workpiece over to cut the other side. Raise the blade or move the fence and repeat the procedure until the tenon fits snug in the groove.

**SIDES.** The sides are made just like the back. Except this time the rails fit *between* the stiles *(Fig. 7)*.

Each side is made up of two stiles (E) and two rails (F) that surround a pegboard panel (G) *(Fig. 7)*.

**Note:** To simplify construction of the cart, I used identical pegboard panels for both the back and the sides.

To create the open space under the top of the cart (for clamps and other tools), I positioned one of the rails (F) 6" down from the top of the stile (E) *(Figs. 7 and 7a)*.

**FILLER STRIPS.** But there's a problem with positioning the rails like this. It leaves an open groove on the inside edge of each stile. To fill these grooves, I used filler strips (H) *(Fig. 7a)*. These are simply cut from some scrap and glued in place.

**ASSEMBLY.** After the filler strips are glued into the grooves, the last step is to assemble the basic cabinet.

To do this, simply glue and clamp the back between the sides so the bottom edges are flush *(Figs. 8 and 8a)*.

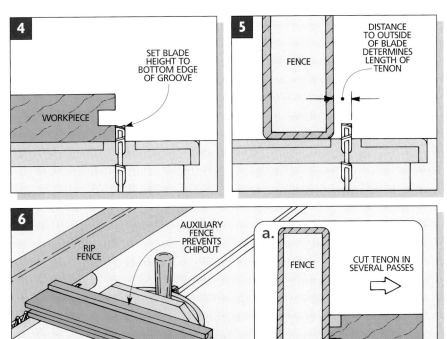

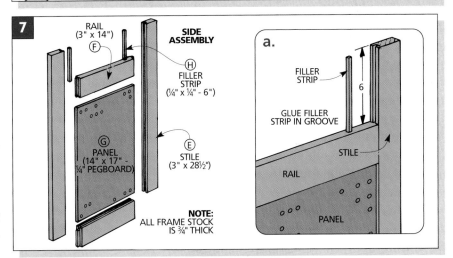

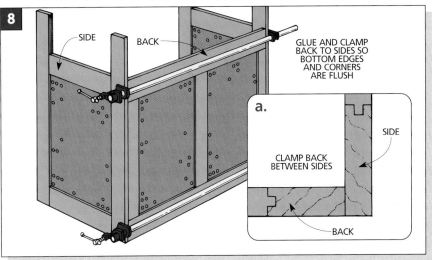

The shelves of the shop cart provide storage space and help strengthen the cabinet (refer to the Exploded View on page 9). The two shelves are identical and easy to build.

**SHELVES.** Each shelf (I) is made from a piece of $\frac{1}{2}$" plywood. Then to prevent the shelf from bowing and to cover the plywood edge, I added a piece of shelf edging (J) *(Fig. 9)*. This is just a piece of $1\frac{1}{2}$"-wide hardwood cut the same length as the shelf.

This edging is joined to the shelf with an offset tongue and groove joint *(Fig. 9a)*. To make this joint, first form the tongue by routing a $\frac{1}{4}$" rabbet $\frac{1}{4}$" deep along the front edge of the shelf. Then cut a groove along the back face of the edging to match the tongue. Make sure you position this groove so the edging sits flush with the top face of the shelf. (If the edging sits a little proud of the shelf, you can plane it flush.) After the joints are cut, the edging is glued and clamped to the shelf.

**SUPPORTS.** To attach the shelves to the cabinet, I fastened shelf supports to their backs and sides *(Fig. 9)*. Then screws are driven through the supports and into the cabinet. The shelves then help reinforce the cabinet.

I cut the side supports (K) and back supports (L) from $\frac{3}{4}$"-thick stock. I found it was easiest to drill shank holes in each one before gluing them to the shelves *(Fig. 9)*.

The side supports (K) are glued to the bottom face of each shelf first, flush with the edges. Then the back support (L) is cut to fit between them *(Fig. 9)*.

**ATTACH SHELVES.** To attach the shelves, screw the lower shelf inside the cabinet so the bottom of the edging strip (J) is flush with the bottom of the cabinet *(Fig. 10)*.

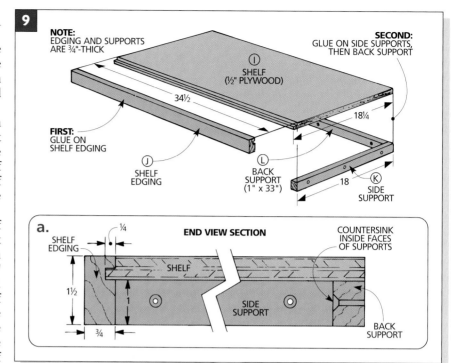

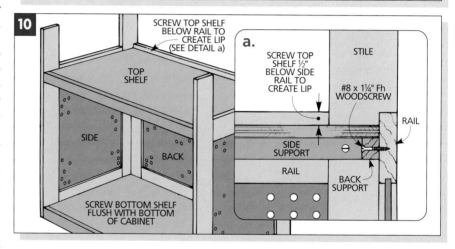

Then to create a lip around the upper shelf (so tools won't roll off), screw the shelf $\frac{1}{2}$" below the top edges of the top rails (A, F) *(Fig. 10a)*.

**CENTER DIVIDER.** The next step is to screw a center divider (M) between the shelves *(Fig. 11)*. The center divider is just a piece of $\frac{1}{2}$" plywood with the top two corners notched to fit around the shelf edging (J) and back support (L) *(Fig. 11)*. To prevent splitting the divider, drill pilot holes in it.

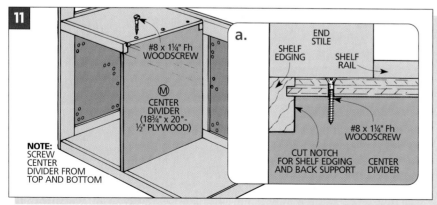

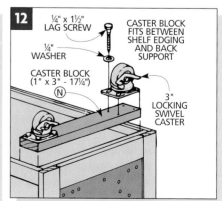

**CASTERS.** Finally, a set of 1"-thick caster blocks (N) are glued under the bottom shelf *(Fig. 12)*. These blocks provide extra holding power for the lag screws that hold the locking swivel casters in place *(Fig. 12)*. (For sources of casters, see page 126.) Once the glue is dry, drill pilot holes for the lag screws and fasten the casters in place.

## TOP

With the center divider and the casters screwed in place, the next step is to build up a solid, durable work surface for the top of the shop cart.

**TWO PIECES.** The top is made by gluing up two plywood top pieces (O). These pieces are cut to match the overall width of the sides (19½") and to a length of 42".

**Note:** The 42" length allows for a 3" overhang on each end.

When you're trying to glue up two large flat surfaces like this, it's not easy to get the edges exactly flush. The pieces tend to slide around on the glue as you clamp them together. The Shop Tip below shows one way around this.

**DADOES.** To "lock" the top in place, I cut dadoes on the underside of the plywood. These are ½" deep and sized to fit over the side stiles (E) *(Fig. 13a)*. Once they're cut, the top pieces are screwed to the cart *(Fig. 14)*.

**TOP COVER.** Since I wanted a hard, smooth surface for the top of the cart, I glued a hardboard top cover (P) on top of the plywood pieces (O) *(Fig. 14)*.

Here again, I cut the top cover slightly oversize, then used a flush trim bit to get all four sides flush.

**Note:** When trimming the top cover, make sure the bit's bearing rides on the top piece of plywood (see drawing in Shop Tip). The edge of the bottom plywood may be uneven across the dadoes.

**TRIM.** The edges of the top are covered with ¾"-thick side trim (Q) and front/back trim (R) *(Fig. 14)*. The side trim's length equals the width of the top. The front/back trim (R) is then cut to length to cover the top's length plus the ends of the side trim *(Fig. 14a)*.

Before I glued the front and back trim (R) to the top, I knocked off the sharp corners by cutting a chamfer on each end *(Fig. 14a)*.

Then, after all of the trim is glued in place, I routed a ¼" chamfer along the top edge *(Fig. 14b)*.

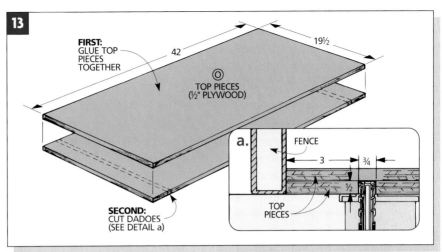

**13**

**FIRST:** GLUE TOP PIECES TOGETHER

42

19½

TOP PIECES (½" PLYWOOD)

**a.** FENCE

3  ¾

½

TOP PIECES

**SECOND:** CUT DADOES (SEE DETAIL a)

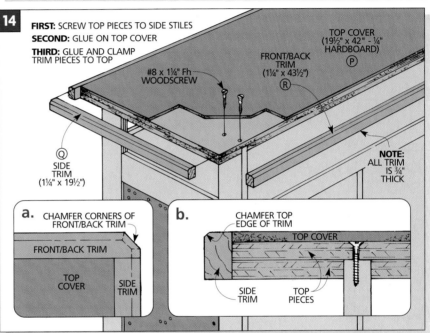

**14**

**FIRST:** SCREW TOP PIECES TO SIDE STILES
**SECOND:** GLUE ON TOP COVER
**THIRD:** GLUE AND CLAMP TRIM PIECES TO TOP

TOP COVER (19½" x 42" - ¼" HARDBOARD) (P)

FRONT/BACK TRIM (1¼" x 43½") (R)

#8 x 1¼" Fh WOODSCREW

SIDE TRIM (1¼" x 19½") (Q)

**NOTE:** ALL TRIM IS ¾" THICK

**a.** CHAMFER CORNERS OF FRONT/BACK TRIM

FRONT/BACK TRIM

TOP COVER

SIDE TRIM

**b.** CHAMFER TOP EDGE OF TRIM

TOP COVER

SIDE TRIM

TOP PIECES

## SHOP TIP . . . . . . . . *Flush Trim Bit*

Trying to get the edges of two workpieces exactly flush can be close to impossible if you just try to position them by hand.

That's why when I need two surfaces perfectly flush, I cut one slightly oversize and then use a flush trim bit to take off the excess after the pieces are glued up (see drawing).

A flush trim bit works because it has a bearing at the end that is right in line with the cutting edge of the bit. As the bearing rolls along one surface, the other surface is trimmed exactly flush with it (see drawing).

For smaller pieces, you can mount your router in the router table and guide the workpiece past the bit. But it's not safe or practical to handle a large workpiece like the top of the shop cart on the router table. In this case, use the flush trim bit in a handheld router.

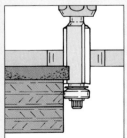

Next, I added a pair of doors. The doors are made just like the rest of the cabinet — a simple frame and panel *(Fig. 15)*.

**FRAMES.** To make the frames, first cut the stiles (S) to match the distance between the bottom of the lower shelf edging and the top of the upper shelf (22" long) *(Fig. 16)*.

The rails (T) are a little trickier. The idea here is to cut them to length so the doors are tight against each other and flush with the sides of the cabinet.

To do this, you'll have to consider the width of the stiles (3"), and the length of the stub tenons ($\frac{1}{4}$"). In my case, the rails (T) measure $12\frac{1}{2}$" long.

**PANELS.** Since I wouldn't be hanging anything on the doors, the panels (U) are cut from hardboard. Here again, they're cut to fit the frames *(Fig. 15)*.

After the doors are glued up, you'll need to plane the stiles to create a $\frac{1}{16}$" gap between the doors.

**MOUNT DOORS.** The next step is to mount the doors to the cabinet with butt hinges *(Fig. 16)*. The easiest way to do this is to cut mortises in the front edge of the side stiles (E) to match the thickness of the hinge *(Fig. 16a)*. The Shop Tip below shows one way to locate the hinge screws in the door.

**HARDWARE.** After the doors are screwed to the cart, I installed a pair of magnetic catches *(Fig. 16b)*.

Next, I drilled centered holes in the door stiles and screwed on a pair of door knobs *(Fig. 16)*.

To complete the cart, brush on two coats of satin polyurethane. ∎

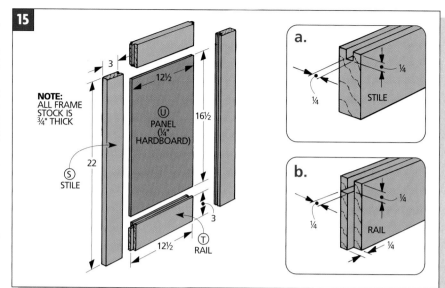

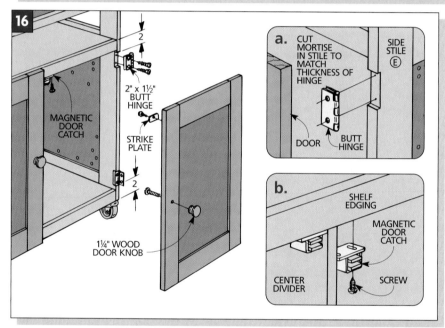

# SHOP TIP . . . . . . . . . . . . . . . . . . . . . . . *Hinge Screw Location*

It's easy to mount the hinges to the stiles. But trying to mark the screw locations in the door can be a challenge.

I used a couple of shop-made pins to help with this. To make the pins, file two brass screws to a point *(Fig. 1)*. (Brass screws file down easily.) Then trap a pin in each of the top and bottom hinges for one door *(Fig. 2)*.

Position the door and press it against the pins to mark the screw locations *(Fig. 2)*.

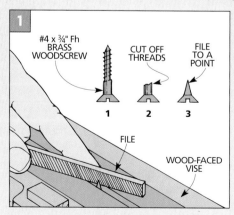

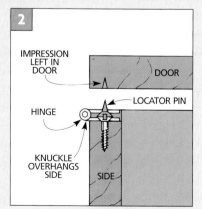

# DESIGNER'S NOTEBOOK

*By adding sliding trays behind the doors, you can make the space suitable for storing smaller items. The trays pull out on full-extension slides to allow easy access to even the farthest corners.*

## CONSTRUCTION NOTES:

■ You can add as many trays as needed to accommodate the items you plan to store in your cabinet.

■ Each tray consists of a front and back (V), a pair of sides (W), and a bottom (X) *(Fig. 1)*. I cut my tray front, back and sides to a width of $2^3/4$". This gave me a $2^1/4$"-deep tray once the bottom was added *(Fig. 1b)*.

■ To determine the length of the front and back pieces (V), first measure the distance from the cabinet stile (E) to the center divider (M). Then subtract 1" to allow $1/2$" clearance for each drawer slide. Cut two pieces to this length for each tray to be built.

■ Next, for each tray, cut two tray sides (W) to a length of $17^1/2$".

■ The frame of the tray is joined together with an easy-to-make rabbet joint *(Fig. 1a)*. To cut this, first mount in the table saw a dado blade set up to cut a $3/4$" dado. Raise the blade to $1/2$" above the table. Then cut a rabbet on each end of the front/back pieces (V).

■ Next, cut a groove $1/4$" deep in each frame piece (V, W) to accept a $1/4$" hardboard bottom (X) *(Fig. 1b)*.

■ To determine the size of the hardboard bottom, dry-assemble the tray and measure the inside dimensions. Add $1/2$" to account for the grooves.

■ Now assemble the five pieces for each tray. Glue the hardboard bottom in place and glue each corner joint. To reinforce the corners, drive two 1" brads into each joint *(Fig. 1)*.

■ The pull-out trays are mounted on full-extension slides. With the type I used, one half of the slide is mounted to the cabinet and the other is screwed to the tray. Follow the instructions that come with your slides. (For sources of drawer slides, see page 126.)

■ I mounted two trays on one side of my cabinet. The upper tray is $9^1/2$" up from the bottom shelf. (I rested each of these slides on a $9^1/2$"-wide plywood spacer while I fastened them in place.) The lower tray is mounted $1/16$" above the bottom shelf *(Fig. 2)*.

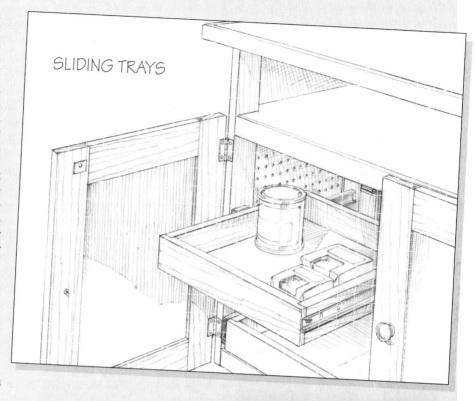

SLIDING TRAYS

## MATERIALS LIST

**NEW PARTS**

| | | |
|---|---|---|
| **V** Front/Backs* | $3/4$ x $2^3/4$ - 16 | |
| **W** Sides* | $3/4$ x $2^3/4$ - $17^1/2$ | |
| **X** Bottoms* | $1/4$ hdbd. - $15^1/4$ $17^1/2$ | |

*Cut two of parts V and W, one of part X for each tray to be built.

**HARDWARE SUPPLIES**

(1 pr.)** 18" drawer slides w/ screws
(8)** 1" brads
** For each tray to be built.

### 1

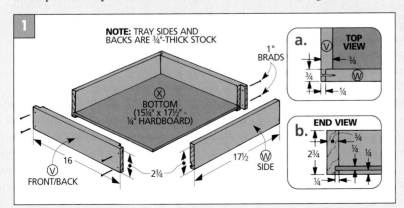

**NOTE:** TRAY SIDES AND BACKS ARE $3/4$"-THICK STOCK

1" BRADS

Ⓧ

BOTTOM ($15^1/4$ x $17^1/2$ - $1/4$" HARDBOARD)

16   Ⓥ FRONT/BACK   $2^3/4$   $17^1/2$   Ⓦ SIDE

**a.** TOP VIEW   Ⓥ   $3/4$   $3/4$   Ⓦ   $1/4$

**b.** END VIEW   $3/4$   $1/4$ $1/4$   $2^3/4$   $1/4$

### 2

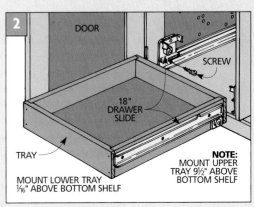

DOOR   SCREW

18" DRAWER SLIDE

TRAY

MOUNT LOWER TRAY $1/16$" ABOVE BOTTOM SHELF

**NOTE:** MOUNT UPPER TRAY $9^1/2$" ABOVE BOTTOM SHELF

# Wall-Hung Tool Cabinet

*Extra-deep doors and an optional drawer unit provide plenty of room for storing tools and hardware. Cutting the strong and attractive box joints is fast and simple with an easy-to-build jig.*

For years, I've been wanting to build this cabinet. It's designed to maximize the one thing that's in short supply in most shops: wall space. The cabinet has a usable depth of 6" — deep enough to hold a variety of hand and power tools.

In addition, the amount of wall space is effectively doubled because the doors also serve as storage compartments. (Both doors are 1¾" deep.)

**DRAWERS.** After completing the main cabinet, I decided to add a case with drawers underneath it. It's the perfect way to keep some of my small hardware and accessories organized and close at hand. Even though the two units are separate, they're fastened together with a spacer between them.

**MATERIALS.** Since this is a shop cabinet, you can build it out of just about any material. I chose birch for the cabinet and door frames, and used ¾" birch plywood for the back panels and the panels for the doors.

Although using ¾"-thick plywood may seem excessive, doors this thick allow you to screw in hooks and racks for various tools.

**BOX JOINTS.** Box joints work well on this project for a couple of reasons. First, it's a strong joint. The fingers of the joint provide plenty of gluing area at all of the corners.

And second, I think the uniform appearance of the joint provides a nice touch of craftsmanship to the case and to the drawers.

**BOX JOINT JIG.** If you've never cut box joints, don't worry. It's automatic once you've built the jig shown on pages 24-25. After the jig is built, you use some scrap to fine tune your setup first. Then simply place your workpieces on the jig and make the cuts. Step-by-step instructions for cutting tight-fitting box joints can be found in the Technique article beginning on page 26.

## EXPLODED VIEW

**OVERALL DIMENSIONS:**
42W x 10D x 35⅞H

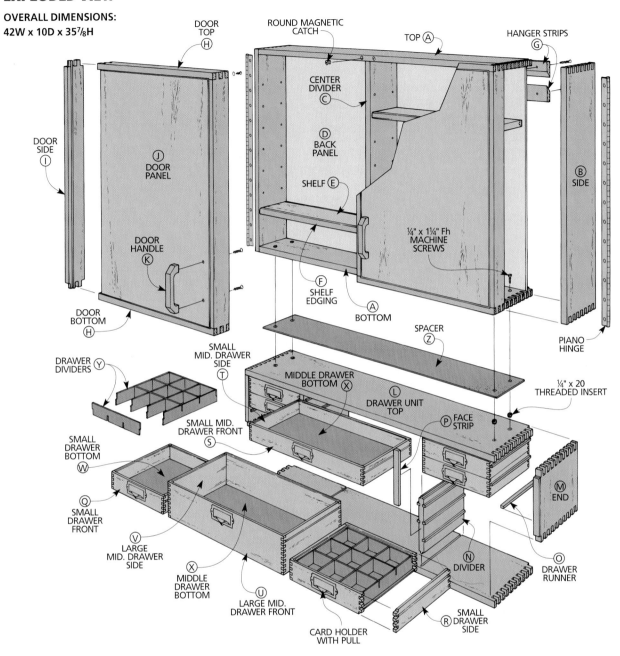

DOOR TOP (H)

ROUND MAGNETIC CATCH

TOP (A)

HANGER STRIPS (G)

DOOR SIDE (I)

DOOR PANEL (J)

CENTER DIVIDER (C)

BACK PANEL (D)

SHELF (E)

¼" x 1¼" Fh MACHINE SCREWS

SIDE (B)

DOOR HANDLE (K)

DOOR BOTTOM (H)

SHELF EDGING (F)

BOTTOM (A)

SPACER (Z)

PIANO HINGE

¼" x 20 THREADED INSERT

DRAWER DIVIDERS (Y)

SMALL MID. DRAWER SIDE (T)

MIDDLE DRAWER BOTTOM (X)

DRAWER UNIT TOP (L)

FACE STRIP (P)

SMALL MID. DRAWER FRONT (S)

SMALL DRAWER BOTTOM (W)

END (M)

SMALL DRAWER FRONT (Q)

LARGE MID. DRAWER SIDE (V)

MIDDLE DRAWER BOTTOM (X)

LARGE MID. DRAWER FRONT (U)

DIVIDER (N)

DRAWER RUNNER (O)

SMALL DRAWER SIDE (R)

CARD HOLDER WITH PULL

---

## MATERIALS LIST

### CABINET

| | | |
|---|---|---|
| **A** | Top/Bottom (2) | ¾ x 7½ - 42 |
| **B** | Sides (2) | ¾ x 7½ - 28 |
| **C** | Center Divider (1) | ¾ x 6 - 27¼ |
| **D** | Back Panel (1) | ¾ ply - 27¼ x 41¼ |
| **E** | Shelves * | ¾ ply - 5 x 19⅝ |
| **F** | Shelf Edging** | ¾ x ¾ - 19⅝ |
| **G** | Hanger Strips (2) | ¾ x 2 - 40½ |
| **H** | Door Top/Bottom (4) | ¾ x 2½ - 20¹⁵⁄₁₆ |
| **I** | Door Sides (4) | ¾ x 2½ - 28 |
| **J** | Door Panels (2) | ¾ ply - 20³⁄₁₆ x 27¼ |
| **K** | Handles (2) | ¾ x 2 - 5 |

*Cut as many as needed. **Cut two per shelf.

### DRAWER UNIT

| | | |
|---|---|---|
| **L** | Top/Bottom (2) | ¾ x 10 - 42 |
| **M** | Ends (2) | ¾ x 10 - 7¾ |
| **N** | Dividers (2) | ¾ x 10 - 7 |
| **O** | Drawer Runners (16) | ⁷⁄₃₂ x ½ - 9⅝ |
| **P** | Face Strips (4) | ⅜ x ¾ - 6¼ |
| **Q** | Sm. Dwr. Fr./Bk. (12) | ⅜ x 2 - 9⅞ |
| **R** | Sm. Dwr. Sides (12) | ⅜ x 2 - 9⅞ |
| **S** | Sm. Mid. Dwr. Fr./Bk. (2) | ⅜ x 2 - 18⅞ |
| **T** | Sm. Mid. Dwr. Sides (2) | ⅜ x 2 - 9⅞ |
| **U** | Lg. Mid. Dwr. Fr./Bk. (2) | ⅜ x 4 - 18⅞ |
| **V** | Lg. Mid. Dwr. Sides (2) | ⅜ x 4 - 9⅞ |
| **W** | Sm. Dwr. Btms. (6) | ⅛ hdbd. - 9½ x 9½ |

| | | |
|---|---|---|
| **X** | Mid. Dwr. Btms. (2) | ⅛ hdbd. - 9½ x 18½ |
| **Y** | Drawer Dividers * | ⅛ hdbd. cut to fit |
| **Z** | Spacer (1) | ⅛ hdbd. - 7 x 39½ |

### HARDWARE SUPPLIES

(8) No. 8 x 1¼" Fh woodscrews
(3) No. 8 x 2" Fh woodscrews
(2) 1½" brass-plated piano hinge
(4) Round magnetic catches
(8) Brass-plated card holders w/ pulls
(4) ¼" x 20 threaded inserts
(4) ¼" x 1¼" Fh machine screws
(2) Oak pulls
(4) ¼" shelf supports

# CUTTING DIAGRAM

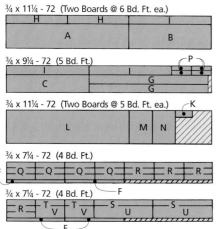

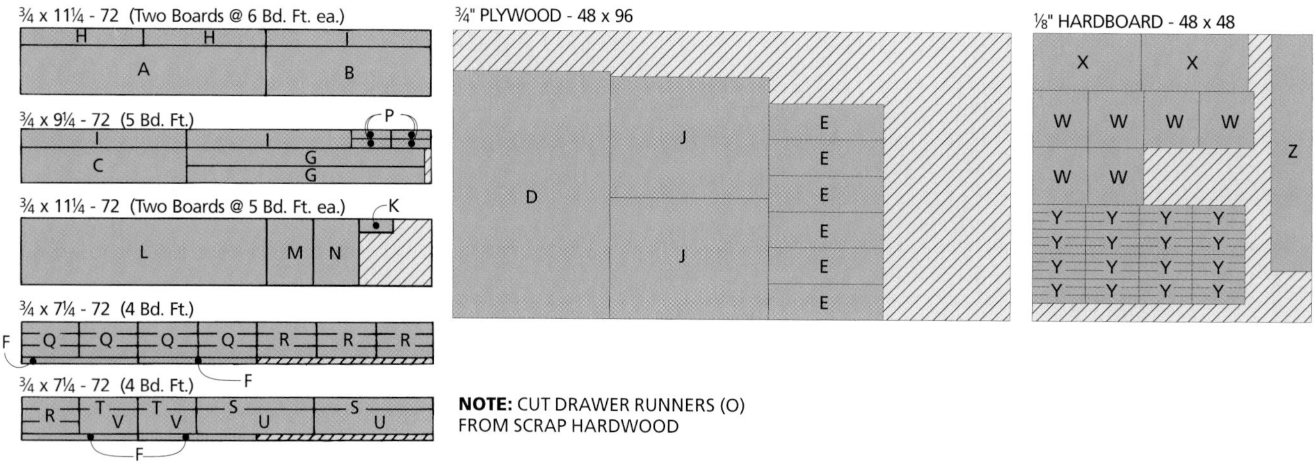

¾ x 11¼ - 72 (Two Boards @ 6 Bd. Ft. ea.)

H | H | I
A | B

¾ x 9¼ - 72 (5 Bd. Ft.)

I | I | P
C | G
G

¾ x 11¼ - 72 (Two Boards @ 5 Bd. Ft. ea.)

K
L | M | N

¾ x 7¼ - 72 (4 Bd. Ft.)

F | Q | Q | Q | Q | R | R | R

¾ x 7¼ - 72 (4 Bd. Ft.) — F

R | T | T | S | S
V | V | U | U
F

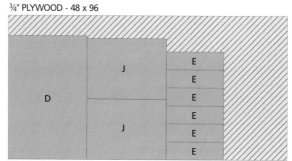

¾" PLYWOOD - 48 x 96

D | J | E
E
J | E
E
E
E

⅛" HARDBOARD - 48 x 48

X | X
W | W | W | W
Z
W | W
Y Y Y Y
Y Y Y Y
Y Y Y Y
Y Y Y Y

**NOTE:** CUT DRAWER RUNNERS (O)
FROM SCRAP HARDWOOD

## CABINET

The cabinet and drawers are all put together with box joints. Building a box joint jig is detailed in the Shop Jig article beginning on page 24. And step-by-step instructions for cutting box joints are in the Technique article on page 26.

**TOP/BOTTOM.** To build the cabinet, first cut the top/bottom (A) and sides (B) to size from ¾"-thick stock *(Fig. 1)*.

**Note:** The final size of these pieces can be altered to suit your needs, but it's nice if they're cut to a width so the joints come out with full pins on the front and back edges *(Fig. 1a)*.

However, just in case there's a little gain when the box joints are cut, I ripped these four pieces a little wide to begin with (to about 7¾"). Then I trimmed them down after the box joint pins and slots were cut.

**BOX JOINTS.** When all the cabinet pieces were cut to size, I used the box joint jig to cut the slots in the ends of each piece. The slots are ½" wide and the depth equals the thickness of the stock (¾" in my case).

First, cut seven slots in the cabinet's side pieces (B) (to produce eight pins) *(Fig. 1a)*. Then cut the mating joints in the top/bottom pieces.

Cutting the box joints on the ends of these long pieces turned out to be easier than I expected. However, to help steady the workpieces I used a 7"-high sliding front fence on the jig.

**Note:** Although the construction of the doors is covered later, it's best to cut the pieces for the door frames now and cut the box joints while the jig is set up. Refer to *Fig. 7* on page 20.

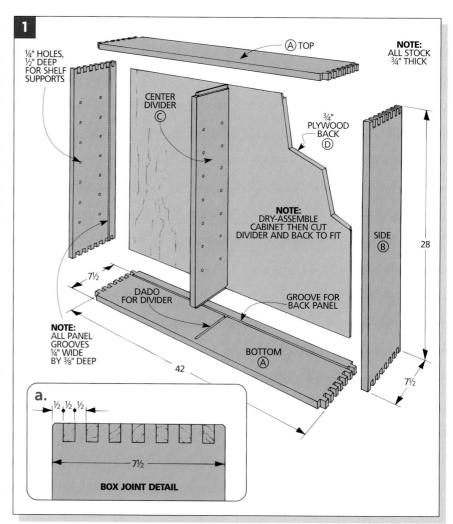

**1**

Ⓐ TOP

**NOTE:**
ALL STOCK
¾" THICK

¼" HOLES,
½" DEEP
FOR SHELF
SUPPORTS

CENTER
DIVIDER
Ⓒ

¾"
PLYWOOD
BACK
Ⓓ

**NOTE:**
DRY-ASSEMBLE
CABINET THEN CUT
DIVIDER AND BACK TO FIT

SIDE
Ⓑ

28

7½

DADO
FOR DIVIDER

GROOVE FOR
BACK PANEL

**NOTE:**
ALL PANEL
GROOVES
¼" WIDE
BY ⅜" DEEP

BOTTOM
Ⓐ

42

7½

**a.**

½" ½" ½"

7½

**BOX JOINT DETAIL**

**GROOVE FOR BACK.** After the box joints are cut, a groove is cut in each piece to accept a tongue cut on the back panel (D). This groove is positioned so it aligns with the second pin from the back of the top/bottom pieces *(Fig. 2)*. (This is 1½" from the back edge to

allow for the ¾"-thick back and ¾" for the cabinet's hanging system.)

Set up the saw to cut a kerf ⅜" deep right next to the edge of the second pin *(Fig. 2a)*. Make this cut on all four pieces before moving the fence to widen the slot to ¼".

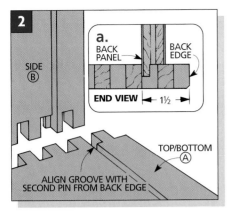

**2**

**a.**

BACK PANEL — BACK EDGE

SIDE (B)

**END VIEW** ← 1½ →

SIDE (B)

ALIGN GROOVE WITH SECOND PIN FROM BACK EDGE

TOP/BOTTOM (A)

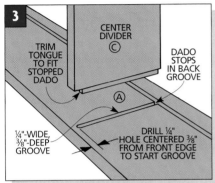

**3**

CENTER DIVIDER (C)

TRIM TONGUE TO FIT STOPPED DADO

DADO STOPS IN BACK GROOVE

(A)

¼"-WIDE, ⅜"-DEEP GROOVE

DRILL ¼" HOLE CENTERED ⅜" FROM FRONT EDGE TO START GROOVE

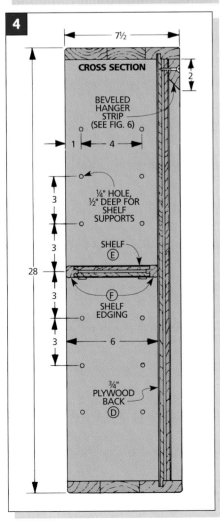

**4**

← 7½ →

**CROSS SECTION**

2

BEVELED HANGER STRIP (SEE FIG. 6)

1 ← 4 →

¼" HOLE, ½" DEEP FOR SHELF SUPPORTS

3

SHELF (E)

3

28

(F) SHELF EDGING

3

← 6 →

3

¾" PLYWOOD BACK (D)

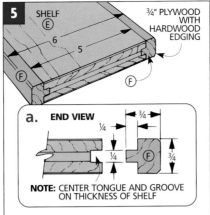

**5**

SHELF (E)

¾" PLYWOOD WITH HARDWOOD EDGING

6

5

(F)

(F)

**a. END VIEW**

¼

¾

¼

(F)

¾

**NOTE:** CENTER TONGUE AND GROOVE ON THICKNESS OF SHELF

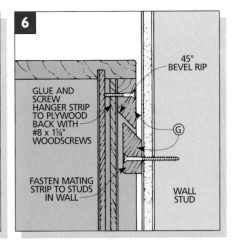

**6**

45° BEVEL RIP

GLUE AND SCREW HANGER STRIP TO PLYWOOD BACK WITH #8 x 1¼" WOODSCREWS

(G)

FASTEN MATING STRIP TO STUDS IN WALL

WALL STUD

**DADO FOR DIVIDER.** Next, ¼"-wide dadoes are cut centered on the length of the top/bottom pieces. A tongue on the center divider (C) will fit into this ⅜"-deep dado *(Fig. 3)*. Since these dadoes are stopped at both ends, I used the router to cut them.

To make sure the dadoes are aligned on both pieces, clamp them together, back edge to back edge with their top and bottom ends flush. Then clamp a fence across both pieces and rout the dado so it starts ⅜" from the front edge of each piece and stops in the groove for the back panel *(Fig. 3)*.

**DIVIDER.** After these dadoes are cut, the center divider (C) can be cut to size. Cut the divider to width to equal the distance from the front edge of the top/bottom pieces (A) to the front edge of the groove that will hold the back panel *(Fig. 3)*.

To determine the length of the center divider, measure the distance from shoulder to shoulder on the side pieces. (This is the distance between the bottoms of the box joint slots on the side pieces.) Then add ¾" for the ⅜"-long tongue on each end.

After the divider is cut to size, cut tongues centered on the ends to fit the dadoes in the top/bottom pieces. Then trim ⅜" from the fronts of the tongues so they match the length of the dadoes in the top and bottom *(Fig. 3)*.

**BACK PANEL.** The last piece needed for the cabinet is the back panel (D). I made this panel out of ¾" birch plywood. To find the size of the panel, measure the shoulder-to-shoulder distance on the sides and the top/bottom pieces, and add ¾" to both dimensions to account for the ⅜"-long tongue on each edge *(Fig. 4)*.

Then cut ⅜"-wide by ½"-deep rabbets on the back face of all four edges of the panel to produce the tongues that fit the grooves in the frame pieces.

**HOLES FOR SHELVES.** Before final assembly, I drilled a series of ¼"-dia. holes in the sides and the center divider for shelf support pins *(Fig. 4)*. I just started with a set of holes centered on the height of the side piece. Then I added holes centered every 3" up and down *(Fig. 4)*.

**ASSEMBLY.** Now the cabinet can be assembled. It takes a little time to apply glue to all the joints, so you may want to enlist a helper. (Using a white or polyurethane glue will also give you more time to work since these glues set up more slowly.)

After the glue is applied, clamp the cabinet together with the back and center divider in place. (The back panel will help pull the frame square, but check to make sure.)

**SHELVES.** Some of the leftover birch plywood can be used to make a few shelves (E). Although it's not necessary, I dressed up the edges by adding birch edging strips (F) *(Fig. 5)*. To help align the edging on the shelf, I cut a groove along each long edge of the plywood. Then I cut a tongue on the shelf edging to fit the groove *(Fig. 5a)*.

**HANGING SYSTEM.** To mount the cabinet to the wall, I made beveled hanging strips (G) *(Fig. 6)*. To do this, cut a 4"-wide blank to length to fit between the cabinet sides (B). Then rip the blank in half at a 45° bevel. Then mount one strip to the wall (make sure you hit studs), and the other to the cabinet.

**CHAMFER EDGES.** The last step on the shelves and the cabinet is to lightly chamfer the edges. I did this with a 45° chamfer bit, chamfering all inside and outside edges of the cabinet.

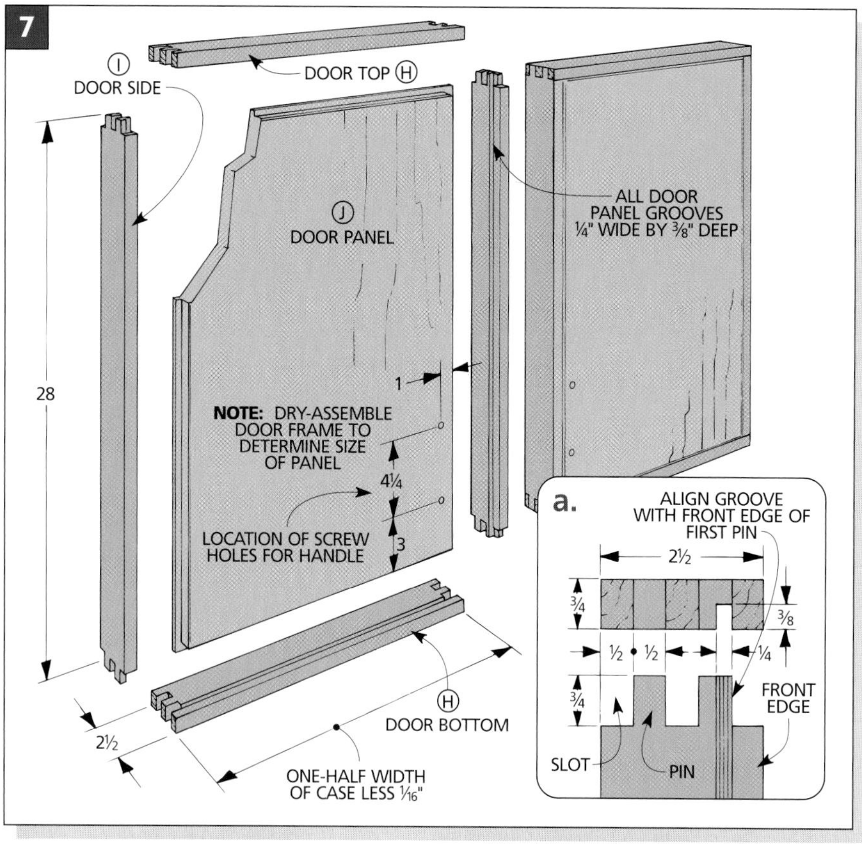
7
DOOR SIDE (I)
DOOR TOP (H)
DOOR PANEL (J)
ALL DOOR PANEL GROOVES ¼" WIDE BY ⅜" DEEP
28
1
NOTE: DRY-ASSEMBLE DOOR FRAME TO DETERMINE SIZE OF PANEL
4¼
LOCATION OF SCREW HOLES FOR HANDLE
3
2½
DOOR BOTTOM (H)
ONE-HALF WIDTH OF CASE LESS 1⁄16"
a.
ALIGN GROOVE WITH FRONT EDGE OF FIRST PIN
2½
¾
⅜
½ ½
¼
FRONT EDGE
SLOT
PIN

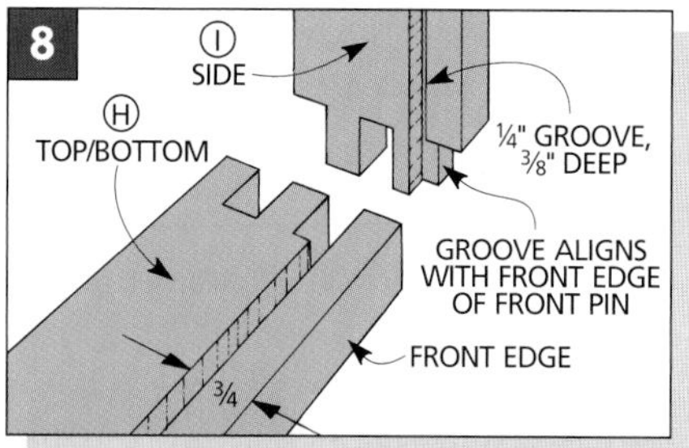
8
SIDE (I)
TOP/BOTTOM (H)
¼" GROOVE, ⅜" DEEP
GROOVE ALIGNS WITH FRONT EDGE OF FRONT PIN
FRONT EDGE
¾

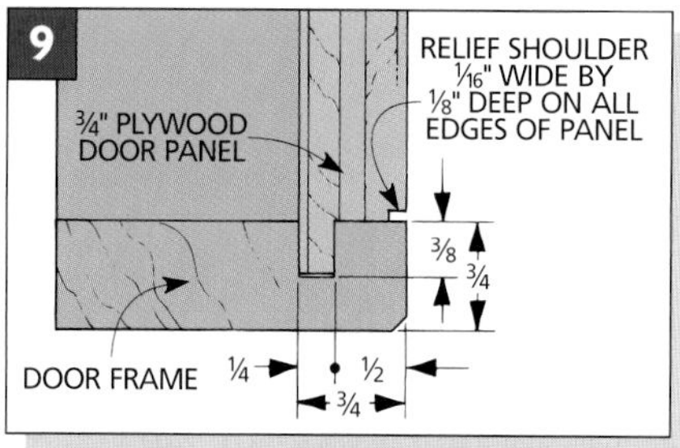
9
RELIEF SHOULDER 1⁄16" WIDE BY ⅛" DEEP ON ALL EDGES OF PANEL
¾" PLYWOOD DOOR PANEL
⅜
¾
DOOR FRAME
¼
½
¾

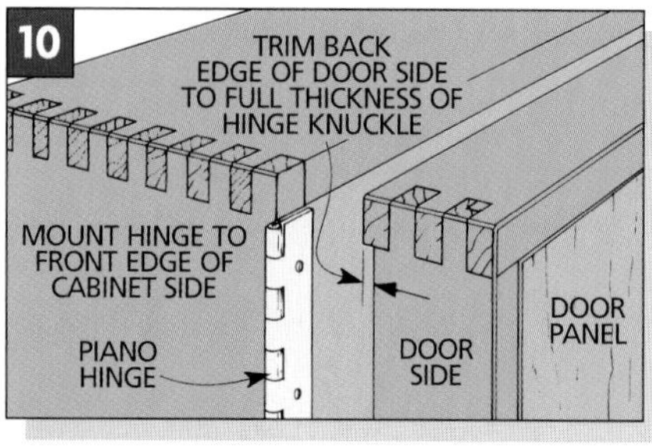
10
TRIM BACK EDGE OF DOOR SIDE TO FULL THICKNESS OF HINGE KNUCKLE
MOUNT HINGE TO FRONT EDGE OF CABINET SIDE
PIANO HINGE
DOOR SIDE
DOOR PANEL

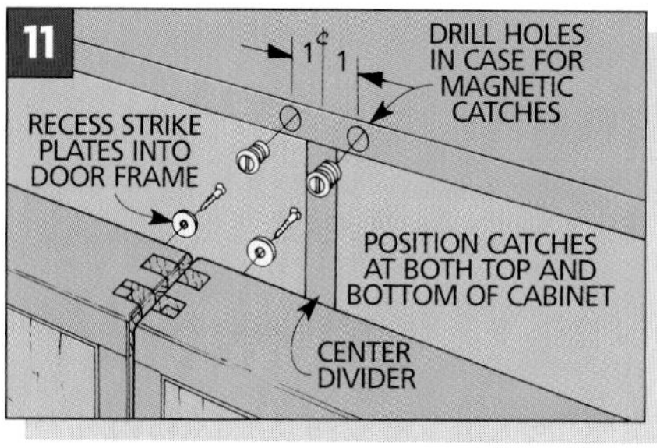
11
DRILL HOLES IN CASE FOR MAGNETIC CATCHES
1
1
RECESS STRIKE PLATES INTO DOOR FRAME
POSITION CATCHES AT BOTH TOP AND BOTTOM OF CABINET
CENTER DIVIDER

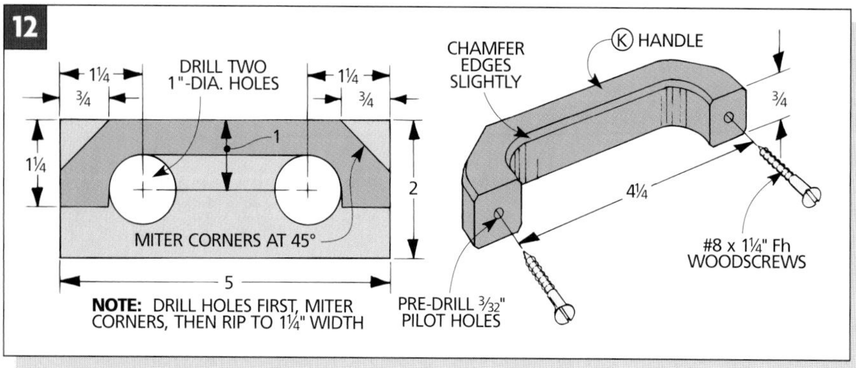
12
1¼
¾
DRILL TWO 1"-DIA. HOLES
1¼
¾
1¼
1
2
MITER CORNERS AT 45°
5
NOTE: DRILL HOLES FIRST, MITER CORNERS, THEN RIP TO 1¼" WIDTH
CHAMFER EDGES SLIGHTLY
(K) HANDLE
¾
4¼
#8 x 1¼" Fh WOODSCREWS
PRE-DRILL 3⁄32" PILOT HOLES

## DOORS

The doors are constructed the same way as the cabinet. Begin by cutting the top/bottom pieces (H) and side pieces (I) to size *(Fig. 7)*. As with the cabinet pieces, the door pieces are cut a little wide to begin with, and trimmed to final width after the box joints are cut.

The length of the door's sides (I) should be exactly the same as the cabinet sides (B). The combined length of the top and bottom pieces (H) should equal the length of the cabinet's top piece (A), less 1/8" (1/16" on each piece) to allow clearance between the doors.

**JOINERY.** As mentioned previously, it's best to cut the box joints on the door pieces at the same time as the cabinet pieces. Start these cuts with the top and bottom pieces, cutting two slots and leaving three pins *(Fig. 8)*.

**DOOR PANEL GROOVE.** After the box joints are cut, you can then cut a groove along the inside edge of each piece for the door panels (J). This groove is positioned so its front edge lines up on the front edge of the first pin on the door side piece *(Figs. 7a and 8)*.

**DOOR PANELS.** Now cut the door panels from 3/4" birch plywood to fit between the bottoms of the grooves in the door frame. Then cut rabbets on the face side of each panel to produce tongues to fit the grooves.

To add an accent to the door, I cut a 1/16"-wide relief shoulder on each rabbeted edge. This provides a "shadow line" that outlines the panel once it's mounted in the frame (*Fig. 9* and the photo on page 16).

**HINGE MORTISE.** Before assembling the doors, I ripped the back edges of the two outer door sides down to make mortises for the piano hinges *(Fig. 10)*. Rip off a width equal to the total thickness of the hinge (at the knuckle).

**ASSEMBLY.** Now glue and clamp the door frames together with the panels in place. When the assembly is dry, mount the doors to the cabinet with piano hinges *(Fig. 10)*.

**CATCHES.** To hold the doors closed, I added magnetic catches to the cabinet. Install one at the top and bottom inside corners of each door *(Fig. 11)*.

**HANDLES.** At first I was going to buy brass handles for the doors. But then I decided to have a little fun and make my own handles. I started with two 2" x 5" blanks of 3/4"-thick birch *(Fig. 12)*.

To form the inside of the handle (K), drill two 1"-dia. holes, centered 1" from the edge of each piece. Next, miter the outside corners at 45°. Then rip the pieces to a finished width of 1¼" and use a bandsaw to cut out the inside shape *(Fig. 12)*. After sanding the handles smooth, chamfer all the edges with a 45° chamfer bit on the router table.

**FINISH.** To complete the cabinet, I chamfered all the outside edges and applied two coats of a tung oil finish.

## DRAWER UNIT

Once the cabinet was complete, I decided to add a drawer unit below it. This is a basic frame (much like the cabinet) that's joined with box joints.

**TOP/BOTTOM.** The two top/bottom pieces (L) are cut to width to match the combined depth of the cabinet and the doors. This should be 10" *(Fig. 13)*. Then cut these two pieces to length to match the length of the cabinet's top/bottom pieces.

**ENDS AND DIVIDERS.** The two ends (M) and two dividers (N) are ripped to the same width as the top/bottom pieces. As for the length, it depends on how many drawers you want and how they're constructed.

Since I wanted to construct these drawers with box joints, I had to plan ahead a little. I wanted the height of the drawers to be an even multiple of the box joint's ¼"-wide pins and slots. Each drawer is 2" in this case *(Fig. 14)*.

Then to determine the height of the opening in the drawer unit, I allowed 6" for three drawers, plus a total of ¼" for clearance (1/16" between each drawer and at the top and bottom) *(Fig. 14)*.

**CUT TO LENGTH.** After the height of the opening is determined, the end pieces (M) can be cut to length. The length of my end pieces was 6¼" (the height of the opening) plus the thickness of the top and bottom pieces (¾" each), for a total of 7¾" *(Fig. 13)*.

**Note:** This makes the end pieces a little odd because they're wider (10") than they are long (7¾").

**DIVIDERS.** The length of the dividers (N) is equal to the height of the opening (6¼") plus ¾" for the two ⅜"-long tongues *(Fig. 13)*.

**BOX JOINTS.** After all these pieces are cut to size, the box joints can be cut to join the top/bottom pieces to the end pieces. Just as I did for the cabinet, I set

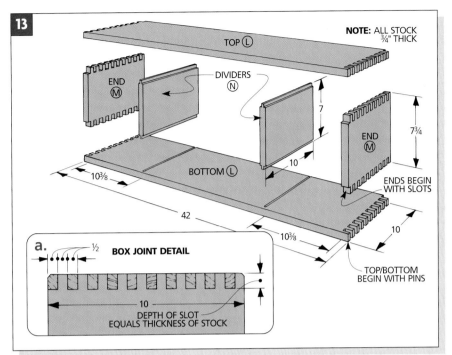

the box joint jig for ½"-wide slots. Then I started by cutting the top/bottom pieces so there would be a pin on the front edge *(Fig. 13)*.

**DADOES FOR DIVIDERS.** After the joints are cut, stopped dadoes are routed on the inside faces of the top and bottom pieces (L). These dadoes accept tongues on the dividers *(Fig. 13)*.

To get the dadoes aligned, I clamped the top and bottom pieces together, back edge to back edge *(Fig. 15)*. Then I marked the centerline of the dadoes 10⅜" from each end (measuring from the bottom of the box joint slots).

Next, drill ¼"-dia. start/stop holes

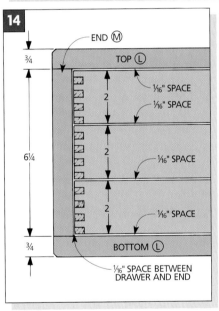
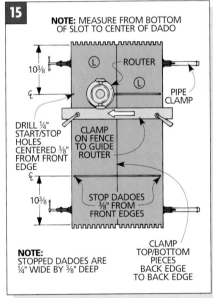

centered ⅜" from the front edges of each piece *(Fig. 15)*.

**Note:** These holes are only as deep as the dado (⅜"). They do not go through the top/bottom pieces.

Now place the router bit in a start hole. Align a fence across both workpieces and clamp it in place. Then rout a ⅜"-deep dado to the stop hole.

**TONGUES ON DIVIDERS.** Finally, cut tongues centered on the thickness of the dividers (N) to fit the stopped dadoes. As with the cabinet's center divider, you'll have to notch one end of each tongue so the divider will sit flush with the edges of the top/bottom (L).

Before assembling the drawer unit, I cut dadoes to mount the drawer runners in the ends (M) and dividers (N).

**POSITION OF DADOES.** The position of the dadoes needs some explanation. When the drawers are built, a groove cut in the drawer's side piece fits over the runner (refer to *Fig. 20*). By putting the runner in a specific position, the groove in the drawer will align with the second slot down in the box joint. When the drawer is assembled, the pin on the drawer front will hide the groove.

**CUT GROOVES.** To position the top dadoes in the end pieces (M), set the distance between the fence and the saw blade to $9/16"$ plus the thickness of the top piece ($15/16"$ total) *(Fig. 15a)*. Then cut a kerf on the inside face of each end piece (M). Next, move the fence to widen the dado to $7/32"$. (I cut these dadoes $1/32"$ less than $1/4"$ so the runners wouldn't bind in the $1/4"$-wide grooves on the drawer sides.)

**REMAINING GROOVES.** After the top dadoes are cut in both end pieces, adjust the fence to cut the remaining dadoes so they're spaced $3 3/8"$ and $5 7/16"$ from the top edge *(Fig. 15a)*.

**DADOES ON DIVIDERS.** Next cut the corresponding dadoes on the dividers (N). This requires different settings because the tongue on the top edge of the divider is only $3/8"$ long *(Fig. 15b)*.

**DRAWER RUNNERS.** After the dadoes are cut on the end pieces and dividers, the runners (O) are cut to thickness so they fit in the dadoes, and to width so they stick out $1/4"$ *(Fig. 16)*.

Since the runners are mounted across the grain of the end pieces and dividers, apply glue only to the front 2" or 3" when gluing them in place. (This is to allow the ends and dividers to expand and contract.)

**FACE STRIPS.** Finally, before assembling the drawer unit, I trimmed $3/8"$ off the front edges of the ends and dividers *(Fig. 16)*. After the case was assembled, I added $3/8"$-thick face strips (P) to hide the dadoes that had cut through the ends of these pieces *(Fig. 17)*.

## DRAWERS

Now that the drawer unit is assembled, the drawers can be built. I started by ripping enough stock for all the drawers to a width of 2" (except for the double-

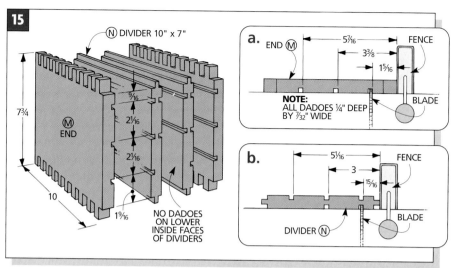

15
N DIVIDER 10" x 7"
M END
7 3/4
10
9/16
2 1/16
2 1/16
1 9/16
NO DADOES ON LOWER INSIDE FACES OF DIVIDERS

a. END M
5 7/16
3 3/8
1 5/16
FENCE
BLADE
NOTE: ALL DADOES 1/4" DEEP BY 7/32" WIDE

b.
5 1/16
3
15/16
FENCE
BLADE
DIVIDER N

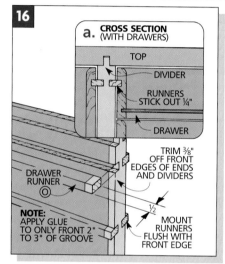

16
a. CROSS SECTION (WITH DRAWERS)
TOP
DIVIDER
RUNNERS STICK OUT 1/4"
DRAWER
DRAWER RUNNER O
NOTE: APPLY GLUE TO ONLY FRONT 2" TO 3" OF GROOVE
TRIM 3/8" OFF FRONT EDGES OF ENDS AND DIVIDERS
1/2
MOUNT RUNNERS FLUSH WITH FRONT EDGE

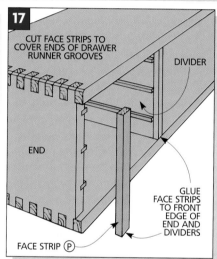

17
CUT FACE STRIPS TO COVER ENDS OF DRAWER RUNNER GROOVES
DIVIDER
END
GLUE FACE STRIPS TO FRONT EDGE OF END AND DIVIDERS
FACE STRIP P

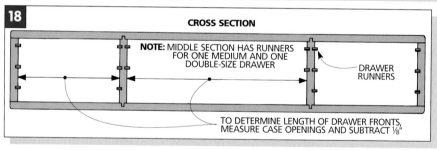

18 CROSS SECTION
NOTE: MIDDLE SECTION HAS RUNNERS FOR ONE MEDIUM AND ONE DOUBLE-SIZE DRAWER
DRAWER RUNNERS
TO DETERMINE LENGTH OF DRAWER FRONTS, MEASURE CASE OPENINGS AND SUBTRACT 1/8"

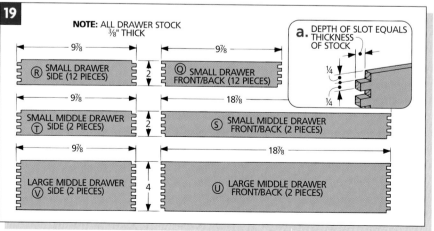

19
NOTE: ALL DRAWER STOCK 3/8" THICK
9 7/8
R SMALL DRAWER SIDE (12 PIECES)
2
9 7/8
Q SMALL DRAWER FRONT/BACK (12 PIECES)
a. DEPTH OF SLOT EQUALS THICKNESS OF STOCK
1/4
1/4
9 7/8
T SMALL MIDDLE DRAWER SIDE (2 PIECES)
2
18 7/8
S SMALL MIDDLE DRAWER FRONT/BACK (2 PIECES)
9 7/8
V LARGE MIDDLE DRAWER SIDE (2 PIECES)
4
18 7/8
U LARGE MIDDLE DRAWER FRONT/BACK (2 PIECES)

size drawer in the center compartment, which is 4" wide). Then all of these pieces are resawn to a thickness of $3/8$".

**FRONT/BACK PIECES.** The drawer front/back pieces (Q, S, U) are cut to length to equal the width of the openings less $1/8$" for clearance ($1/16$" on each side) *(Figs. 18 and 19)*.

**SIDE PIECES.** I cut all the drawer side pieces (R, T, V) to the same length as the front and back pieces (Q) on the small drawers *(Fig. 19)*.

**BOX JOINTS.** The drawers are joined with $1/4$"-wide box joints. After the joints are made, cut grooves for the drawer bottom and the runners *(Fig. 20)*. Then hardboard bottoms (W, X) are cut and the drawers are assembled.

## DIVIDER SYSTEM

In some of the drawers I added an interlocking divider system. Before cutting the stock for the dividers, I rounded over the inside top edges of the drawers *(Figs. 20a and 20b)*.

The dividers (Y) can be made from leftover hardwood stock or from $1/8$" hardboard. Either way, the dividers must be the same thickness as the width of the slot cut by the saw blade.

**CUT TO SIZE.** Cut the dividers to width to equal the distance from the drawer bottom to where the roundover starts *(Fig. 20a)*. Then cut them to length to match the width and depth of the inside of the drawer.

**CUT JOINTS.** To make the interlocking joints, start by cutting a notch on each end of each divider *(Fig. 21a)*. Then cut notches $2^7/8$" from each end *(Fig. 21b)*. After the joints are cut, just slide the dividers together and place them in the drawers.

## MOUNT DRAWER UNIT

With the drawers complete, I mounted the drawer unit to the bottom of the cabinet. A $1/8$" hardboard spacer (Z) between the two units allows clearance for the doors to swing open *(Fig. 22)*.

Drill $1/4$" holes through the bottom of the cabinet, stopping when the bit just touches the top of the drawer unit. Then drill holes at these points for $1/4$"-inside dia. threaded inserts.

Mount threaded inserts in the holes in the drawer unit. Then fasten the cabinet and drawer unit together with $1/4$" flathead machine screws. ∎

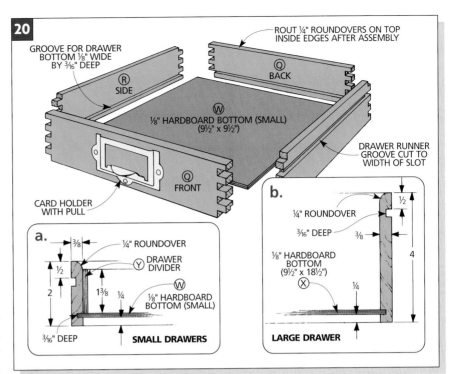

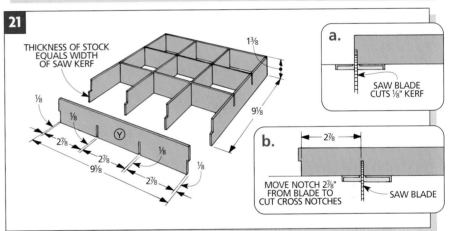

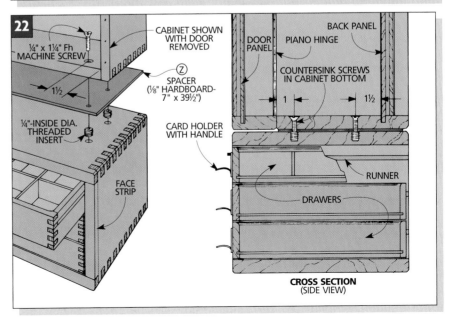

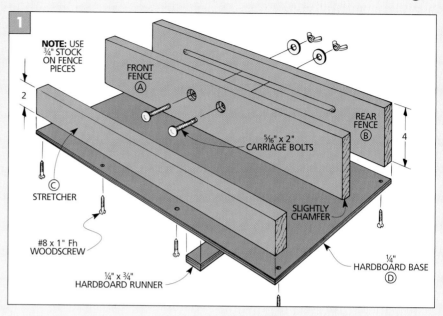

A s I was working on the Wall-Hung Tool Cabinet, I had to cut a lot of box joints. To cut this joint accurately, you have to meet two criteria: 1) the pins and slots have to be exactly the same width, and 2) all slots must be the same depth.

In order to do this, I use a jig to support and align the workpieces. This jig incorporates a two-part sliding fence that allows the micro-adjustments that match the pins to the slots. And a 1/4" hardboard base provides a stable, even platform for the workpiece to rest on as it passes over the blade (or bit).

## MAKE THE JIG

To make this jig, I cut the 1/4" hardboard base (D) to a size of 12" by 24". After the base is cut, the fence can be added.

This fence consists of a front fence (A) that slides against a stationary rear fence (B) *(Fig. 1)*. Rip both fences to a width of 4" out of 3/4"-thick hardwood and cut them to a length of 24" *(Fig. 2)*.

**FRONT FENCE.** The front fence slides on the back fence by means of two 5/16" carriage bolts. Mark the position of these bolts 1 1/2" down from the top edge and centered 3" apart *(Fig. 2)*.

After marking the position of the holes, drill two 3/4"-dia. counterbores 3/8" deep to recess the head of the carriage bolts. Then drill 5/16" shank holes the rest of the way through the front fence *(Fig. 2a)*.

**REAR FENCE.** To allow the front fence to slide, a 3/8"-wide slot is cut in the rear fence so it's centered 1 1/2" down from the top edge of the fence *(Fig. 2)*.

To cut this slot, first drill 3/8"-dia. start and stop holes 4" from each end of the workpiece. Then position the start hole over a 3/8" straight bit on the router table *(Fig. 3)*.

When the workpiece is positioned, slide the router table's fence against the workpiece and tighten it down. Then rout the slot between the two holes *(Fig. 3)*. Rout this slot in several successively deeper passes.

**FASTEN FENCE TO BASE.** After the groove is routed, screw and glue the rear fence flush with the back edge of the base *(Fig. 1)*. Then mount the front fence to the rear fence with carriage bolts, wing nuts and washers.

**STRETCHER.** Later, a slot will be cut through the base (refer to *Fig. 5*). To keep the base together, I glued and screwed a 2"-high stretcher (C) to the front edge of the base *(Fig. 1)*.

**RUNNER.** I also added a runner to the bottom of the base to guide the jig in the miter gauge slot in the table saw. Rip a 12"-long runner out of 1/4" hardboard so it's wide enough to slide smoothly in the slot. Then use a square to align the runner 4" from the left edge of the jig base, and glue it in place *(Fig. 4)*.

## INDEXING KEY

Now an indexing key is mounted in a notch in the bottom edge of the front fence. This key maintains even spacing of the slots.

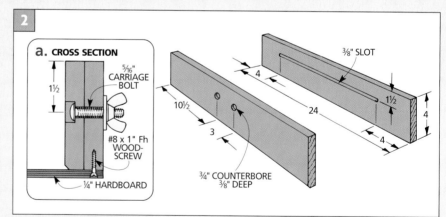

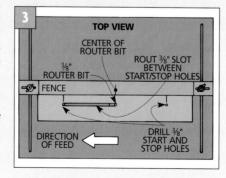

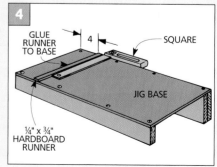

**CUT KEY NOTCH.** To cut the notch for this key, set the dado blade to the width you want for the box joint pins and slots. Then adjust the blade height to just over $1/4$" and cut a slot through the hardboard base *(Fig. 5)*.

Now you can raise the blade height (measuring from the surface of the hardboard) so it's about $1/16$" less than the thickness of the stock being joined with box joints *(Fig. 6)*. This $1/16$" reduction makes the notch and thus the key shorter to allow clearance when the joint is cut (refer to *Fig. 2* on page 26). Now cut through the fences to form the notch for the key.

**INDEX KEY.** After the notch is cut, cut the index key from a scrap of hardwood to fit tightly in the notch. Cut the strip 4" to 6" long and then cut off a 2"-long piece for the key and glue it into the notch in the front fence *(Fig. 7)*. (Save the leftover strip for the next step.)

**ADJUST FENCE.** To adjust the fence for the pin spacing, align the leftover strip with the edge of the slot in the base and adjust the front fence until the key contacts the strip *(Fig. 8)*.

Then, before cutting the box joints, raise the blade to a height to match the thickness of the stock *(Fig. 9)*.

And one more tip. The index pin will probably need slight adjustments to get the proper spacing for the pins and slots. To help gauge my adjustments, I scribed a line across both fences so it would be easier to see how far I was moving the front fence *(Fig. 10)*.

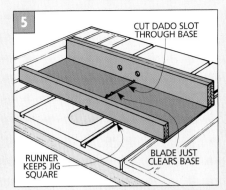

CUT DADO SLOT THROUGH BASE

RUNNER KEEPS JIG SQUARE

BLADE JUST CLEARS BASE

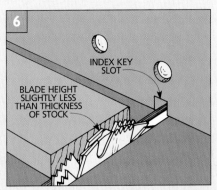

INDEX KEY SLOT

BLADE HEIGHT SLIGHTLY LESS THAN THICKNESS OF STOCK

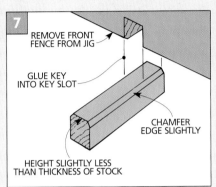

REMOVE FRONT FENCE FROM JIG

GLUE KEY INTO KEY SLOT

CHAMFER EDGE SLIGHTLY

HEIGHT SLIGHTLY LESS THAN THICKNESS OF STOCK

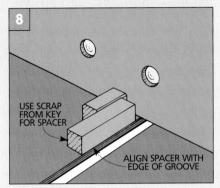

USE SCRAP FROM KEY FOR SPACER

ALIGN SPACER WITH EDGE OF GROOVE

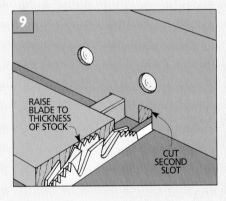

RAISE BLADE TO THICKNESS OF STOCK

CUT SECOND SLOT

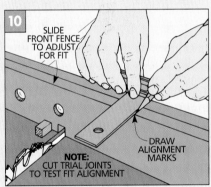

SLIDE FRONT FENCE TO ADJUST FOR FIT

NOTE: CUT TRIAL JOINTS TO TEST FIT ALIGNMENT

DRAW ALIGNMENT MARKS

## BOX JOINTS ON THE ROUTER TABLE

The box joint jig can be modified for use on a router table. However, on the router table, the slot in the workpiece must be cut in one pass, so it's best suited for making joints that require slots less than $3/8$" by $3/8$".

To modify the jig, cut the base so it's 3" wider than the front-to-back measurement of your router table. This allows for a $1^1/2$"-wide runner added to each side of the base *(Fig. 11)*.

Cut and assemble the jig as shown above. Then screw one runner to one edge of the base. Place the jig on the router table with this runner butted tightly against the edge and mark the position of the other runner. Screw the second runner in place, then wax the bottom of the base and the sides of the runners so the jig slides smoothly.

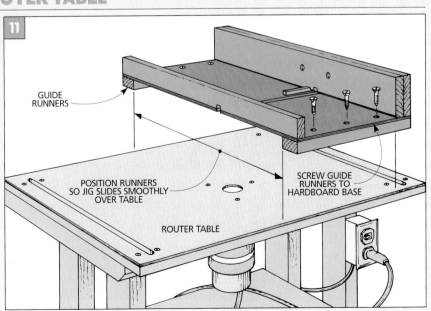

GUIDE RUNNERS

POSITION RUNNERS SO JIG SLIDES SMOOTHLY OVER TABLE

SCREW GUIDE RUNNERS TO HARDBOARD BASE

ROUTER TABLE

# TECHNIQUE ....... *Box Joint Drawers*

The box joint jig shown on the previous two pages makes good, tight-fitting joints. But tight joints are just part of building a drawer. Getting the drawers to fit properly in their case means planning ahead.

The problem is that the pins and slots must be cut in a specific sequence so the grooves for the drawer bottom and the runners can be positioned properly.

## CUT STOCK TO SIZE

To make the tool cabinet drawers, I started by resawing ³/₄"-thick stock to ³/₈" for the drawer fronts, backs, and sides. Then I cut the pieces to finished length and width, making sure the ends were square.

**Note:** I usually cut the stock wider than necessary to allow for what I call "creep." If the slots and pins aren't exactly what they're supposed to be, the finished joint ends up slightly narrower or wider than I planned. In that case, I trim the pieces *after* cutting the box joints so the top and bottom pins are equal thickness. This is what I did for the tool cabinet.

But, the *drawers* for the tool cabinet must fit a specific opening. So I cut the pieces to final size and risked the width of the bottom pin being slightly off.

## CUT THE BOX JOINTS

After the stock is cut to size, mark the top edges of all pieces. Then the box joints can be cut on the table saw or on the router table.

The procedure is the same on both, but I used a straight bit in the router table to give me a flat-bottomed groove. (See the bottom of page 27 for tips on getting the same results using a dado blade in the table saw.)

**SET THE JIG.** To make sure the pins are cut to the correct length, set the bit height to the exact thickness of the stock. An easy way to gauge this is to lay a piece of stock on the base of the jig next to the bit.

**FRONT/BACK.** Before making cuts on the drawer pieces, you'll need to make a trial joint on two test pieces. Start by placing the top edge of the front/back test piece against the index key. Then rout the first slot *(Fig. 1)*. Now move the piece so the slot straddles the key and cut the next slot. Repeat until slots have been cut across the workpiece *(Fig. 2)*.

**CUT JOINTS IN SIDES.** Next, cut slots in a side test piece. This piece starts with a slot to mate with the pin on the front/back piece. To set the width of this slot, flip the front/back piece around and place it on the jig so its top pin is between the key and the bit *(Fig. 3)*.

Now press the top edge of the side piece tight against the front/back piece and cut the top notch in the side piece.

After the top notch is cut, remove the front/back piece and slide the side piece over so the just-cut notch is over the key. Then cut the remaining slots just as you did for the front/back piece.

**TEST FIT.** Now test the fit of this trial joint. It should be a friction fit — just loose enough to allow for swelling when the glue is applied. If the joint doesn't fit well, try the following adjustments.

**LOOSE JOINT.** For a loose joint, move the key *away* from the blade.

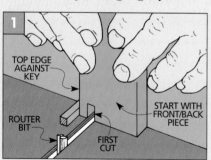

**1** — TOP EDGE AGAINST KEY / ROUTER BIT / FIRST CUT / START WITH FRONT/BACK PIECE

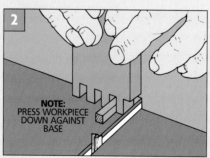

**2** — NOTE: PRESS WORKPIECE DOWN AGAINST BASE

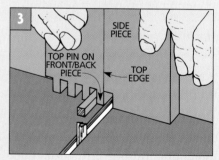

**3** — SIDE PIECE / TOP PIN ON FRONT/BACK PIECE / TOP EDGE

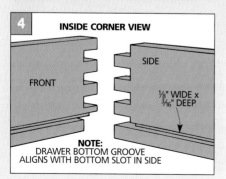

**4** — INSIDE CORNER VIEW / FRONT / SIDE / ¹/₈" WIDE x ³/₁₆" DEEP / NOTE: DRAWER BOTTOM GROOVE ALIGNS WITH BOTTOM SLOT IN SIDE

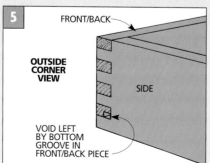

**5** — FRONT/BACK / OUTSIDE CORNER VIEW / SIDE / VOID LEFT BY BOTTOM GROOVE IN FRONT/BACK PIECE

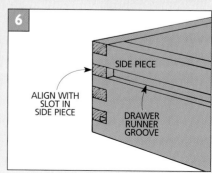

**6** — SIDE PIECE / ALIGN WITH SLOT IN SIDE PIECE / DRAWER RUNNER GROOVE

**TIGHT JOINT.** For a too-tight joint, move the key *toward* the blade.

**LONG PINS.** If the pins stand proud of the mating piece, lower the bit.

**SHORT PINS.** Pins that are too short mean you should raise the bit.

Once your test pieces fit well, you can cut the joints on the drawer pieces.

## CUT THE GROOVES

Once the joints are cut on the drawer parts, grooves are cut in all pieces to accept the bottom panel.

**BOTTOM GROOVE.** To make sure the groove doesn't show from the front of the drawer, set the rip fence so the saw blade aligns with the bottom edge of the bottom slot in a side piece *(Fig. 4)*. This way, when the groove is cut in the front piece, it will only be visible on the drawer's side *(Fig. 5)*.

After the saw fence is positioned, cut grooves in all four pieces.

**MAKE DRAWER BOTTOMS.** Now cut the bottoms out of ⅛" hardboard to fit between the bottoms of the grooves. Cut the bottom just a tad undersized so it doesn't get hung up during assembly.

**DRAWER RUNNER GROOVE.** Before assembly, the ³⁄₁₆"-deep grooves for the drawer runners are cut on the outer surface of the side pieces. To cut these grooves, adjust the fence so the blade aligns with the upper edge of the second slot on the side piece *(Fig. 6)*.

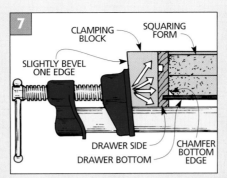

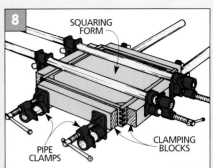

Now make the first pass on the outside face of each piece. Then widen the grooves by making repeated passes until the grooves are exactly the width of the slot.

## ASSEMBLY

Now the drawer can be assembled. To simplify this process, I used a "squaring form" and beveled clamping blocks.

**SQUARING FORM.** The squaring form is made from two pieces of plywood or particleboard cut to fit snug inside the drawer *(Fig. 7)*. This form keeps the sides from buckling in when the clamps are tightened. Rout a ¼" chamfer on the bottom edges so it doesn't get glued to the bottom panel or drawer sides.

**CLAMPING BLOCKS.** To make sure the clamping pressure is evenly distributed along the joints, I cut some beveled clamping blocks from scrap *(Fig. 7)*.

**ACTUAL ASSEMBLY.** To assemble the

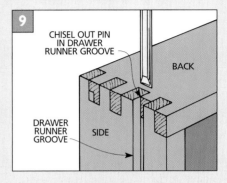

drawer, first brush glue on the pins and slots and join both side pieces to the drawer's back. Slide the bottom into place, then put the front in place.

With the squaring form inside, draw the clamps up tight *(Fig. 8)*.

**FINAL TOUCHES.** After the glue is dry, chisel out the pin blocking the rear of the runner groove *(Fig. 9)*.

Next, fill the voids in the sides (created by the grooves for the bottom). This can be done with a piece of scrap.

## BOX JOINTS ON THE TABLE SAW

Box joints cut on the router table have a nice, flat-bottomed slot. But it's not safe to cut slots larger than ⅜" by ⅜".

To cut larger box joints, you can use a dado blade in the table saw. However, these slots might require some "touch-up" for a tight fit.

The reason is that most dado blades don't cut a smooth-bottomed groove

(see photos). To get around this, cut in a scrap piece a dado the same width as the slots. Glue in a tongue with a piece

of self-adhesive sandpaper on it. The tongue should match the depth of the slots *(Fig. 10)*. Sand the bottoms flat.

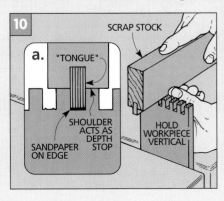

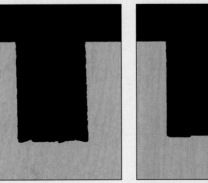

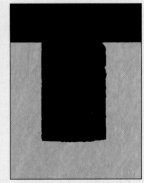

**RAGGED BOTTOM.** *The dado blade that cut this slot left a ragged bottom. Slight gaps would be visible across the width of each slot.*

**STEPPED BOTTOM.** *The outside corners of the slot are square, but the blade left a ridge in the middle. This would cause gaps at the outside of the slot.*

**CURVED BOTTOM.** *Cut by a wobble dado blade, this slot has a slight curve along the bottom. The joint will have a gap at the center of the slot.*

# Classic Workbench

*The base of this workbench offers more than just a solid foundation for the hard maple top.*
*An extra-wide drawer and two pull-out trays store a shop's worth of tools — all within easy reach.*

**M**ost shops can always use more storage space. So why not build a workbench where the base not only supports the top but also provides some valuable storage inside for your power and hand tools? That's the idea behind this workbench.

To make every inch of this storage space usable, a drawer and two trays ride on full-extension slides. This keeps all of your tools accessible.

**TOP.** Then there's the top. This laminated, hard maple top adds considerable weight to a storage cabinet already filled with tools. When you combine the two, you end up with a "rock-solid"

workbench capable of handling most any project you decide to take on.

**DRAWER AND TRAYS.** The drawer and trays make the bench a great place to store tools. The full-extension slides allow you access to even the back corners. The trays are joined together with rabbeted corners. On the drawer, you can exercise your craftsmanship with hand-cut dovetails.

**VISE.** To hold your projects on the bench, there's a metal woodworking vise attached to one corner with a thick, maple block covering the front jaw. A pair of dog holes in the block line up with the holes in the bench top so bench

dogs can be used to hold big projects. And the vise is easy to install. Just four lag screws hold it in place.

**FRAME AND PANEL.** The front and back of the bench's base (including the doors) consist of $\frac{1}{4}$" plywood panels held in frames. These front and rear frame assemblies are then joined with sturdy sides cut from $\frac{3}{4}$" plywood.

**MATERIALS.** I used solid cherry and cherry plywood to provide a contrast to the light maple used for the benchtop. *Woodsmith Project Supplies* offers a kit with all the hardware you need to make this bench (except the vise). See page 126 for more information.

# EXPLODED VIEW

**OVERALL DIMENSIONS:**
62W x 25¼D x 36H

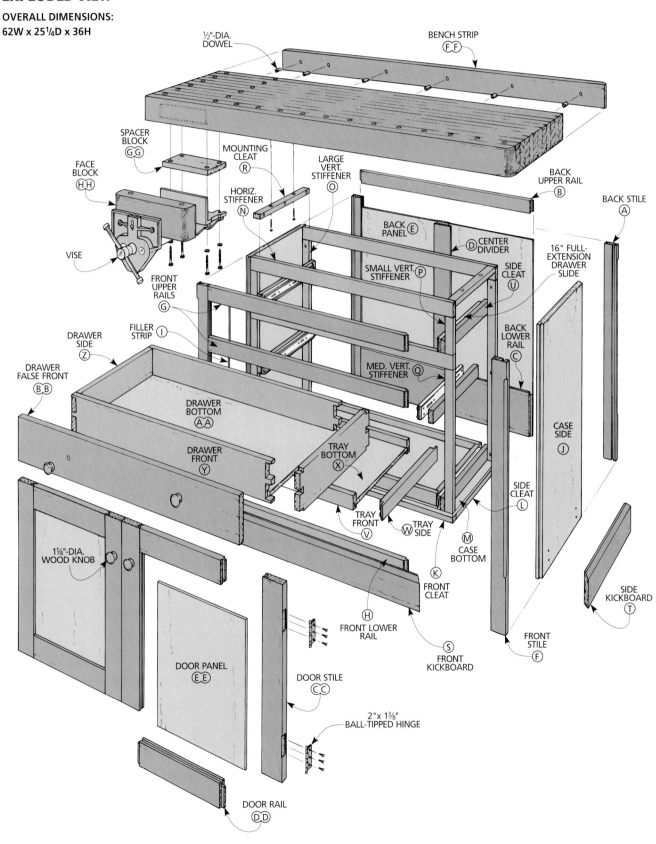

½"-DIA. DOWEL

BENCH STRIP
FF

SPACER BLOCK
GG

MOUNTING CLEAT
R

LARGE VERT. STIFFENER
O

BACK UPPER RAIL
B

BACK STILE
A

FACE BLOCK
HH

HORIZ. STIFFENER
N

BACK PANEL
E

CENTER DIVIDER
D

16" FULL-EXTENSION DRAWER SLIDE

VISE

SMALL VERT. STIFFENER
P

SIDE CLEAT
U

FRONT UPPER RAILS
G

BACK LOWER RAIL
C

FILLER STRIP
I

MED. VERT. STIFFENER
Q

DRAWER SIDE
Z

DRAWER FALSE FRONT
BB

DRAWER BOTTOM
AA

CASE SIDE
J

DRAWER FRONT
Y

TRAY BOTTOM
X

1¼"-DIA. WOOD KNOB

TRAY FRONT
V

TRAY SIDE
W

SIDE CLEAT
L

CASE BOTTOM
M

FRONT CLEAT
K

SIDE KICKBOARD
T

FRONT LOWER RAIL
H

FRONT KICKBOARD
S

FRONT STILE
F

DOOR PANEL
EE

DOOR STILE
CC

2"x 1⅜" BALL-TIPPED HINGE

DOOR RAIL
DD

# CUTTING DIAGRAM

¾ x 9 - 96 CHERRY (6 Bd. Ft.)

¾ x 7 - 96 MAPLE (4.7 Bd. Ft.)

¾ x 4 - 96 MAPLE (2.7 Bd. Ft.)

¾ x 6 - 96 MAPLE (4 Bd. Ft.)

¾ x 5 - 72 CHERRY (2.5 Bd. Ft.)

¾ x 7 - 72 CHERRY (3.5 Bd. Ft.)

¾ x 5 - 72 CHERRY (2.5 Bd. Ft.)

¾ x 6 - 72 CHERRY (3 Bd. Ft.)

1¾ x 5 - 96 MAPLE (6.7 Bd. Ft.)

1¾ x 8 - 72 MAPLE (6 Boards @ 7.5 Bd. Ft. ea.)

**ALSO NEED:**
¼" x 48" x 48"
CHERRY PLYWOOD

½" x 48" x 48"
MAPLE PLYWOOD

¾" x 48" x 48"
CHERRY PLYWOOD

RESAW TO
¾" THICKNESS

RESAW TO
¾" THICKNESS

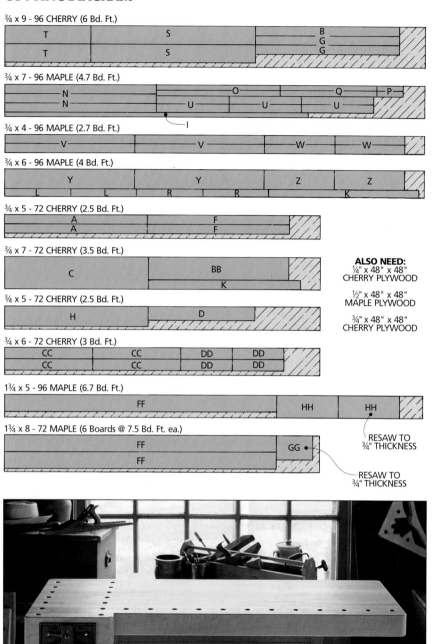

The cabinet for this workbench is a large wooden case consisting of two frames (front and rear) held together by a pair of plywood sides.

**REAR FRAME.** I started with the rear frame. It's just a pair of ¾"-thick stiles and rails that surround two ¼"-thick plywood panels and a center divider (*Fig. 1*). I cut the stiles (A) to size first.

## MATERIALS LIST

**CASE**

| | | |
|---|---|---|
| A | Back Stiles (2) | ¾ x 2 - 32½ |
| B | Back Upper Rail (1) | ¾ x 2 - 32¾ |
| C | Bk. Lower Rail (1) | ¾ x 6⅞ - 32¾ |
| D | Center Divider (1) | ¾ x 3 - 24⅜ |
| E | Back Panels (2) | ¼ ply - 15¼ x 24⅜ |
| F | Front Stiles (2) | ¾ x 2 - 32½ |
| G | Fr. Upper Rails (2) | ¾ x 2 - 32¾ |
| H | Fr. Lower Rail (1) | ¾ x 4⅜ - 32¾ |
| I | Filler Strips (1) | ¼ x ⅜ - 60 (rgh) |
| J | Case Sides (2) | ¾ ply - 17¼ x 32½ |
| K | Fr./Bk. Cleats (2) | ¾ x 1¼ - 34½ |
| L | Side Cleats (2) | ¾ x 1¼ - 14 |
| M | Case Bottom (1) | ½ ply - 16½ x 34½ |
| N | Horiz. Stiffeners (3) | ¾ x 2 - 34½ |
| O | Lg. Vert. Stfnrs. (2) | ¾ x 1¼ - 26⅛ |
| P | Sm. Vert. Stfnrs. (2) | ¾ x 1¼ - 5 |
| Q | Md. Vert. Stfnrs. (2) | ¾ x 1¼ - 19⅛ |
| R | Mntg. Cleats (2) | ¾ x 1¼ - 15 |
| S | Fr./Bk. Kickbds. (2) | ¾ x 4 - 37½ |
| T | Side Kickboards (2) | ¾ x 4 - 19½ |
| U | Slide Cleats (6) | ¾ x 1¾ - 16⁷⁄₁₆ |
| V | Tray Front/Back (4) | ¾ x 1¾ - 29 |
| W | Tray Sides (4) | ¾ x 1¾ - 16 |
| X | Tray Bottoms (2) | ½ ply - 15¼ x 28¾ |
| Y | Drawer Fr./Bk. (2) | ¾ x 4⅜ - 29½ |
| Z | Drawer Sides (2) | ¾ x 4⅜ - 16 |
| AA | Drawer Bottom (1) | ½ ply - 15¼ x 28¾ |
| BB | Dwr. False Front (1) | ¾ x 4⅞ - 31⅞ |
| CC | Door Stiles (4) | ¾ x 2½ - 19⅛ |
| DD | Door Rails (4) | ¾ x 2½ - 11¾ |
| EE | Door Panels (2) | ¼ ply - 11¾ x 14⅞ |

**BENCH TOP**

| | | |
|---|---|---|
| FF | Bench Strips (13) | 1¾ x 3⁹⁄₁₆ - 62 |
| GG | Spacer Block (1) | ¾ x 5 - 9 |
| HH | Face Block (1) | 2½ x 4⅝ - 14 |

## HARDWARE SUPPLIES

(8) No. 4 x ½" Fh woodscrews
(16) No. 8 x 1" Fh woodscrews
(36) No. 8 x 1¼" Fh woodscrews
(20) No. 8 x 1¾" Fh woodscrews
(2) No. 14 x 2" Rh woodscrews
(4) ¼" x 3" lag screws
(4) ½" x 3" lag screws
(4) ¼" washers
(4) ½" washers
(3) ½" dowel x 48"
(3 pr.) 16" full-extension drawer slides
(4) 1¼"-dia. wood knobs
(2 pr.) 2" x 1⅜" ball-tipped hinges
(2) Ball catches
(1) Record No. 52½ ED vise

Next, cut a couple of grooves in each one. The first (centered on the edge) holds the plywood panels and the stub tenons on the rails *(Figs. 1 and 1a)*. A second groove on the inside face holds a $3/8$"-long tongue cut on the case side.

Once the grooves are complete, the upper rail (B) and lower rail (C) can be cut. Both rails are the same length, have a $3/8$" stub tenon cut on each end and a groove cut in one edge. The only difference is their widths. The upper rail is 2" wide. The lower rail is $6^7/8$".

I dry-assembled the stiles and rails next to measure the opening for a center divider and two plywood panels.

The center divider (D) is just a 3"-wide piece of stock with stub tenons on the ends and a groove on each edge *(Fig. 1b)*. It fits between the upper and lower rails and splits the opening in half.

To find the size of the back panels (E), measure between the frame pieces and center divider and add $3/4$" for the grooves *(Fig. 1)*. Then glue and clamp the panels and frame pieces together.

**FRONT FRAME.** Like the back frame, the front frame is built with stiles and rails. But you won't need the plywood panels. Instead, the frame pieces create openings for a drawer and two doors.

Once again, there's a pair of identical stiles (F) with grooves on one edge and on the inside face *(Fig. 1)*. But instead of two rails, the front frame has three.

There's a pair of identical upper rails (G) with stub tenons on the ends. They frame the drawer opening. There's also a lower rail (H) cut to the same length,

but it's wider. Since there are no panels, you don't need grooves on the rails. Just glue the front frame together *(Fig. 1)*.

But the grooves in the stiles between the rails need to be filled. So I added small filler strips (I) *(Fig. 2)*.

With the front and back frames complete, a pair of case sides (J) are cut next *(Fig. 3)*. These are just $3/4$"-thick pieces

of plywood with $3/8$" rabbets cut on both long edges. Each rabbet forms a tongue that fits into the groove already cut in the stile *(Fig. 3a)*.

Then glue and clamp the sides and frames together to assemble the case.

**CHAMFER STILES.** Next, to ease the sharp edges, I routed stopped chamfers on all four corners *(Fig. 4)*.

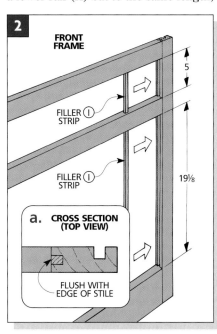

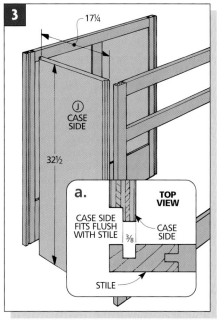

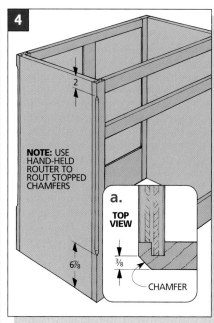

Next, I turned my attention to the inside of the case, starting at the bottom and working my way up.

**CLEATS.** First, I cut a pair of front and back cleats (K) and a pair of side cleats (L) to fit inside the case *(Fig. 5)*. These 1¼"-wide cleats are positioned so the case bottom (added next) will fit flush with the top edge of the lower rail on the front frame *(Fig. 5a)*. To help position the cleats properly, I used a simple trick. To hold them at the proper height, I cut a spacer to rest them on while I drilled the screw holes.

**BOTTOM.** After the four cleats are installed, the case bottom (M) can be cut to size *(Fig. 5)*. This piece of ½"-thick plywood rests on the cleats and helps strengthen the cabinet once the plywood is glued and screwed in place.

**STIFFENERS.** On most projects, I'd be finished with the cabinet once the bottom was installed. But not here. Instead, to make the case stronger, I added horizontal and vertical frame stiffeners (N, O, P, Q).

These ¾"-thick pieces of maple do two things. First, the horizontal stiffeners lap over the joint lines where a rail meets a stile *(Fig. 7)*. It's an easy way to strengthen the stub tenon joints. And second, the stiffeners provide more bulk for the frame so it resists racking.

I started by cutting three horizontal stiffeners (N) to fit inside the top of the case *(Fig. 6)*. Two of them fit behind the top rails on the front frame *(Fig. 6a)*. The third is glued to the top rail of the back frame. These stiffeners are ripped to match the width of the top rails.

Next, I added the vertical stiffeners. First, the long vertical stiffeners (O) are glued and screwed to the back two corners of the case between the horizontal

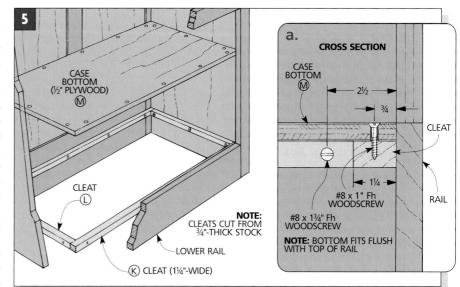

**5**

CASE BOTTOM (½" PLYWOOD) Ⓜ

CLEAT Ⓛ

LOWER RAIL

Ⓚ CLEAT (1¼"-WIDE)

**NOTE:** CLEATS CUT FROM ¾"-THICK STOCK

**a.** CROSS SECTION

CASE BOTTOM Ⓜ

2½

¾

CLEAT

RAIL

1¼

#8 x 1" Fh WOODSCREW

#8 x 1¾" Fh WOODSCREW

**NOTE:** BOTTOM FITS FLUSH WITH TOP OF RAIL

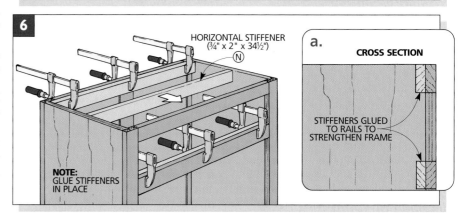

**6**

HORIZONTAL STIFFENER (¾" x 2" x 34½") Ⓝ

**NOTE:** GLUE STIFFENERS IN PLACE

**a.** CROSS SECTION

STIFFENERS GLUED TO RAILS TO STRENGTHEN FRAME

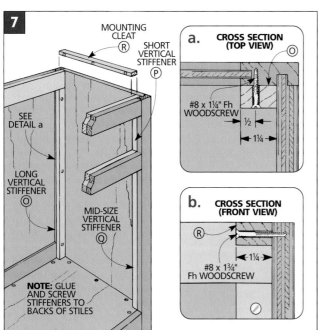

**7**

MOUNTING CLEAT Ⓡ

SHORT VERTICAL STIFFENER Ⓟ

SEE DETAIL a

LONG VERTICAL STIFFENER Ⓞ

MID-SIZE VERTICAL STIFFENER Ⓠ

**NOTE:** GLUE AND SCREW STIFFENERS TO BACKS OF STILES

**a.** CROSS SECTION (TOP VIEW) Ⓞ

#8 x 1¼" Fh WOODSCREW

½

1¼

**b.** CROSS SECTION (FRONT VIEW)

Ⓡ

1¼

#8 x 1¾" Fh WOODSCREW

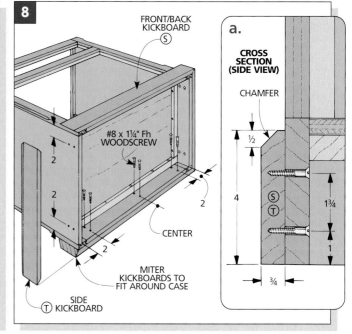

**8**

FRONT/BACK KICKBOARD Ⓢ

#8 x 1¼" Fh WOODSCREW

2

2

2

CENTER

2

MITER KICKBOARDS TO FIT AROUND CASE

SIDE Ⓣ KICKBOARD

**a.** CROSS SECTION (SIDE VIEW)

CHAMFER

½

4

Ⓢ Ⓣ

1¾

1

¾

stiffener and the case bottom *(Figs. 7 and 7a)*. Short vertical stiffeners (P) fit along the sides of the drawer opening between the horizontal stiffeners. And finally, two mid-size stiffeners (Q) are glued and screwed behind the front frame alongside the door openings.

**MOUNTING CLEATS.** Now to hold the top in place later, I added a pair of mounting cleats (R) *(Figs. 7 and 7b)*. These are just ³⁄₄"-thick pieces of stock glued and screwed flush with the tops of the case sides.

**KICKBOARD.** To complete the case, all that's left is to install a kickboard around the bottom.

First, I cut the stock to its finished width (4"). Next I routed a ¹⁄₂" chamfer along the top edge *(Fig. 8a)*. Then the front/back kickboards (S) and side kickboards (T) are mitered to fit around the base and are glued and screwed in place *(Figs. 8 and 8a)*.

**Note:** Start with the front kickboard, then add the sides before attaching the back piece. This allows you to get the best fitting miters up front.

## TRAYS

A wide drawer at the top and a pair of pull-out trays behind the doors provide plenty of storage space in the cabinet. I started work on the trays next.

**CLEATS.** I planned on using full-extension slides for the drawer and trays. That way, every inch of them would be accessible. But the slides couldn't be screwed to the case sides because the frame stiffeners got in the way. So I added slide cleats (U) to provide a mounting surface for the slides *(Fig. 9)*.

These cleats are ³⁄₄"-thick pieces of stock screwed to the frame stiffeners. The cleats don't extend all the way to the front of the case, though. If they did,

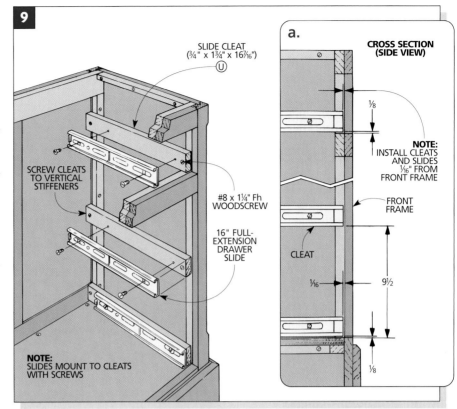

**9**

SLIDE CLEAT
(³⁄₄" x 1³⁄₄" x 16⁷⁄₁₆")
U

SCREW CLEATS
TO VERTICAL
STIFFENERS

#8 x 1¹⁄₄" Fh
WOODSCREW

16" FULL-
EXTENSION
DRAWER
SLIDE

**NOTE:**
SLIDES MOUNT TO CLEATS
WITH SCREWS

**a.**
CROSS SECTION
(SIDE VIEW)

¹⁄₈

**NOTE:**
INSTALL CLEATS
AND SLIDES
¹⁄₁₆" FROM
FRONT FRAME

FRONT
FRAME

CLEAT

¹⁄₁₆   9¹⁄₂

¹⁄₈

the doors and drawer wouldn't close fully *(Fig. 9a)*. To get the needed clearance, I installed the cleats ¹⁄₁₆" back from the inside face of the front frame.

**TRAYS.** With the cleats installed in the case, I started building the trays. I decided to use pull-out trays in the bottom of the cabinet because it makes it a lot easier to get at your tools — especially the ones at the back.

To find the size of the front/back tray pieces, first measure the opening between the cleats (mine was 30¹⁄₂"). Then subtract 1" for the thickness of two slides and ¹⁄₂" for the lap joints at the corners. Determining the size of the tray sides is easier. It matches the length of your slides (16").

I used these measurements to cut the tray front/back (V) and sides (W) to finished size *(Fig. 10)*. (My tray was 16" deep and 29¹⁄₂" wide.) Next, I cut ³⁄₄"-wide rabbets at both ends of the sides for the lap joints that join the tray pieces *(Fig. 10a)*. Then ³⁄₈"-deep grooves can be routed on the inside faces of all the tray pieces to hold a ¹⁄₂" plywood bottom *(Fig. 10b)*. (When the tray is assembled, the half-laps cover the grooves in the front/back pieces.)

Usually, I use ¹⁄₄"-thick material for a drawer bottom. But making the tray bottom (X) from ¹⁄₂" plywood keeps it from sagging when loaded with tools. It should fit snug in the tray pieces before you glue the tray together.

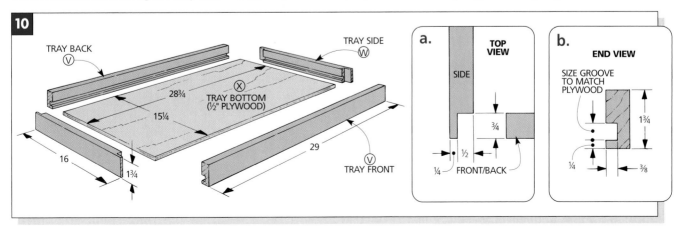

**10**

TRAY BACK
V

TRAY SIDE
W

28³⁄₄   TRAY BOTTOM
(¹⁄₂" PLYWOOD)   X

15¹⁄₄

16   1³⁄₄

29

TRAY FRONT
V

**a.**   TOP
VIEW

SIDE

³⁄₄

¹⁄₂

¹⁄₄   FRONT/BACK

**b.**   END VIEW

SIZE GROOVE
TO MATCH
PLYWOOD

1³⁄₄

¹⁄₄   ³⁄₈

With the trays complete, the drawer is built next. It has hand-cut dovetails for strength and durability.

First, measure the opening. The length of the front/back pieces (Y) will be $2\frac{1}{2}$" less than the drawer opening's width. The length of the sides (Z) is the same as the tray sides (W) (16"). Cut the drawer pieces to size and lay out and cut the dovetails *(Figs. 11 and 11a)*. (The Shop Jig box below shows how to build and use a guide to help you accurately cut dovetails.)

Now rout a groove for a $\frac{1}{2}$"-thick plywood drawer bottom *(Fig. 11b)*. Then cut the bottom (AA) to fit and glue the drawer together.

You'll probably notice the groove cut for the drawer bottom is still visible on the drawer front. But don't worry. It'll be hidden by a false front added later.

**SLIDE INSTALLATION.** The next step is to install the full-extension drawer slides. I used a pair of 16" slides for the drawer and for each tray. (Hardware sources are listed on page 126.)

Installing the slides is a two-step process. First, one half of the slide is

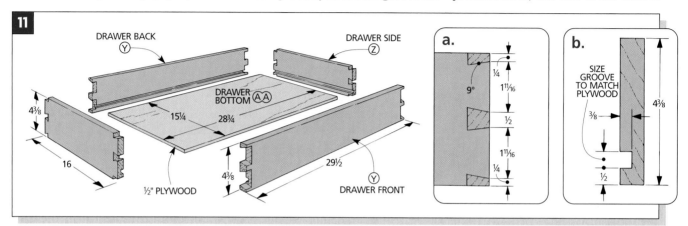

**11**

DRAWER BACK (Y)
DRAWER SIDE (Z)
DRAWER BOTTOM (AA)
$4\frac{3}{8}$
$15\frac{1}{4}$
$28\frac{3}{4}$
16
$\frac{1}{2}$" PLYWOOD
$4\frac{3}{8}$
$29\frac{1}{2}$
DRAWER FRONT (Y)

**a.**
$9°$
$\frac{1}{4}$
$1\frac{11}{16}$
$\frac{1}{2}$
$1\frac{11}{16}$
$\frac{1}{4}$

**b.**
SIZE GROOVE TO MATCH PLYWOOD
$\frac{3}{8}$
$4\frac{3}{8}$
$\frac{1}{2}$

## SHOP JIG ............................................. *Dovetail Jig*

This two-piece jig helps keep the saw aligned with the layout lines when making the cuts on a dovetail joint. There's a block to guide the saw, and a clamping bar to hold the jig in place.

Once you've decided on the dovetail angle (I used 9° for the drawer on the workbench), it's easy to build the jig. Start with the guide block *(Fig. 1)*. Both the sides and kerfs use the same angle. The block is beveled on the sides for cutting the tails. And it has two angled kerfs for cutting the pins.

Then glue and screw the guide block to the clamping bar *(Fig. 2)*. But don't cut off the waste just yet. It keeps all the pieces of the guide block positioned correctly on the clamping bar until the glue is completely dry.

To use the jig, first lay out the tails and pins on your workpieces. Then clamp the jig to the end of a workpiece and start on the pins *(Fig. 3)*. Just make sure the saw blade stays tight against the guide block.

You cut the tails on the mating piece the same way. Except this time, you'll press the saw blade against the bevel on the side of the block to help keep the saw at the proper angle *(Fig. 4)*.

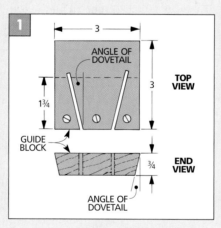

**1**
3
ANGLE OF DOVETAIL
3
$1\frac{3}{4}$
GUIDE BLOCK
TOP VIEW
END VIEW
$\frac{3}{4}$
ANGLE OF DOVETAIL

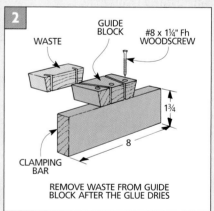

**2**
WASTE
GUIDE BLOCK
#8 x $1\frac{1}{4}$" Fh WOODSCREW
$1\frac{3}{4}$
8
CLAMPING BAR
REMOVE WASTE FROM GUIDE BLOCK AFTER THE GLUE DRIES

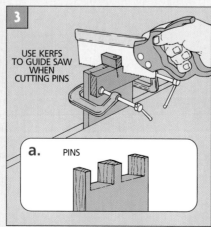

**3**
USE KERFS TO GUIDE SAW WHEN CUTTING PINS
**a.** PINS

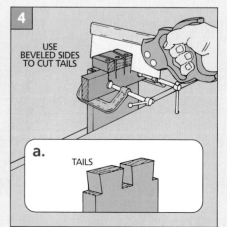

**4**
USE BEVELED SIDES TO CUT TAILS
**a.** TAILS

screwed to the slide cleat (U) in the case (refer to *Fig. 9* on page 33). Then the other half is mounted to the drawer or tray *(Figs. 12 and 12a)*. (For more about full-extension slides, see Shop Info on page 86.)

**FALSE FRONT.** After the drawer is installed in the case, a false front (BB) is added. This is just a ³⁄₄"-thick piece of stock that fits in the case with ¹⁄₁₆" clearance all around *(Fig. 13a)*.

Before screwing the false front to the drawer, I drilled a pair of ¹⁄₂"-dia. holes for some wood knobs *(Fig. 13)*. Then install the false front, and glue the knobs in the holes.

## DOORS

The last thing to add to the cabinet is a set of doors. The doors are cut to fit tight, then are trimmed for clearance.

The goal here is to have ¹⁄₁₆" of clearance around each edge of the doors *(Fig. 15)*. You also need the same clearance between the doors. So I measured the opening in the frame first (19¹⁄₈" x 32") and then cut the stiles (CC) and rails (DD) for a tight fit *(Fig. 14)*. But remember to allow for the tenons when cutting the rails to length.

Next, a groove is routed in each frame piece to match the thickness of the center panel *(Fig. 14a)*. And to hold the frame together, tenons are cut on

the ends of the rails to fit snug in the grooves *(Fig. 14b)*. Then a door panel (EE) is cut to fit in each frame before gluing the door together.

After the doors are assembled, you can trim them for the ¹⁄₁₆" clearance.

Now hinges can be installed on each

door by mortising them into the front frame and door stiles *(Figs. 14 and 15)*. While installing the doors, I used pennies for spacers *(Figs. 15a and 15b)*.

Finally, a pair of knobs is attached to the doors. And ball catches are installed in the cabinet to hold the doors closed.

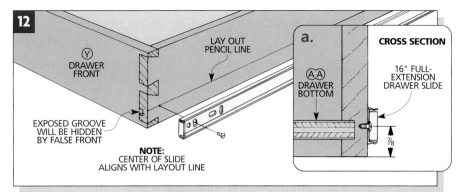

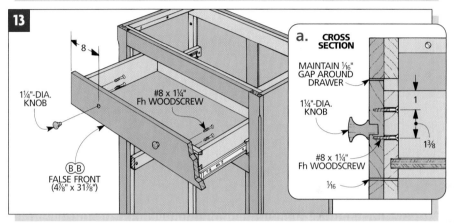

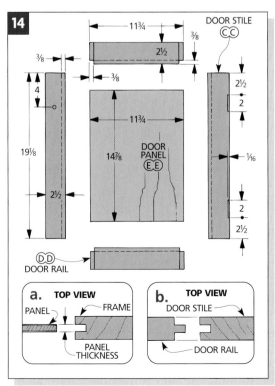

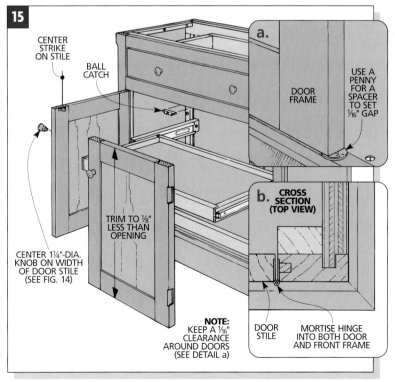

After the cabinet was completed, I started work on the bench top.

**Note:** For details on building laminated tops, refer to page 38.

**STRIPS.** This laminated top consists of 13 bench top strips (FF). These strips are 1¾"-thick pieces of stock cut to a finished length of 62" and a rough width of 3⁹⁄₁₆" (*Fig. 16*).

**ALIGNMENT HOLES.** To keep all the strips aligned when gluing them up, I drilled holes for short lengths of ½"-dia. dowels (*Figs. 16 and 16a*). But remember, the two outside strips only have holes on one face.

**DOG HOLES.** Before gluing the bench top strips together, there are still a few things left to do.

First, drill a series of ¾"-dia. dog holes in the top (*Fig. 16b*). (Shop Info on page 37 has more about bench dogs.) Then rout a ⅛" chamfer around each hole to soften the edges.

**ROUNDOVER.** Next, three of the corners on the outside strips are rounded over (*Figs. 16 and 16c*).

**Note:** Don't round the corner at the end where the vise will be mounted.

**NOTCH.** Now before gluing the top together, rout and chisel a pocket in the front bench top strip for mounting a metal vise. After the top is assembled, the back jaw of the vise slips into this pocket (*Figs. 17 and 20*).

**GLUE-UP.** With the pocket routed, the bench top strips can be glued together (*Fig. 18*). Later, I used a belt sander to sand the top and bottom faces smooth and to final width (3½").

**BENCH TOP INSTALLATION.** Once the top is sanded, it can be attached to the cabinet. But first I routed a ⅛" chamfer on the bottom edge (*Fig. 19*). Then center the top side-to-side with a 1¼" overhang on the back (*Fig. 19a*). Now drill shank holes through the cleats in the cabinet and use 3" lag screws with washers to hold the bench top in place.

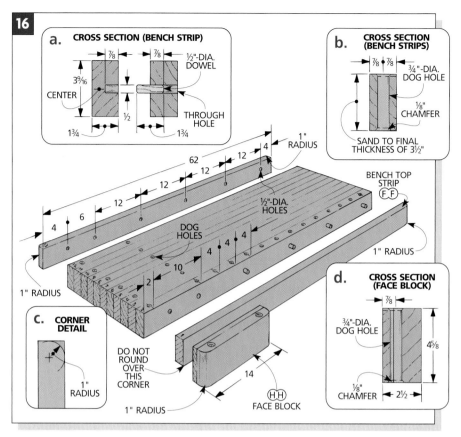

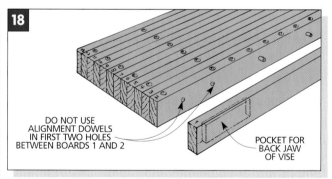

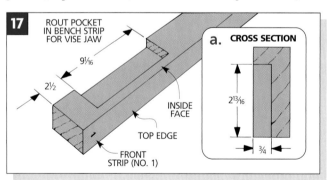

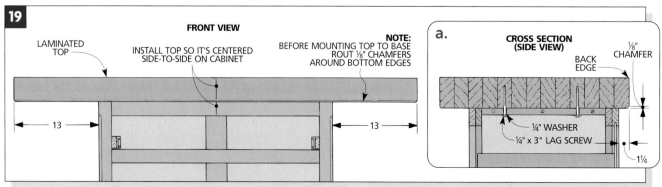

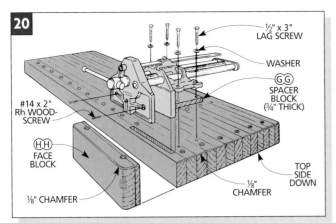

**20**

½" x 3" LAG SCREW

WASHER

G G SPACER BLOCK (¾" THICK)

#14 x 2" Rh WOOD SCREW

H H FACE BLOCK

⅛" CHAMFER

⅛" CHAMFER

TOP SIDE DOWN

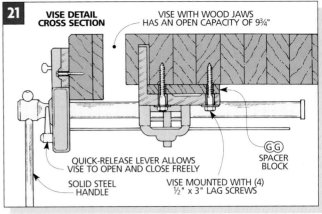

**21**

VISE DETAIL CROSS SECTION

VISE WITH WOOD JAWS HAS AN OPEN CAPACITY OF 9¾"

QUICK-RELEASE LEVER ALLOWS VISE TO OPEN AND CLOSE FREELY

SOLID STEEL HANDLE

VISE MOUNTED WITH (4) ½" x 3" LAG SCREWS

G G SPACER BLOCK

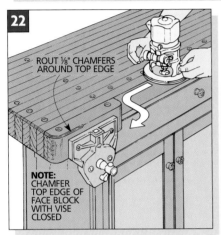

**22**

ROUT ⅛" CHAMFERS AROUND TOP EDGE

NOTE: CHAMFER TOP EDGE OF FACE BLOCK WITH VISE CLOSED

## VISE

With the top secured to the cabinet, the vise can be installed next. (I used a Record vise, model #52½ ED. See page 126 for sources.)

**VISE INSTALLATION.** Before installing the vise, I added a spacer block (GG) to make the top of the face block (added next) level with the bench top. This ¾"-thick piece of stock is cut to match the mounting plate on the vise (*Fig. 21*). Then drill ½"-dia. holes through the spacer block and screw the block and vise to the bench top.

**FACE BLOCK.** After installing the vise, I covered the front jaw with a thick maple block.

To make the face block (HH), glue together a couple pieces of stock to create a 2½"-thick laminated piece (*Figs. 21 and 16d*). Then drill two ¾"-dia. dog holes in the face block and round over the two outside corners. Now rout a ⅛" chamfer on the bottom edge and attach the face block to the vise (*Fig. 21*).

To complete the bench top, I routed a ⅛" chamfer around the top edge (including the vise) (*Fig. 22*). ■

---

## SHOP INFO .................................... Bench Dogs

One way to improve the versatility of a workbench is to add holdfasts and bench dogs. These fit into the ¾"-dia. holes drilled in the bench top.

Holdfasts secure items down on the bench (see left photo). Bench dogs clamp your work from the sides (see middle and right photos). This allows you to work on the entire work surface (like for planing). Brass bench dogs are easier on plane blades and chisels. See page 126 for sources of these items.

**Holdfast.** *A holdfast is one of the simplest ways to secure a workpiece to a bench. (The one pictured holds stock up to 4" thick.) Simply drive the head down to jamb the holdfast into the hole, and it won't let up until you dislodge it with a sideways tap.*

**Bench Dog.** *Bench dogs are used with a woodworking vise. Some bench dogs are square, but these are round (see photo at right also). Press the dog into a hole and a thin metal spring presses against the side of the hole to keep the dog at a specific height.*

**Wonder Dog.** *A Wonder Dog is like a bench dog with a vise built in. The body is round, but it also has a 6"-long steel thread attached to a brass head, so you can apply pressure just like a vise or a clamp. As shown here, it can be used in place of an end vise.*

# TECHNIQUE ......... *Laminated Top*

**B**uilding a laminated top may seem a little intimidating at first. But with a few tricks, it's easy to lay out the boards and glue them together without any gaps.

## LAYOUT

Like drawing and discarding playing cards to get a better hand, the boards need to be sorted for the best fit and appearance. Start by checking for crook and bow.

**CROOK.** The crook of a board can cause you more trouble than its bow. So check for crook first.

Crook is warpage across the width of a board running from end-to-end *(Fig. 1* and the Shop Tip below). It can be difficult to straighten a crooked board. So if there's more than 1/8" of crook, I'll cut it into shorter pieces for another project.

Boards with less than 1/8" of crook can be used — if they've been sorted first. I arrange them so the crooks oppose each other *(Fig. 1)*. This way when the pieces are forced flat, the crook is canceled. To keep track of the direction as I'm sorting, I'll mark an arrow on each board pointing to the high side of the crook *(Fig. 1)*.

**BOW.** Next, you can sort the boards to minimize bow. Bow is warpage along the edge from end-to-end *(Fig. 2)*. Unlike crooked boards, you can usually straighten a bowed board.

Here again, arrange your boards so the bows oppose each other. I put my straightest boards on the outside to help pull the rest of the bowed pieces straight.

**Note:** While rearranging the boards for bow, remember to keep the crooks opposed.

**APPEARANCE.** With the pieces sorted for crook and bow, you still need to consider how the boards will look when glued together. Small blemishes will be sanded out when the top is leveled. But for larger defects you should shuffle the boards again.

**LABEL PIECES.** Once you have the boards arranged, dry-clamp them together *(Fig. 3)*. Then number the pieces along one end. After all, you want to be sure you can get them back together correctly.

I'll also mark an arrow next to the number. This arrow points to the face that fits in an alignment jig used to drill guide holes. (This jig is built next.)

**Note:** The arrow on the last board (No. 13) points to the opposite face from the others. That's because the holes in this piece must be drilled from the opposite side.

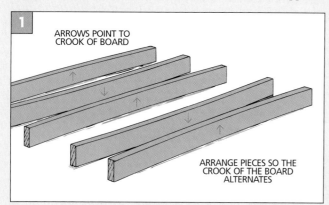

**1**
ARROWS POINT TO CROOK OF BOARD
ARRANGE PIECES SO THE CROOK OF THE BOARD ALTERNATES

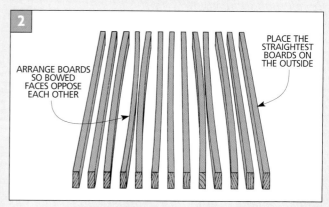

**2**
ARRANGE BOARDS SO BOWED FACES OPPOSE EACH OTHER
PLACE THE STRAIGHTEST BOARDS ON THE OUTSIDE

## SHOP TIP ...... *Measuring Crook*

A simple way to measure crook is to use a string and some tape.

Just stretch the string from end-to-end and tape it in place. Then at the center, measure the gap between the string and the board.

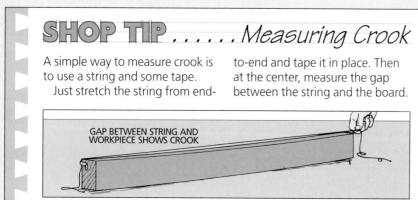

GAP BETWEEN STRING AND WORKPIECE SHOWS CROOK

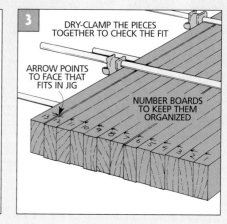

**3**
DRY-CLAMP THE PIECES TOGETHER TO CHECK THE FIT
ARROW POINTS TO FACE THAT FITS IN JIG
NUMBER BOARDS TO KEEP THEM ORGANIZED

It can be a challenge keeping your boards aligned during glue-up. Splines or biscuits can help. But I prefer to use short pieces of dowel to help keep the top flat and the ends aligned.

**DRILLING JIG.** To drill the dowel holes, I made a simple jig. It fits over the workpiece so I could drill accurate "starter holes" with a hand drill. Then the workpiece is moved to the drill press where the holes are made large enough to hold the dowels. Drilling starter holes first ensures the dowel holes in each workpiece will be aligned. Plus, they help guide the larger drill bit.

The jig consists of three pieces: a guide block with $1/16$"-dia. guide holes, a top cap, and an end cap (*Fig. 4*).

**USING THE JIG.** To use this jig, it needs to be clamped to your workpiece. To do this, position the jig against the face indicated by the arrow on the top edge, keeping the numbered end tight against the end cap (*Fig. 5*). Now clamp the top cap first. This forces the jig to follow any crook in the board. Once that's done, clamp the jig to the face of the workpiece.

Next, drill the $1/16$"-dia. starter holes in each piece (*Fig. 5a*).

**Note:** The jig fits on the same side of all pieces except the last one (No. 13).

**DOWEL HOLES.** With the guide holes drilled, the dowel holes are drilled next. I used a $1/2$"-dia. brad point bit in the drill press (*Figs. 6 and 6a*). Just make sure the dowels you plan on using fit snug in the holes bored by the bit.

**Note:** The dowel holes in the first and last boards (1 and 13) don't go all the way through.

**GLUE-UP.** Gluing up a laminated top isn't hard. It just takes a lot of glue and a little muscle. A trick I'll use is to glue up the top in sections instead of trying to do the whole thing at once (*Fig. 7*).

The goal is to join two halves. To do that, I'll glue together smaller segments (the three or four outside boards) first. Since these are my straightest boards (they were sorted that way), they form a straight base to build on. Then put a liberal amount of glue on one face of each board, insert the dowels, and clamp the sections together (see the photo on the opposite page).

With the first sections dry, add more boards to both sections until you have two halves. Finally, glue these halves together to complete the top (*Fig. 8*).

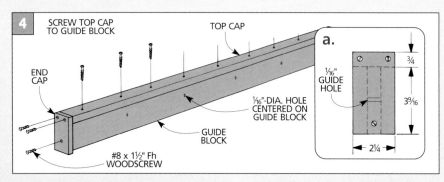

4 SCREW TOP CAP TO GUIDE BLOCK · TOP CAP · END CAP · $1/16$"-DIA. HOLE CENTERED ON GUIDE BLOCK · GUIDE BLOCK · #8 x $1\frac{1}{2}$" Fh WOODSCREW

a. $1/16$" GUIDE HOLE · $3/4$ · $3\frac{9}{16}$ · $2\frac{1}{4}$

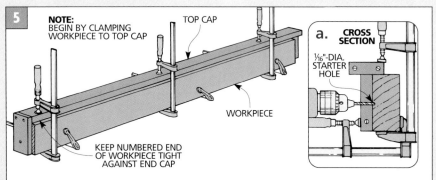

5 **NOTE:** BEGIN BY CLAMPING WORKPIECE TO TOP CAP · TOP CAP · WORKPIECE · KEEP NUMBERED END OF WORKPIECE TIGHT AGAINST END CAP

a. **CROSS SECTION** · $1/16$"-DIA. STARTER HOLE

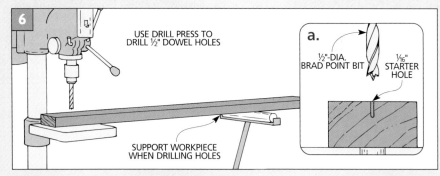

6 USE DRILL PRESS TO DRILL $1/2$" DOWEL HOLES · SUPPORT WORKPIECE WHEN DRILLING HOLES

a. $1/2$"-DIA. BRAD POINT BIT · $1/16$" STARTER HOLE

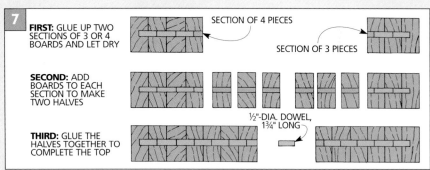

7 **FIRST:** GLUE UP TWO SECTIONS OF 3 OR 4 BOARDS AND LET DRY · SECTION OF 4 PIECES · SECTION OF 3 PIECES

**SECOND:** ADD BOARDS TO EACH SECTION TO MAKE TWO HALVES

**THIRD:** GLUE THE HALVES TOGETHER TO COMPLETE THE TOP · $1/2$"-DIA. DOWEL, $1\frac{3}{4}$" LONG

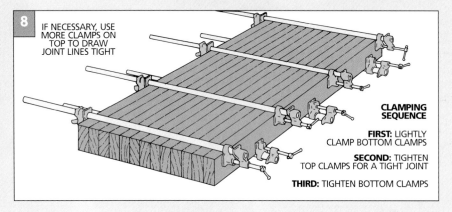

8 IF NECESSARY, USE MORE CLAMPS ON TOP TO DRAW JOINT LINES TIGHT

**CLAMPING SEQUENCE**

**FIRST:** LIGHTLY CLAMP BOTTOM CLAMPS

**SECOND:** TIGHTEN TOP CLAMPS FOR A TIGHT JOINT

**THIRD:** TIGHTEN BOTTOM CLAMPS

# STORAGE CABINETS

**S**torage cabinets don't have to hold every tool and accessory you own. In fact, they can be more efficient if you design cabinets for specific purposes.

The hardware storage cabinet takes up a minimal amount of floor space, and offers many shallow drawers with optional dividers to organize your hardware and small tools.

The drill bit cabinet is also a space saver, with tilt-out trays and an optional drawer. And you can keep all your blades in order with the simple saw blade storage cabinet.

The drafting cabinet has a tilt-down drawing surface and an optional bulletin board and storage rack inside. Finally, the mobile finishing cabinet combines several storage features with a convenient turntable work surface.

# Hardware Storage Cabinet

*It doesn't take up much floor space, but this cabinet will provide plenty of storage for your hardware. And the drawer sizes, positions, and dividers can all be customized to fit your individual needs.*

One day as I was going through my monthly "clean everything in the shop" routine, I was getting frustrated with little plastic drawers that don't hold enough, and big workbench drawers that force me to pile tools on top of tools. I needed a better way to store and organize small tools and pieces of hardware.

I decided to build this Hardware Storage Cabinet. It takes up less than two square feet of floor space (about the same as a three-drawer file cabinet), yet there's almost 13 square feet of storage.

**DRAWERS.** The cabinet shown here has 12 drawers: six small, five medium, and one large. However, the size and number of the drawers can be altered to suit your needs. A medium-size drawer takes up exactly twice the space of a small drawer. And a large drawer is a little taller than one medium plus one small drawer.

Actually, if I were to build another cabinet, I'd alter the measurements to replace the large drawer with three small ones (these small drawers are really handy for all sorts of things). But you might want a different combination, depending on what you're storing.

**MULTIPLE CUTS.** Also, these drawers are designed to take full advantage of multiple cutting techniques. Once you make a setting for one drawer, it's the same on all the drawers (no matter what size they are).

**DIVIDERS.** If you'd like to separate your hardware even more, you can build a series of dividers and mini-dividers that can be moved or removed as your needs change. For details, see the Designer's Notebook on page 47.

**MATERIALS.** The dimensions of the drawers allow you to cut all the pieces from standard construction lumber (1x4s and 1x8s) with very little waste (see the Cutting Diagram on the opposite page). ³⁄₄" plywood and ¹⁄₄" hardboard are also used for the cabinet.

## EXPLODED VIEW

**OVERALL DIMENSIONS:**
$16^7/_8$W x $15^1/_2$D x 35H

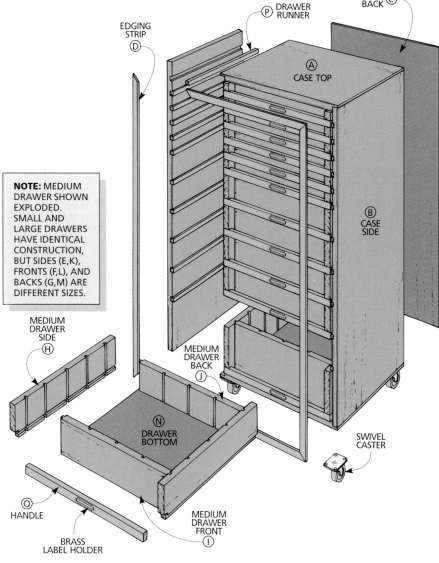

CASE BACK (C)

DRAWER RUNNER (P)

EDGING STRIP (D)

CASE TOP (A)

CASE SIDE (B)

MEDIUM DRAWER SIDE (H)

MEDIUM DRAWER BACK (J)

DRAWER BOTTOM (N)

MEDIUM DRAWER FRONT (I)

HANDLE (O)

BRASS LABEL HOLDER

SWIVEL CASTER

**NOTE:** MEDIUM DRAWER SHOWN EXPLODED. SMALL AND LARGE DRAWERS HAVE IDENTICAL CONSTRUCTION, BUT SIDES (E,K), FRONTS (F,L), AND BACKS (G,M) ARE DIFFERENT SIZES.

### MATERIALS LIST

**CASE**

| | | |
|---|---|---|
| **A** | Top/Bottom (2) | $3/_4$ ply - $15^1/_4$ x $16^7/_8$ |
| **B** | Sides (2) | $3/_4$ ply - $15^1/_2$ x $34^1/_2$ |
| **C** | Case Back (1) | $1/_4$ hdbd. - $34^1/_2$ x $16^7/_8$ |
| **D** | Edging Strips (4) | $1/_2$ x cut to fit |

**DRAWERS**

| | | |
|---|---|---|
| **E** | Small Sides (12) | $3/_4$ x $1^{11}/_{16}$ - $15^1/_4$ |
| **F** | Small Fronts (6) | $3/_4$ x $1^{11}/_{16}$ - $14^1/_4$ |
| **G** | Small Backs (6) | $3/_4$ x $1^{11}/_{16}$ - $14^1/_4$ |
| **H** | Md. Sides (10) | $3/_4$ x $3^7/_{16}$ - $15^1/_4$ |
| **I** | Md. Fronts (5) | $3/_4$ x $3^7/_{16}$ - $14^1/_4$ |
| **J** | Md. Backs (5) | $3/_4$ x $3^7/_{16}$ - $14^1/_4$ |
| **K** | Large Sides (2) | $3/_4$ x $5^7/_{16}$ - $15^1/_4$ |
| **L** | Large Front (1) | $3/_4$ x $5^7/_{16}$ - $14^1/_4$ |
| **M** | Large Back (1) | $3/_4$ x $5^7/_{16}$ - $14^1/_4$ |
| **N** | Bottoms (12) | $1/_4$ hdbd. - $14^1/_4$ x $11^3/_4$ |
| **O** | Handles (12) | $3/_4$ x $1/_2$ - $15^1/_4$ |
| **P** | Runners (24) | $1/_2$ x $1/_2$ - 15 |

**HARDWARE SUPPLIES**

(48) No. 18 x 1" wire brads
(84) 3d finish nails
(4) Swivel casters w/ screws
(12) $1/_2$" brass label holders

## CUTTING DIAGRAM

$3/_4$ x $7^1/_4$ - 96 (5 Bd. Ft.)

$3/_4$ x $3^1/_2$ - 96 (2.3 Bd. Ft.)

$3/_4$" PLYWOOD - 48 x 48    $1/_4$" HARDBOARD - 48 x 96

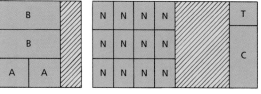

**NOTE:** CUT EDGING STRIPS (D) FROM EXTRA $3/_4$" STOCK. PARTS Q, R, S, T ARE OPTIONAL DIVIDERS (SEE DESIGNER'S NOTEBOOK ON PAGE 47).

Normally, you would decide the size of the cabinet first, and then build the drawers to fit. But since there are so many drawers here, I wanted to simplify the construction as much as possible.

So I chose the final dimensions of the drawers (for ease of cutting), and then built the cabinet to accept them. I found it works best if the outside dimensions of the drawers are $15^1/4$" x $15^1/4$". This gave me the dimensions for the cabinet.

**TOP/BOTTOM.** First cut two pieces for the top and bottom (A) of the cabinet $15^1/4$" wide (this is the depth of the drawers). Their length is $16^7/8$" (to allow $15^1/4$" for the drawer width, $1/8$" clearance on the sides, and $1^1/2$" for rabbets used to attach the cabinet sides.)

Then cut $1/2$" x $3/4$" rabbets on the ends of both pieces (*Fig. 1*). Also cut a $1/4$" x $1/2$" rabbet on the back edge (to attach the cabinet's back).

**SIDES.** The sides (B) have grooves for the drawer runners (*Fig. 2*). To make sure they lined up perfectly on both sides, I cut a piece of plywood to the final length of the sides, but twice the width (plus a little extra for trim). This way I could cut all the grooves in one double-wide piece, then rip the workpiece to get two matched sides.

First, I cut the workpiece to a rough width of 32" and to the final length of the side pieces ($34^1/2$") (*Fig. 2*). This length allows for the 12 drawers (including clearance) plus 1" for the two $1/2$"-deep rabbets on the top and bottom (A).

**DADOES FOR RUNNERS.** Now the dadoes for the runners can be cut $1/2$" wide by $1/4$" deep. I cut these on a table saw with a dado blade. Their measurements (shown in *Fig. 2*) are the distance from the fence to the "beginning" edge of the dado.

I'm using the term "beginning" edge because the six dadoes at the top of the cabinet are cut with the *top* edge of the workpiece against the fence. But the lower five dadoes are cut with the *bottom* edge against the fence.

**Note:** There's no need for a dado (or a runner) for the bottom drawer.

**RIP TO WIDTH.** After the dadoes are cut in the workpiece, rip the sides to final width to match the top and bottom. Then cut rabbets on the back edges of both pieces for the cabinet back (*Fig. 2*).

**ASSEMBLY.** Before the case is assembled, I cut the $1/4$" hardboard back (C) to

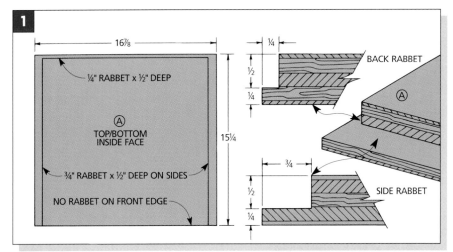

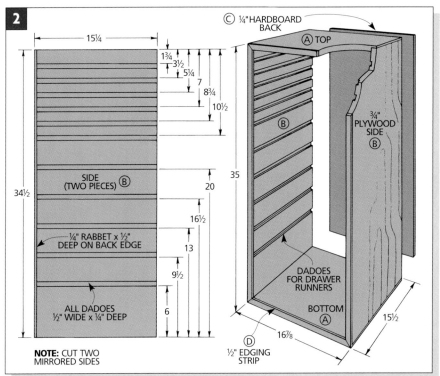

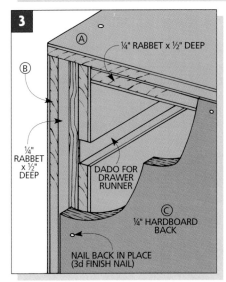

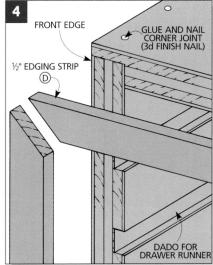

final size. Then glue and nail the four pieces for the cabinet together, and also glue and nail the back in place *(Fig. 3)*. (The back holds the assembly square.)

Finally, I added edging strips (D) to the front of the cabinet (to cover the exposed plywood edges) *(Fig. 4)*.

## DRAWERS

The drawer design is a little out of the ordinary in that the sides extend beyond the drawer front and back. This was done for two reasons. First, I needed a little extra "meat" at the front and back to strengthen the tongue and groove joint.

Second, I didn't want to put stops on the drawers (so I can take one wherever I need it), but I also didn't want to pull one out too far and have it fall on my toe.

So I extended the sides beyond the back. As the drawer pulls out, you naturally stop when you see the back, but even if you pull too far, there's enough left on the sides so they don't fall out.

**CUTTING SEQUENCE.** Now cut all the pieces for the 12 drawers. To speed things along, I made multiple cuts. Once the saw was set up to make a cut, I made the cut on all pieces. I used the following sequence.

**CUT TO ROUGH LENGTH.** I find things go much easier if I'm working with small pieces. So cut enough pieces for the sides (E, H K), fronts (F, I, L), and backs (G, J, M) (plus a few extra test pieces) to a rough length of $15^7/8$".

This length accommodates the final lengths needed for all the pieces, and also allows you to get six blanks out of an 8' board (allowing $1/8$" for kerfs).

**Note:** You can also cut pieces for the optional dividers while you're set up (see the Designer's Notebook on page 47).

**TRIM TO LENGTH.** Next, I used a cut-off jig (see page 46) to trim all these pieces to their final length *(Fig. 5)*.

**RIP TO WIDTH.** All of these rough pieces are ripped to final width to get the four basic pieces for each drawer (the front, the back, and the two sides).

**SELECTION.** When the pieces are cut to final width and length, mark what each piece is (to avoid confusion), and also mark the inside face of each piece.

**DADOES.** Now, a series of $1/4$" x $1/4$" dadoes is cut. The positions of the dadoes are such that you can set the distance from the fence to the inside of the blade, make a cut on one end, and then turn the piece around and cut the other end.

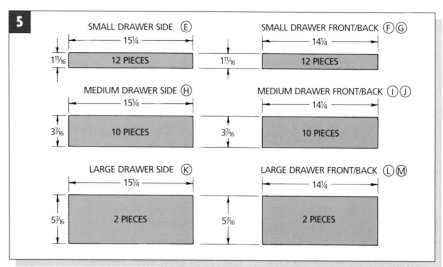

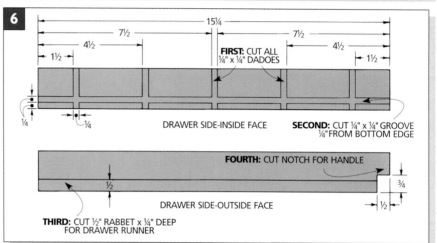

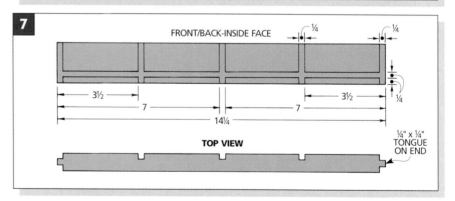

I worked on all the side pieces first *(Fig. 6)*. After that, the dadoes on the front and back pieces are cut *(Fig. 7)*.

**TONGUES.** Next, I cut the tongues on the ends of the front and back to fit snugly in the dadoes. This just means cutting two rabbets on each end *(Fig. 7)*.

Cut a tongue on a scrap piece first to check the width. (This test assembly should fit between the sides of the cabinet with about $1/8$" of clearance.)

**GROOVE FOR BOTTOM.** Cut a groove for the drawer bottom on the inside edge of each of the fronts, backs and sides. This groove starts $1/4$" from the bottom edge and is wide enough to accept a $1/4$" hardboard bottom.

**RABBET FOR RUNNER.** Next, rabbets are cut on the outside bottom edges of the sides to fit the runners. To get a smooth cut here, I cut these rabbets on the router table with a straight bit.

**NOTCH FOR HANDLE.** Match up pairs of sides and mark the fronts. Then cut a $1/2$"-deep by $3/4$"-high notch on the front of each side for a drawer handle.

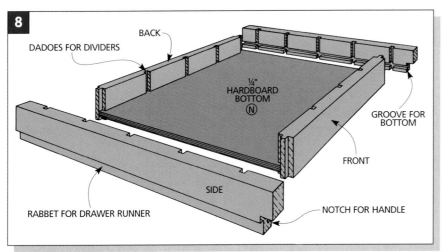

**8**

DADOES FOR DIVIDERS

BACK

¼"
HARDBOARD
BOTTOM
(N)

GROOVE FOR
BOTTOM

FRONT

SIDE

RABBET FOR DRAWER RUNNER

NOTCH FOR HANDLE

**DRAWER BOTTOMS.** Once notches for the handles are cut, you can dry-assemble the four pieces for each drawer to get the measurements for the drawer bottom (N). (I cut all the bottoms out of ¼" hardboard.)

**ASSEMBLY.** Finally, the drawers can be assembled. First, apply glue to the tongue and groove joints and join the four pieces and the drawer bottom. I tacked a small brad through the drawer side to hold each joint together while the glue dried.

**DRAWER HANDLES.** The drawer handles (O) are ripped to a width of ½" from some of the remaining stock. Then they're glued and nailed into the notches on the front edges of the drawer's sides *(Fig. 9)*.

**RUNNERS.** If all has gone well, the drawers will fit in the cabinet with a total of ⅛" of play. All you need now are the runners (P). To make these, I ripped ½"-wide strips from some of the remaining stock. Then I resawed each strip so there would be about 1/16" clear-

---

## SHOP JIG ............................ *Panel Cut-off Jig*

For the drawer parts on the Hardware Storage Cabinet, I wanted to be able to cut several pieces to identical length. There are 12 drawers in the cabinet, so to make this easier, I made a simple cut-off jig that includes a moveable stop block *(Fig. 1)*.

**CONSTRUCTION.** The basic jig is very easy to make. Cut a piece of ½" plywood for the base about 16" wide and long enough to extend 12" past the wing of the table saw.

The base is guided with two runners. The first runner is cut to fit the miter gauge channel. The second runner is mounted to the outside edge of the plywood base so it rides against the edge of the extension wing.

**Note:** Some table saw extension wings have bolts along the edges, so you may want to add a wooden strip to the edge of the wing.

**ASSEMBLY.** To assemble the jig, place the first runner in the miter gauge channel and spread a thin bead of glue along the top of it. Then position the plywood base over the runner so the "working" end of the plywood extends into the path of the blade.

Temporarily tack the plywood to the runner with small brads. Then pick up the base and turn it over to drill pilot holes and drive screws to secure the runner to the base. Return this assembly to the saw and mount the out-

side runner so it fits snugly against the wing (or the wooden strip on the end of the extension wing).

Now trim the working end of the plywood base square by pushing it through the saw blade. (This way you will know the end of the base is exactly on the path of the blade.)

**THE FENCE.** Finally, add a ¾" x 1½" fence to the trailing edge of the base *(Figs. 1 and 2)*. Chamfer the inside edge of this fence to create a sawdust relief *(Fig. 2)*. Then use a large framing square to position the fence square with the working edge (and the blade), and glue and nail it in place.

**STOP BLOCK.** Then I added a moveable stop to the fence. This is simply a matter of cutting another strip the same size as the fence *(Fig. 2)*.

Before adding this second strip, cut two small squares of ¼" plywood. Glue

a plywood square to each end of the first fence, and then add the top strip. This will form a ¼" groove for a carriage bolt that holds the wooden stop block to the fence *(Fig. 2)*.

**USING THE JIG.** To get the best (cleanest) cuts when using this jig, I use a three-cut procedure.

First, cut all of the pieces to rough length (about ½" longer than needed).

Second, cut a clean end on one end of each rough piece.

Last, mark the final length on one of the pieces (measuring from the clean end), and adjust the stop block so the cut is made on this mark. Be sure to check the fit of this piece.

Now all the remaining pieces (like the drawer pieces for the hardware storage cabinet) can be cut to identical lengths using the block as a sure stop for the final length.

**1**

¼" SPACERS BETWEEN FENCES

RUNNER

ADJUSTABLE STOP

PANEL

SLOT

PLYWOOD BASE

RUNNER

GUIDE BOLTED TO WING

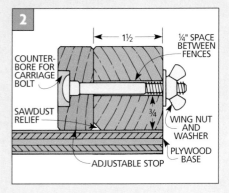

**2**

1½

¼" SPACE BETWEEN FENCES

COUNTER-BORE FOR CARRIAGE BOLT

SAWDUST RELIEF

¾

WING NUT AND WASHER

ADJUSTABLE STOP

PLYWOOD BASE

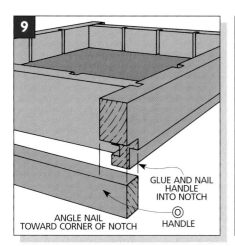

**9**

GLUE AND NAIL
HANDLE
INTO NOTCH

ANGLE NAIL
TOWARD CORNER OF NOTCH

Ⓞ HANDLE

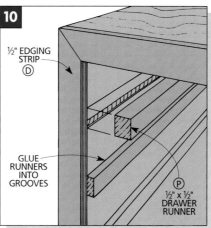

**10**

½" EDGING
STRIP
Ⓓ

GLUE
RUNNERS
INTO
GROOVES

Ⓟ ½" x ½"
DRAWER
RUNNER

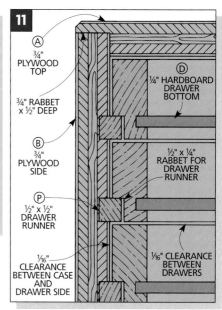

**11**

Ⓐ ¾"
PLYWOOD
TOP

¾" RABBET
x ½" DEEP

Ⓑ ¾"
PLYWOOD
SIDE

Ⓟ ½" x ½"
DRAWER
RUNNER

1/16"
CLEARANCE
BETWEEN CASE
AND
DRAWER SIDE

Ⓓ ¼" HARDBOARD
DRAWER
BOTTOM

½" x ¼"
RABBET FOR
DRAWER
RUNNER

1/16" CLEARANCE
BETWEEN
DRAWERS

ance between the runner and the rabbet on the drawer side *(Fig. 11)*.

**DIVIDERS.** You can add dividers and mini-dividers to the drawers if you like

(see the Designer's Notebook below).

**HARDWARE.** To complete the cabinet, I added swivel casters to the bottom and label holders to the drawer fronts. ∎

# DESIGNER'S NOTEBOOK

*Adding a series of custom drawer dividers helps you organize and separate hardware and supplies.*

## DRAWER DIVIDERS

■ Cut the dividers (Q, R, S) to rough length and final width *(Fig. 1)*. They're 9/16" narrower than the drawer pieces to allow 1/16" clearance below the tops of the drawer sides.

■ Cut dadoes (that same way you did on the front and back) on *both* sides of the dividers *(Fig. 2)*.

■ Now cut the tongues on the dividers the same as on the front and back, but reset the saw so they will fit loosely in the side dadoes (so you'll be able to remove them easily).

■ After making the dividers, use the left-over hardboard to cut mini-dividers (T). These are the same width as the drawer dividers and cut to custom lengths to fit

between the drawer dividers.

■ Now it's just a matter of arranging the dividers and mini-dividers to suit your individual needs. Some options are shown in the photos at right.

### MATERIALS LIST

**NEW PARTS**

| | | |
|---|---|---|
| Q | Small Dividers | ¾ x 1⅛ - 14¼ |
| R | Medium Dividers | ¾ x 2⅞ - 14¼ |
| S | Large Divider | ¾ x 4⅞ - 14¼ |
| T | Mini-Dividers | ¼ hdbd. x cut to fit |

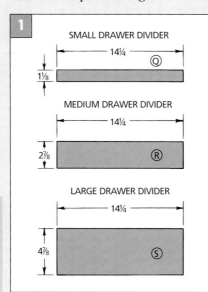

**1**

SMALL DRAWER DIVIDER
14¼
Ⓠ
1⅛

MEDIUM DRAWER DIVIDER
14¼
Ⓡ
2⅞

LARGE DRAWER DIVIDER
14¼
Ⓢ
4⅞

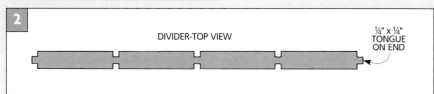

**2**

DIVIDER-TOP VIEW

¼" x ¼"
TONGUE
ON END

# Drill Bit Cabinet

*Customizable tilt-out trays, extra shelves, and an optional drawer help you store and organize all your drill bits and accessories in one convenient place. And it's small enough to fit anywhere in your shop.*

Sometimes it just seems like there's a black hole in my shop where the one drill bit I need always disappears. Although the right bit eventually turns up, it's usually only after a frustrating search of all the different places I use to store them. It's a waste of time and effort, so I decided to do something about it.

To organize all of my drill bits and accessories in one convenient place (and keep them from getting nicked or damaged), I built this simple cabinet. It's designed with one thing in mind — lots of storage in a compact space.

**STORAGE.** In spite of its small size, this cabinet provides all the storage space I need.

The back part of the cabinet houses two tilt-out trays that provide easy access to my bits. And there are two shelves inside the door with holes drilled to fit your small accessories.

**OPTIONAL DRAWER.** There's even a drawer that can be added underneath the cabinet if you need additional storage. This drawer is optional, but I've found it comes in pretty handy for extra bits, accessories, or odds and ends.

**CUSTOM TRAYS.** Not every drill bit will fit into the same type of storage tray. But with these plans, you can customize your trays to hold Forstner bits, brad point bits, and spade bits. For more on this, see the Designer's Notebook on page 53.

**MATERIALS AND HARDWARE.** For a small shop project like this, you can use just about any type of wood. You may even have enough leftovers lying around your shop to make most of the parts of the cabinet.

This cabinet was made entirely from $3/4$" and $1/2$" hardwood stock, $1/2$" ply-

wood, and $1/8$" hardboard.

Along with making use of readily available materials, this project also doesn't require a lot of special hardware.

Aside from the common woodscrews, all you'll need is a $1^1/_2$" x $19^1/_2$" piano hinge for the case, and two 1"-dia. wood knobs (for the door and drawer).

# EXPLODED VIEW

**OVERALL DIMENSIONS:**
10W x 7D x 23⁵/₈H

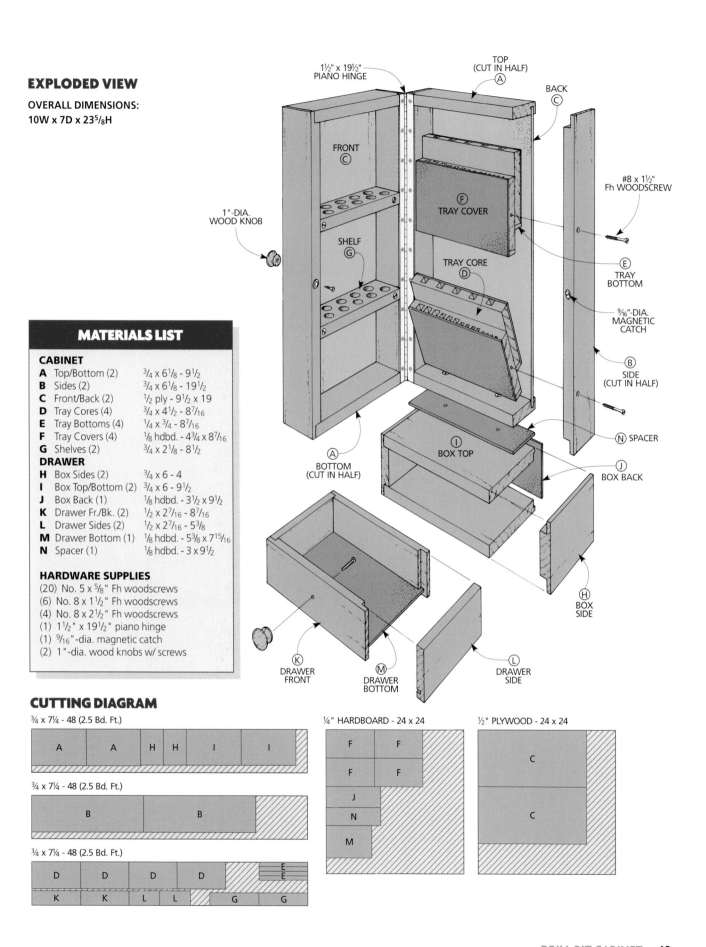

**1½" x 19½" PIANO HINGE**

**TOP (CUT IN HALF)** Ⓐ

**BACK** Ⓒ

**FRONT** Ⓒ

**#8 x 1½" Fh WOODSCREW**

**1"-DIA. WOOD KNOB**

**TRAY COVER** Ⓕ

**SHELF** Ⓖ

**TRAY CORE** Ⓓ

Ⓔ **TRAY BOTTOM**

**⁹/₁₆"-DIA. MAGNETIC CATCH**

Ⓑ **SIDE (CUT IN HALF)**

**BOX TOP** Ⓘ

Ⓐ **BOTTOM (CUT IN HALF)**

Ⓝ **SPACER**

Ⓙ **BOX BACK**

Ⓗ **BOX SIDE**

Ⓚ **DRAWER FRONT**

Ⓜ **DRAWER BOTTOM**

Ⓛ **DRAWER SIDE**

## MATERIALS LIST

### CABINET

| | | |
|---|---|---|
| **A** | Top/Bottom (2) | ³/₄ x 6¹/₈ - 9¹/₂ |
| **B** | Sides (2) | ³/₄ x 6¹/₈ - 19¹/₂ |
| **C** | Front/Back (2) | ¹/₂ ply - 9¹/₂ x 19 |
| **D** | Tray Cores (4) | ³/₄ x 4¹/₂ - 8⁷/₁₆ |
| **E** | Tray Bottoms (4) | ¹/₄ x ³/₄ - 8⁷/₁₆ |
| **F** | Tray Covers (4) | ¹/₈ hdbd. - 4³/₄ x 8⁷/₁₆ |
| **G** | Shelves (2) | ³/₄ x 2¹/₈ - 8¹/₂ |

### DRAWER

| | | |
|---|---|---|
| **H** | Box Sides (2) | ³/₄ x 6 - 4 |
| **I** | Box Top/Bottom (2) | ³/₄ x 6 - 9¹/₂ |
| **J** | Box Back (1) | ¹/₈ hdbd. - 3¹/₂ x 9¹/₂ |
| **K** | Drawer Fr./Bk. (2) | ¹/₂ x 2⁷/₁₆ - 8⁷/₁₆ |
| **L** | Drawer Sides (2) | ¹/₂ x 2⁷/₁₆ - 5³/₈ |
| **M** | Drawer Bottom (1) | ¹/₈ hdbd. - 5³/₈ x 7¹⁵/₁₆ |
| **N** | Spacer (1) | ¹/₈ hdbd. - 3 x 9¹/₂ |

### HARDWARE SUPPLIES

(20) No. 5 x ⁵/₈" Fh woodscrews
(6) No. 8 x 1¹/₂" Fh woodscrews
(4) No. 8 x 2¹/₂" Fh woodscrews
(1) 1¹/₂" x 19¹/₂" piano hinge
(1) ⁹/₁₆"-dia. magnetic catch
(2) 1"-dia. wood knobs w/ screws

## CUTTING DIAGRAM

**³/₄ x 7¹/₄ - 48 (2.5 Bd. Ft.)**

| A | A | H | H | I | I |

**³/₄ x 7¹/₄ - 48 (2.5 Bd. Ft.)**

| B | B |

**³/₄ x 7¹/₄ - 48 (2.5 Bd. Ft.)**

| D | D | D | D | E / E |
| K | K | L | L | G | G |

**¹/₄" HARDBOARD - 24 x 24**

| F | F |
| F | F |
| J | |
| N | |
| M | |

**¹/₂" PLYWOOD - 24 x 24**

| C |
| C |

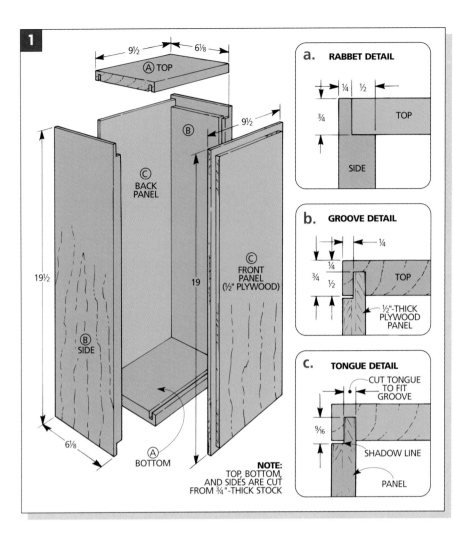

**1**

9½  6⅛

(A) TOP

9½

(B)

(C)
BACK
PANEL

19½

(C)
FRONT
PANEL
(½" PLYWOOD)

19

(B)
SIDE

6⅛

(A)
BOTTOM

**NOTE:**
TOP, BOTTOM,
AND SIDES ARE CUT
FROM ¾"-THICK STOCK

**a.  RABBET DETAIL**

¼  ½

¾

TOP

SIDE

**b.  GROOVE DETAIL**

¼

¼

¾

½

TOP

½"-THICK
PLYWOOD
PANEL

**c.  TONGUE DETAIL**

CUT TONGUE
TO FIT
GROOVE

9⁄16

SHADOW LINE

PANEL

## CASE

There's nothing complicated about building the case for the Drill Bit Cabinet. It starts off as a simple wood box. Then it's cut apart to form two identical halves. So rather than a simple flat door whose only purpose is to keep the cabinet closed, this design provides storage *inside* the door as well as within the cabinet itself.

The case consists of a top and bottom (A) that are held together by two side pieces (B) *(Fig. 1)*.

**Note:** I used ¾"-thick maple for the top, bottom, and sides of my drill bit cabinet, although any ¾"-thick hardwood will work.

To accept the top and bottom, ½"-deep rabbets are cut on each end of the side pieces *(Fig. 1a)*. Then two grooves are cut in each of the case pieces to accept a pair of plywood panels that are added next *(Fig. 1b)*.

**PANELS.** The front and back panels (C) are made from ½"-thick plywood. Normally, ¼" plywood might suffice for the front and back of a cabinet like this. But I needed enough "thickness" to screw into when attaching the storage shelves (and also for mounting the cabinet to a wall, if you decide you want a hanging version).

---

**SHOP TIP** . . . . . . . . . . . . . . . . . . . . . *Cutting a Box In Two*

Like a lot of woodworking tasks, cutting a box into two parts looks more complicated than it is. All it takes is the right cutting sequence and a simple trick.

First, cut two opposite sides of the box *(Step 1)*. The problem is when you cut the next two sides, the saw kerfs can pinch the blade and cause kickback.

To prevent the kerfs from closing, slip a pair of spacers through the box *(Step 2)*.

After making the final two cuts, remove the tape and separate the two halves.

**NOTE:**
RUN SAME
SIDE AGAINST
FENCE FOR
EACH PASS

**1** To cut a box into two halves, first you need to adjust the height of the table saw blade to cut through the thickness of the box sides. After the blade is set up, make a pass on opposite sides (or ends) of the box. Just be sure to run the same side against the fence for each pass. This way, if the cuts end up a little off-center, they will still be aligned with each other.

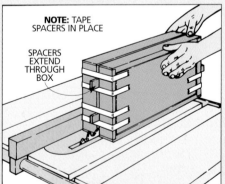

**NOTE:** TAPE
SPACERS IN PLACE

SPACERS
EXTEND
THROUGH
BOX

**2** Once the initial cuts have been made, you need to take the proper precautions to avoid a kickback accident. To prevent the saw kerfs from closing up and pinching the blade, cut a pair of spacers from ⅛" hardboard and slip them through the box. I use strips of masking tape to hold the spacers in place (you don't want them falling into the blade during a cut).

**Note:** Unfortunately, $1/2$" maple plywood isn't always easy to come by. If you can't find any locally, you can glue up two pieces of $1/4$"-thick birch plywood as a substitute to make the front and back panels.

**RABBETS.** With the front and back panels both cut to size, the next step is to cut rabbets around all their edges. This forms tongues to fit in the grooves you already cut in the top, bottom, and sides *(Fig. 1c)*.

The main idea here is to cut the rabbets deep enough so the tongue fits the groove. But it should also be *wide* enough to produce a slight "shadow line" between the sides and the panels. (I cut $9/16$"-wide rabbets on my panels, which produced a $1/16$" gap all the way around each one.)

**GLUE-UP.** After dry-assembling all the pieces, you're ready to glue and clamp the case together. Then, after the glue is dry, it's just a matter of separating the case into two equal parts. (For instructions on cutting a box into two halves, see the Shop Tip on the opposite page.)

**HINGE.** The next step is to hinge the two halves of the cabinet together. To make it easy to install, I screwed a piano hinge into a shallow rabbet that's cut in one edge of each of the side pieces *(Figs. 2 and 2a)*. (For sources of hardware, see page 126.)

**CATCH.** After installing the hinge, a magnetic catch and strike plate are

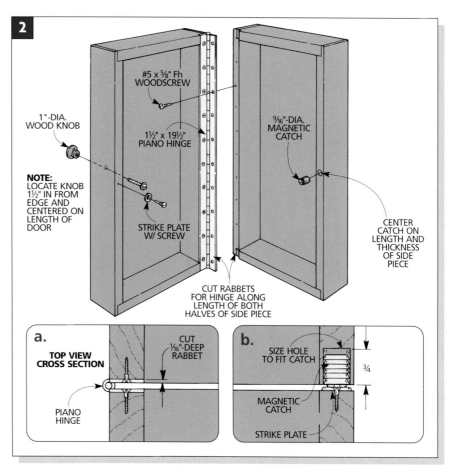

**2**

#5 x $5/8$" Fh WOODSCREW

1"-DIA. WOOD KNOB

$1\frac{1}{2}$" x $19\frac{1}{2}$" PIANO HINGE

$9/16$"-DIA. MAGNETIC CATCH

**NOTE:** LOCATE KNOB $1\frac{1}{2}$" IN FROM EDGE AND CENTERED ON LENGTH OF DOOR

STRIKE PLATE W/ SCREW

CENTER CATCH ON LENGTH AND THICKNESS OF SIDE PIECE

CUT RABBETS FOR HINGE ALONG LENGTH OF BOTH HALVES OF SIDE PIECE

**a.**
TOP VIEW CROSS SECTION

CUT $1/16$"-DEEP RABBET

PIANO HINGE

**b.**
SIZE HOLE TO FIT CATCH

$3/4$

MAGNETIC CATCH

STRIKE PLATE

added to keep the door of the cabinet closed tight *(Fig. 2)*.

The catch fits in a hole that's drilled in the side piece on the back part of the cabinet *(Fig. 2b)*. And the strike plate is screwed to the edge of the door. (For

more on installing magnetic catches, see the Shop Tip below.)

**KNOB.** All that's left to complete the case is to add a 1"-diameter wood knob. It's simply screwed in place on the door of the cabinet *(Fig. 2)*.

---

**SHOP TIP** . . . . . . . . . . . . . . . *Installing Magnetic Catches*

Magnetic catches are generally fairly simple to install. But especially on a project with a narrow wood surface (like the $3/4$" on the Drill Bit Cabinet), you need to be able to install one accurately.

The one I used, like most, consists of two parts: a magnet and a catch plate (or screw). To install one properly, two things must be done. First, the magnet has to be seated straight in the hole and flush with the work surface. To do this, I guide

the magnet in the hole with a square, flat block of wood *(Fig. 1)*.

Second, in order for the door to stay closed, the

catch must align with the magnet. To ensure it does, I place the screw on the magnet, close the door, and tap the door with a

no-mar hammer *(Fig. 2)*. Then when you open the door, the mark left behind will indicate where to mount the catch.

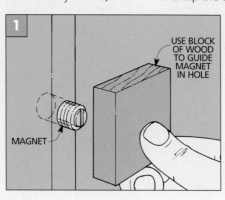

**1**

USE BLOCK OF WOOD TO GUIDE MAGNET IN HOLE

MAGNET

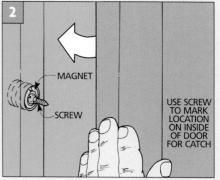

**2**

MAGNET

SCREW

USE SCREW TO MARK LOCATION ON INSIDE OF DOOR FOR CATCH

## TRAYS

The back of the cabinet holds two trays for storing drill bits. To make it easy to remove a bit, these trays tilt forward.

**STAIRSTEP.** Each tray organizes the bits in two "stairstep" sections. After building each section (I made four altogether) as a separate unit, they're glued together in pairs to form the trays.

**CORE.** Each section starts off as a core piece (D) made from $^3/_4$"-thick hardwood *(Fig. 4)*. To allow the tray to tip out of the cabinet without binding, I cut each core piece $^1/_{16}$" narrower (shorter) than the cabinet opening.

**DADOES.** To provide a separate compartment for each bit, there's a series of dadoes cut in each core piece. The size and spacing of these dadoes will vary, depending on the bits you plan on storing (see the Designer's Notebook on the opposite page).

**BOTTOM AND COVER.** Next, to keep the drill bits from falling out of the tray, glue on a $^1/_4$"-thick hardwood bottom (E), and a cover (F) cut from a piece of $^1/_8$"-thick hardboard *(Fig. 4)*.

**ASSEMBLY.** With each of the sections complete, you're ready to assemble them in pairs *(Fig. 4a)*.

**Note:** To provide plenty of finger room when removing a bit, the sections are glued together back to back.

**INSTALL TRAYS.** Now you can install the trays. A screw on each side holds the tray in place and acts as a pivot point to allow it to tip out *(Figs. 3a and 4a)*. To keep the bits upright when the trays are pushed back in, a wood block is glued onto the back of each tray.

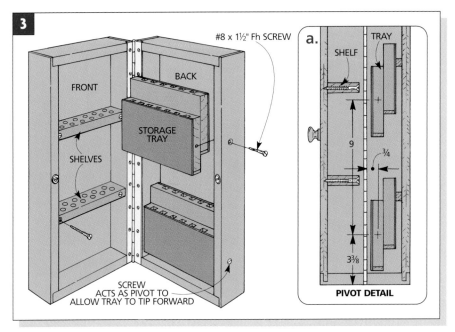

## SHELVES

To take advantage of the space inside the door, I added a pair of hardwood shelves for my accessories. Along with the shelves, I installed the index for my twist bits in the bottom of the door (refer to the photo on page 48).

**CUSTOMIZE SHELVES.** As with the storage trays, you'll need to customize the shelves (G) for your accessories *(Fig. 5)*. All I did was drill holes to accommodate my countersinks, plug cutters, and special drill bits.

**ATTACH SHELVES.** After locating the shelves so there's plenty of clearance to lift everything out, drill countersunk shank holes through the edges and screw the shelves to the front panel.

## DRAWER

As an option, you can add a drawer to store small accessories. The drawer fits inside a wood box that's attached to the bottom of the cabinet (see photo on opposite page).

**BOX.** Like the cabinet, the box has two sides (H) that are rabbeted at each end to accept a top and bottom (I) *(Figs. 6 and 1a)*. Before gluing the box together, you'll need to cut a shallow rabbet along the back edges of these four pieces for a $^1/_8$"-thick hardboard back (J) *(Fig. 6a)*.

**DRAWER.** The next step is to build a drawer to fit inside the box. The drawer shown opposite is designed to fit flush with the front of the cabinet with a $^1/_{16}$"

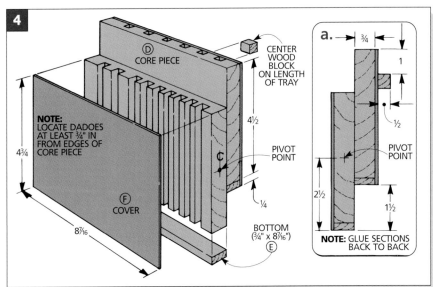

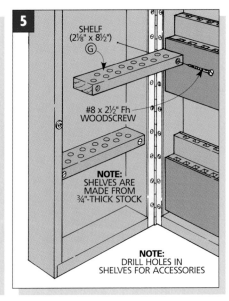

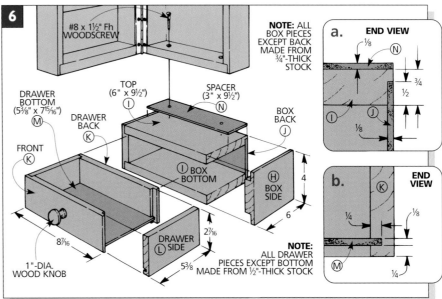

gap on the top and a $1/32$" gap on each side of the opening in the box.

The drawer consists of a front and back piece (K) that are $1/2$" thick and rabbeted at the ends for the two sides (L) *(Fig. 6)*. Grooves cut in each piece accept a bottom (M) made from $1/8$"-thick hardboard *(Fig. 6b)*. After gluing up the drawer, I screwed on a wood knob to match the one on the door.

**SPACER.** Before attaching the drawer box, I added a spacer (N) to keep the door from dragging across the box.

This is a piece of $1/8$"-thick hardboard that's cut to fit the bottom (A) of the back of the cabinet and glued in place.

**ATTACH BOX.** Now attach the box to the bottom of the cabinet. After locating the box flush with the back and sides of the cabinet, it's glued and screwed through the bottom of the cabinet. ■

# DESIGNER'S NOTEBOOK

*Taking extra time now to customize your drill bit trays will save you some headaches later.*

## CUSTOMIZED TRAYS

■ Not every drill bit fits in the same type of storage tray. So while you're building trays for the cabinet, it's worth it to take time to customize them for your bits.

■ To do this, it's just adjust the size and spacing of the dadoes in the core pieces (D) (see drawings below).

**Note:** In some cases, you may also need to adjust the *length* of the dadoes by adding wood "stops."

■ See below to adapt your storage trays for Forstner, brad point, and spade bits.

■ Also see the tip at right to help keep your spade bits aligned.

*A V-shaped groove routed in the top edge of the tray will keep the paddles of all your spade bits facing forward.*

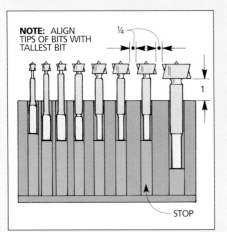

**Forstner Bits.** *To separate your Forstner bits, space them $1/4$" apart. Then to get the bits to stick up an equal amount, glue a wood "stop" in each dado.*

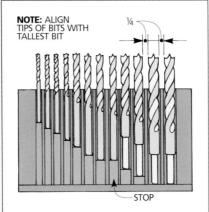

**Brad Point Bits.** *To keep brad point bits from rattling around, cut the dadoes $1/16$" deeper and wider than the bit diameters. Again, "stops" align the tips.*

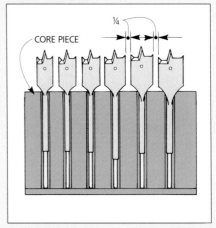

**Spade Bits.** *To prevent the "paddles" of your spade bits from hitting each other, space them $1/4$" apart. Then cut dadoes $1/16$" deeper and wider than the shanks.*

# Saw Blade Storage

*Rather than waste your shop's wall space and risk damaging your saw blades, you can build this compact cabinet that stores, organizes, and protects all your blades in one place.*

The simplest way to store a saw blade is to hang it on a nail in the wall of your shop. But if you have as many blades as I do, there's a problem. You can either hang them all on the same nail and run the risk of damaging the teeth. Or you can hang them on separate nails and lose valuable wall space.

To solve both of these problems, I built a saw blade storage cabinet that can sit on a workbench or be screwed to a wall. It has nine single trays that can each handle a 10" (or smaller) saw blade. And it also has one double-size tray that can store a dado blade.

**IDENTICAL PARTS.** The hardboard bottoms for the trays are all identical (with the same pattern routed into the front for a pull). So you can save time by making a template and routing all the patterns at once. See the Shop Tip on page 57 for more on this.

The nine regular drawer fronts are also identical, so you can set up your saw once and cut them all in succession.

**MATERIALS.** Although there are many identical parts in this cabinet, it's still designed to be inexpensive and practical to build.

Most of the main parts of the cabinet are made from ³/₄"-thick plywood and

¹/₄" hardboard. The casing strips and tray fronts are ³/₄"-thick hardwood.

**BLADE SELECTION.** Building a small but versatile blade storage cabinet like this one got me thinking about how to best go about selecting the types of saw blades to keep in my shop.

There are several kinds of blades to choose from, and depending on your budget and the types of projects you build, your selection can vary quite a bit from another woodworker's. But there are some things to look for, and I've outlined some of the important ones here. See the Shop Info section on pages 58-59 for more on selecting saw blades.

## EXPLODED VIEW

**OVERALL DIMENSIONS:**
$12^1/_{16}$W x $11^1/_2$D x $15^1/_2$H

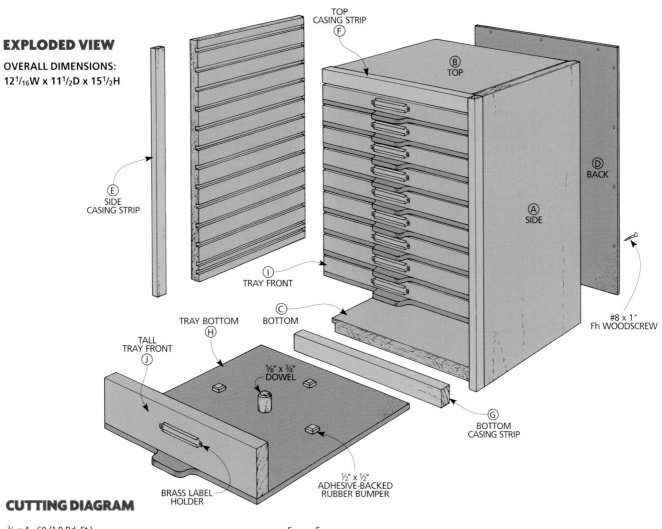

TOP CASING STRIP
F

B
TOP

D
BACK

A
SIDE

E
SIDE CASING STRIP

I
TRAY FRONT

#8 x 1"
Fh WOODSCREW

C
BOTTOM

TRAY BOTTOM
H

TALL TRAY FRONT
J

$^5/_8$" x $^3/_4$"
DOWEL

G
BOTTOM CASING STRIP

BRASS LABEL HOLDER

$^1/_2$" x $^1/_2$"
ADHESIVE-BACKED RUBBER BUMPER

## CUTTING DIAGRAM

$^3/_4$ x 4 - 60 (1.9 Bd. Ft.)

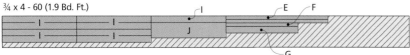

I   I   I   J   E   F   G

$^3/_4$" PLYWOOD - 24 x 48

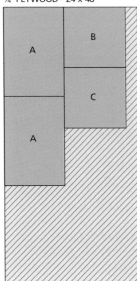

A   B   C   A

$^1/_4$" HARDBOARD - 48 x 48

H H H
H H H
H H H
H D

---

### MATERIALS LIST

**WOOD**

| | | |
|---|---|---|
| **A** | Sides (2) | $^3/_4$ ply - $15^1/_2$ x $10^3/_4$ |
| **B** | Top (1) | $^3/_4$ ply - $11^1/_{16}$ x $10^1/_2$ |
| **C** | Bottom (1) | $^3/_4$ ply - $11^1/_{16}$ x $10^1/_2$ |
| **D** | Back (1) | $^1/_4$ hdbd. - $11^9/_{16}$ x $15^1/_2$ |
| **E** | Side Casing Strips (2) | $^3/_4$ x $^1/_2$ - $15^1/_2$ |
| **F** | Top Casing Strip (1) | $^3/_4$ x $^3/_4$ - $10^9/_{16}$ |
| **G** | Btm. Casing Strip (1) | $^3/_4$ x $^{15}/_{16}$ - $10^9/_{16}$ |
| **H** | Tray Bottoms (10) | $^1/_4$ hdbd. - 11 x 12 |
| **I** | Tray Fronts (9) | $^3/_4$ x $^{15}/_{16}$ - 11 |
| **J** | Tall Tray Front (1) | $^3/_4$ x $2^3/_{16}$ - 11 |

**HARDWARE SUPPLIES**

(50) No. 8 x $^3/_4$" Fh woodscrews
(12) No. 8 x 1" Fh woodscrews
(40) $^1/_2$" rubber bumpers
(10) $^1/_2$" brass label holders
(10) $^5/_8$" x $^3/_4$" dowels

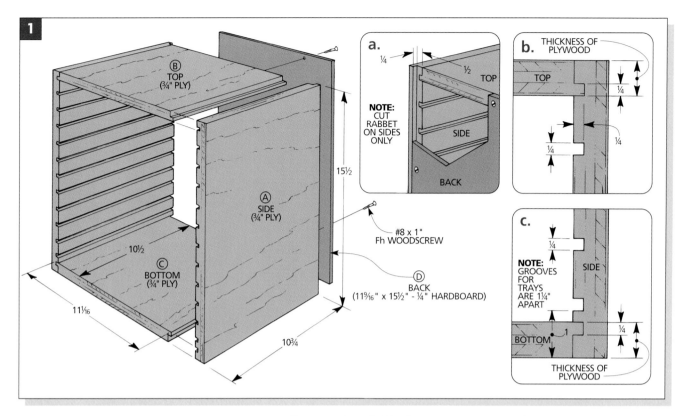

## SIDES

I began by building the cabinet that holds the pullout trays. It's just an open plywood box with grooves cut in the sides for the trays *(Fig. 1)*.

**SIDES.** When laying out the sides (A), I oriented the grain to run the same direction as the grooves *(Fig. 1)*. This way, there's less chance of chipping the plywood's face veneer later when the grooves are cut.

Cut the sides to a width (distance across the grain) of $15^1/_2$" and a length (distance with the grain) of $10^3/_4$".

**GROOVES.** After the sides are cut to size, there are two sets of $1/_4$"-wide grooves to cut. The first set of grooves forms half of a locking rabbet that joins the top and bottom to the sides *(Figs. 1*

*and 1b)*. The second set holds the saw blade trays *(Fig. 1c)*.

I cut all of these grooves with a dado blade in the table saw.

**Note:** To match up the grooves in each side piece, I used the rip fence as a stop and the same setup for each opposing groove before moving on to the next set.

**RABBETS FOR BACK.** In addition to the grooves, a rabbet is cut in the back edge of each side piece. This rabbet accepts a back that's added later *(Fig. 1a)*.

## TOP & BOTTOM

Now work can begin on the top (B) and bottom (C) *(Fig. 1)*. To leave room for the back, the length (depth) of each piece is $1/_4$" less than the sides ($10^1/_2$")

*(Fig. 1)*. And they're both cut to a width of $11^1/_{16}$".

**Note:** For appearance, the grain direction of the top and bottom should match that of the sides *(Fig. 1)*.

To complete the top and bottom, rabbets are cut in the ends of each. These rabbets form tongues to fit the grooves cut earlier *(Figs. 1b and 1c)*.

## BACK & CASING STRIPS

After gluing and clamping the cabinet together, cut a back (D) from $1/_4$" hardboard to fit between the rabbets in the sides *(Figs. 1 and 1a)*. The back is simply screwed in place.

**CASING STRIPS.** To complete the cabinet, I covered the plywood edges with casing strips cut from $3/_4$"-thick maple *(Figs. 2 and 3)*. Start by gluing on the side casing strips (E). Then cut a top casing strip (F) and bottom casing strip (G) to fit, and glue them in place.

## TRAYS

Now the cabinet is ready for the trays. Whether you're building regular trays for single blades or a double-size tray for a dado blade, each is made up of a bottom and a tray front *(Fig. 4)*. The only difference is the tray for the dado blade has a taller front.

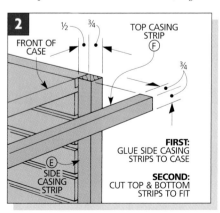

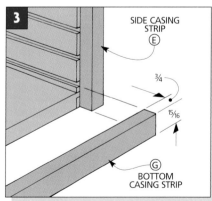

# EXPLODED VIEW

**OVERALL DIMENSIONS:**
**30¹⁄₂W x 7¹⁄₄D x 30H**

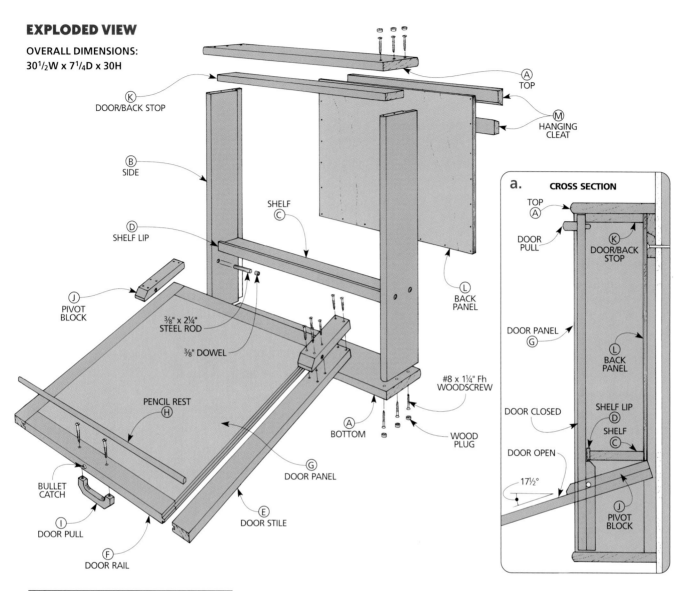

K **DOOR/BACK STOP**

B **SIDE**

C **SHELF**

D **SHELF LIP**

J **PIVOT BLOCK**

³⁄₈" x 2¹⁄₄" **STEEL ROD**

³⁄₈" **DOWEL**

H **PENCIL REST**

I **DOOR PULL**

BULLET CATCH

F **DOOR RAIL**

E **DOOR STILE**

G **DOOR PANEL**

A **BOTTOM**

#8 x 1¹⁄₄" Fh **WOODSCREW**

WOOD PLUG

L **BACK PANEL**

A **TOP**

M **HANGING CLEAT**

**a. CROSS SECTION**

TOP A

DOOR PULL

K DOOR/BACK STOP

DOOR PANEL G

L BACK PANEL

DOOR CLOSED

SHELF LIP D

SHELF C

DOOR OPEN

17¹⁄₂°

J PIVOT BLOCK

---

## MATERIALS LIST

### WOOD

| | | |
|---|---|---|
| **A** | Top/Bottom (2) | ³⁄₄ x 7¹⁄₄ - 30¹⁄₂ |
| **B** | Sides (2) | ³⁄₄ x 7 - 28¹⁄₂ |
| **C** | Shelf (1) | ³⁄₄ x 4⁵⁄₈ - 28¹⁄₂ |
| **D** | Shelf Lip (1) | ¹⁄₄ x 1 - 28¹⁄₂ |
| **E** | Door Stiles (2) | ³⁄₄ x 2¹⁄₈ - 28¹⁄₄ rgh. |
| **F** | Door Rails (2) | ³⁄₄ x 2¹⁄₈ - 24³⁄₄ rgh. |
| **G** | Door Panel (1) | ³⁄₄ ply - 24³⁄₄ x 24³⁄₄ |
| **H** | Pencil Rest (1) | ¹⁄₂ x ¹⁄₂ - 28¹⁄₄ |
| **I** | Door Pull (1) | ³⁄₄ x 1¹⁄₄ - 5 |
| **J** | Pivot Blocks (2) | ³⁄₄ x 2 - 7¹⁄₂ |
| **K** | Door/Back Stop (1) | ³⁄₄ x 5 - 28¹⁄₂ |
| **L** | Back Panel (1) | ¹⁄₄ ply - 29¹⁄₂ x 20³⁄₄ |
| **M** | Hanging Cleat (1) | ³⁄₄ x 4¹⁄₂ - 29¹⁄₂ rgh. |

### HARDWARE SUPPLIES

(30) No. 8 x 1¹⁄₄" Fh woodscrews
(28) ³⁄₄" wire nails
(2) ³⁄₈" x 2¹⁄₄" steel rods
(1) ³⁄₈" x ⁵⁄₈" bullet catch
(1) ³⁄₈" x 3 ft. dowel rod (or 16 wood plugs)

---

## CUTTING DIAGRAM

**ALSO NEED:** ONE 4' x 4' SHEET ³⁄₄" PLYWOOD, PLUS ONE 4' x 4' SHEET ¹⁄₄" PLYWOOD

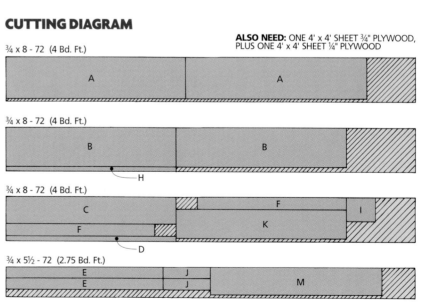

³⁄₄ x 8 - 72 (4 Bd. Ft.)

A   A

³⁄₄ x 8 - 72 (4 Bd. Ft.)

B   B   H

³⁄₄ x 8 - 72 (4 Bd. Ft.)

C   F   I
F   K   D

³⁄₄ x 5¹⁄₂ - 72 (2.75 Bd. Ft.)

E   J
E   J   M

The Drafting Cabinet has two main components — a rectangular cabinet with a narrow shelf inside, and a pivot-down door.

I started by building the cabinet.

**CUT PARTS TO SIZE.** First, I ripped two pieces of stock to finished width ($7^1/_4$") for the cabinet top/bottom (A) *(Fig. 1)*.

Next, rip two pieces for the cabinet sides (B) *(Fig. 1)*. These side pieces are ripped $^1/_4$" narrower than the top and bottom to allow for a bullnose that will be routed on the front edge of the top and bottom.

The last piece to rip to width ($4^5/_8$") is the inside shelf (C).

When all five pieces are ripped to width, you can cut them to their finished lengths *(Fig. 1)*.

**RABBETS.** The plywood back for this cabinet fits into a pair of rabbets that are cut along the back edge of the cabinet sides *(Fig. 1)*. In addition to the back, there's also a hanging cleat (M) for mounting the cabinet to the wall (refer to the Exploded View on page 61).

To accept both the back and the cleat, the rabbets have to be cut wider than usual. I cut them in two steps using a combination blade in the table saw.

The first cut is made with the piece lying on its face *(Fig. 2)*. This cut establishes the shoulder.

To complete the rabbet, reposition the rip fence and raise the blade height to make a second pass with the workpiece standing on edge *(Fig. 3)*.

**BULLNOSE EDGES.** Just because this Drafting Cabinet is designed for use in the shop doesn't mean it has to look rough. To make it look a little nicer, I used a $^1/_2$" roundover bit to rout a bull-nose on the front edge of all four cabinet pieces, and also on the ends of the top

and bottom pieces *(Fig. 3)*.

**DRILL SCREW HOLES.** Other than the rabbets for the back, there's no fancy joinery on this cabinet. All five pieces are joined with butt joints and held together with woodscrews.

To locate all the screwholes for attaching the top and bottom to the cabinet sides, first clamp these four outside pieces together.

**Note:** The top and bottom are positioned so there's a $^1/_4$" overhang on the sides and front edges *(Fig. 1a)*.

**ASSEMBLE CABINET.** When the cabinet is clamped together, drill pilot holes

and counterbores for the screws. Also drill a hole in both side pieces for the pivot pins *(Fig. 1)*. Then the cabinet can be assembled with screws and glue.

Next, the shelf can be installed. I used a pair of spacer blocks to hold the shelf in place while drilling the screw holes *(Fig. 5)*.

After the shelf has been screwed to the cabinet, the screw holes can be plugged with short lengths of $^3/_8$" dowel or wood plugs.

Finally, cut and glue a $^1/_4$"-thick shelf lip (D) to fit on the front edge of the shelf *(Fig. 1)*.

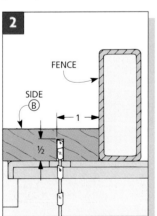

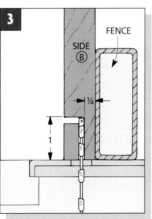

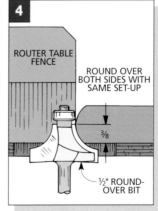

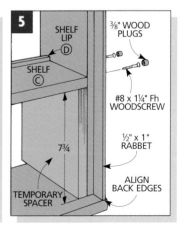

## BUILDING THE DOOR

The work surface is a door that folds down. It consists of a $3/4$" plywood panel surrounded by a hardwood frame. I started by cutting the frame pieces.

**EQUAL GAP.** To operate smoothly, the door fits in the cabinet with a $1/8$" gap all around. But it's easiest to build the door to fit the opening tightly. You can trim the door to achieve a uniform gap later.

**RAILS AND STILES.** First, rip four pieces of $3/4$" stock to a rough width of $2^1/8$".

**Note:** For the best fit between the frame and panel, start with frame pieces the exact thickness of the plywood.

Then cut two door stiles (E) to length so they fit tightly between the top and bottom of the cabinet *(Fig. 6)*.

With the stiles in place, measure between them to determine the rough length of the rails. Add $1/2$" (for $1/4$"-long stub tenons on the ends) and cut two door rails (F) to this length *(Fig. 6)*.

**GROOVES.** The panel is joined to the frame with tongue and groove joints *(Fig. 7)*. I made a $1/4$"-wide groove centered on the inside edge of each piece by making two passes on the table saw.

**PLYWOOD.** Now cut the plywood panel (G) to fit inside the frame *(Fig. 6)*. Add $1/2$" to each dimension for the $1/4$"-long tongues that are cut next.

**TONGUES.** Next, just cut centered tongues on all four edges of the panel.

## SHOP TIP ............ Door Pull

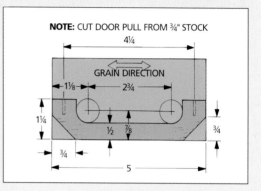

You can use almost any door pull to open the Drafting Cabinet. But to get one that matches the cabinet, I made my own from a piece of scrap birch.

Start with a 5"-long blank cut extra wide (see drawing). First lay out the dimensions for the holes on the inside, and the "ears" on the outside corners.

Then drill the holes that define the arcs, and use a band saw to cut off the ears.

To soften the outside edges, I used a $1/2$"

roundover bit and routed a bullnose profile — like on the edges of the cabinet *(refer to Fig. 4)*.

Now rip the pull to finished width from the oversized blank, and clean out the waste area between the holes.

**NOTE:** CUT DOOR PULL FROM $3/4$" STOCK

4$1/4$
GRAIN DIRECTION
1$1/8$  2$3/4$
1$1/4$  $1/2$  $7/8$  $3/4$
$3/4$
5

**Note:** Sneak up on the tongue's thickness until it just fits the grooves *(Fig. 6a)*.

Cut tongues on the ends of the door rails (F) to fit the same grooves *(Fig. 7)*.

Now glue the door frame around the panel. Then drill a pair of holes centered on the width of one rail for attaching the door pull *(Figs. 6 and 8a)*.

**TRIM DOOR EDGES.** To make the door open and close smoothly, just trim an

equal amount ($1/8$", or one blade's width) off all four edges.

**PENCIL REST.** Before mounting the door, cut a pencil rest (H) *(Fig. 8)*. Round over the top two edges using a $1/4$" roundover bit in the router table.

The pencil rest hides the screw holes for the door pull. But don't glue it in place just yet — first make the pull (see the Shop Tip above).

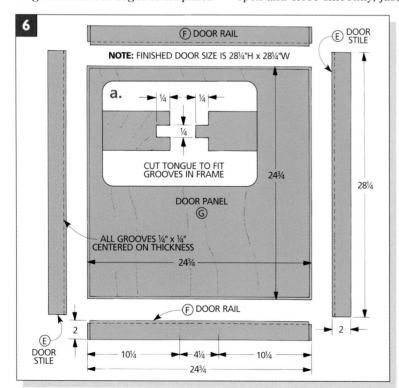

**6**

(F) DOOR RAIL    (E) DOOR STILE

**NOTE:** FINISHED DOOR SIZE IS 28$1/4$"H x 28$1/4$"W

**a.**  $1/4$  $1/4$  $1/4$
CUT TONGUE TO FIT GROOVES IN FRAME

DOOR PANEL (G)

24$3/4$
28$1/4$

ALL GROOVES $1/4$" x $1/4$" CENTERED ON THICKNESS

24$3/4$

(F) DOOR RAIL

2    10$1/4$  4$1/4$  10$1/4$    2
24$3/4$

(E) DOOR STILE

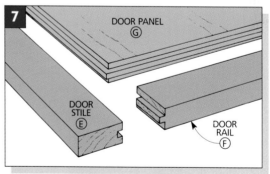

**7**  DOOR PANEL (G)

DOOR STILE (E)    DOOR RAIL (F)

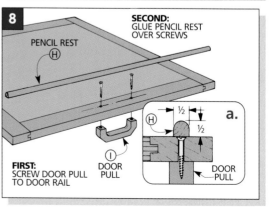

**8**

SECOND: GLUE PENCIL REST OVER SCREWS

PENCIL REST (H)

**a.**  (H)  $1/2$  $1/2$

FIRST: SCREW DOOR PULL TO DOOR RAIL

(I) DOOR PULL    DOOR PULL

## INSTALLING THE DOOR

After the cabinet and door are built, the door can be installed. It's held in by two pivot pins that serve as door hinges.

**PIVOT BLOCKS.** One end of each pivot pin fits in a hole in the cabinet, the other in the door. But for added strength, the pin doesn't go into the door frame — it fits in a hole in a pivot block *(Fig. 10)*.

To make the pivot blocks (J), cut two pieces of $3/4$"-thick stock to finished width and length *(Fig. 9)*. Then cut a 45° bevel across the front of each block, leaving a $1/4$"-wide decorative edge.

**PIVOT PIN HOLES.** Drilling holes for the pivot pins can be tricky, because the holes must be as close to the inside edge as possible (about $1/16$"), yet completely within the pivot block.

To drill the holes, place a temporary fence on a drill press table. Then lower the bit and slide the fence up to it. Now, back the fence $1/16$" away from the bit and clamp it to the table *(Fig. 9a)*.

**Note:** To ensure that the holes are drilled exactly the same distance from the end of each block, I used a stop block clamped to the fence.

**SCREW HOLES.** After the pivot holes have been drilled, the next step is to drill countersunk shank holes for the screws that attach the blocks to the door frame *(Fig. 10)*.

**DOOR STOP.** Before mounting the door in the cabinet, I cut a stop (K) for the door and plywood back *(Fig. 12)*. The purpose of this piece is to create a pair of rabbets on the underside of the cabinet top. The plywood back (L) fits against the back edge of the stop, and the pivoting door closes against the front edge of the stop.

To make the door/back stop (K), first crosscut a piece of stock so it fits tightly inside the cabinet from side to side. Sneak up on the width of the stop so when it's positioned flush with the rabbets on the back of the cabinet sides, the stop extends to a point 1" from front of the cabinet side *(Fig. 12)*.

**INSTALL DOOR.** After the door/back stop is glued in place, the door is installed. This is a two-step process. First, the pivot blocks are screwed to the back inside corners of the door *(Fig. 10)*.

Second, position the door inside the cabinet and tap the pivot pins into the

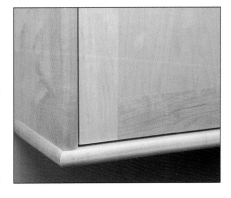

holes in the cabinet sides *(Fig. 11)*.

When both pins are fully seated in the holes in the cabinet, adjust the door for an equal gap on both sides. Now, with a temporary spacer holding the door in this position, tap a length of $3/8$" dowel into the holes *(Fig. 11a)*. Then trim the dowels flush.

**BULLET CATCH.** To keep the door "locked" in the closed (up) position, I installed a bullet catch centered on the top edge of the door *(Fig. 12)*.

When the door is closed, the bullet catch fits into a "dimple" in a strike plate that's attached to the underside of the cabinet top *(Fig. 12a)*.

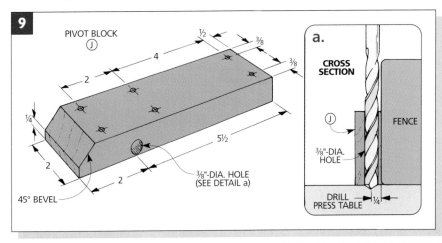

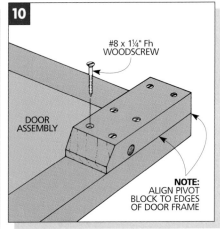

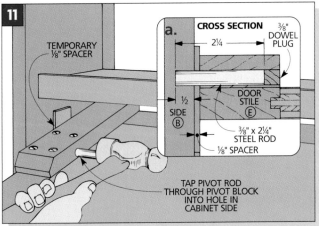

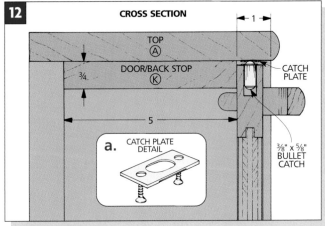

## INSTALLING THE BACK

Before hanging the drafting cabinet in your workshop (or wherever else you want it), there are a couple more things to be done. First, a piece of plywood is installed in the back.

**PLYWOOD BACK.** The plywood back fits in the rabbets cut on the inside edges of the cabinet sides. But the back doesn't have to extend all the way to the bottom of the cabinet. You can't see below the shelf when the door is open anyway (refer to the photo on page 60).

So I cut the ¼" back panel (L) to width to fit in the rabbets from left to right *(Fig. 13)*. But I cut it to length so it extends from the cabinet top just to the bottom edge of the shelf. Then it can be glued and nailed into the rabbets on the back of the cabinet.

**HANGING CLEAT.** The last thing that needs to be done before hanging the cabinet is to make the cleat that holds it to the wall. To make the hanging cleat (M), start out with a piece of ¾"-thick stock at least 4½" wide *(Fig. 13a)*.

Cut this blank to length to fit across the back of the cabinet.

After the blank is cut to length, adjust the table saw blade for a 30°

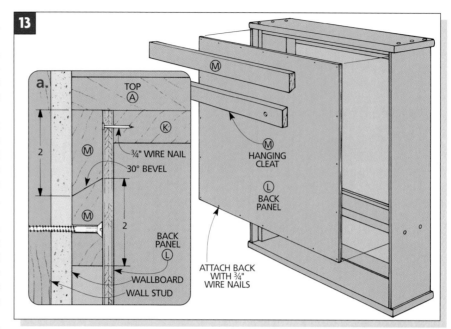

bevel, and rip the cleat blank to produce two 2"-wide hanging cleats.

**Note:** It's easier to hang the cabinet if this second cleat is cut a little shorter than the one attached to the cabinet.

Now glue one of the cleats to the top of the cabinet at the back *(Fig. 13)*.

Then drill a pair of countersunk shank holes in the other cleat *(Fig. 13)*.

Now screw the second cleat into a pair of wall studs so the door is at a height that's comfortable for drawing. (Refer to the Shop Tip below for information on determining the most comfortable height for you.)

Finally, hang the cabinet on the wall carefully, making sure the mating cleats interlock *(Fig. 13a)*. ∎

---

## SHOP TIP ......................................... *Mounting Height*

Since the Drafting Cabinet is designed to hang on the wall, there's a decision to make. How high off the floor should you mount it? You'll have to experiment with what's most comfortable for you, but here are some guidelines to help you decide. The first decision to make is what feels best — sitting or standing.

If you'll use the cabinet mostly for quick sketches, you may want to mount the cabinet for standing.

But, if you'll be using the cabinet to design a lot of projects, you may prefer to mount it so it's comfortable for sitting.

To find the best height for *sitting*, the first consideration should be elbow

height. The idea is to mount the cabinet so the drawing surface is at a height equal to the bottom of your elbow when your arm is bent *(Fig. 1)*. This should leave about 10" (or a range of between 8" and 12") as

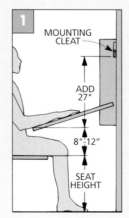

clearance for your knees.

An average-height person sitting in a typical 17" chair should be comfortable when the elbow is about 27" from the floor.

This means the cleat should be screwed into the wall with the bottom edge about 54" off the floor. (See above for more on the mounting system.)

The rule for mounting the cabinet for *standing* is the same as for sitting — position it in relation to your elbow. If you've built the cabinet as specified in the plans, you'll probably find the most comfortable height to be where the wall cleat is mounted about eye level *(Fig. 2)*.

Again, you may want to

experiment. And if you want to switch from sitting to standing, no problem. Just mount two cleats — one for each position.

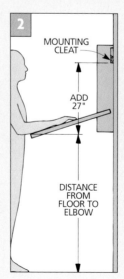

# DESIGNER'S NOTEBOOK

*Adding a bulletin board and a storage rack helps you organize and store your drafting materials.*

## OPTIONAL COMPONENTS

■ The Drafting Cabinet doesn't have to be just a hanging box with a fold-down drawing surface. There's quite a bit of room inside, so it's a natural place for things to accumulate. To organize the inside, I added a couple of optional components. First I installed a bulletin board in the back of the cabinet (*Fig. 1*).

■ To make your own bulletin board, fasten a piece of acoustic ceiling tile to the plywood cabinet back. Then cover it with a 1/8"-thick sheet of cork (*Fig. 2*).

■ If you don't want to make your own bulletin board, an easier (and probably cheaper) way is to buy a ready-made bulletin board with a frame around it. Then you can cut away the frame and fit the board inside the cabinet.

■ Either way, the bulletin board will have to be held in place. To do this, make stop molding (*Figs. 2 and 2a*). Just two strips of molding — one on each side of the bulletin board — are enough to hold the board in place.

■ A storage rack is also a handy thing to have inside the cabinet. It can hold a pad of standard-size (14" x 17") drawing paper, a 24" T-square, triangles, and other drafting materials (*Fig. 1*).

■ The storage rack resembles a corral fence — it's simply a pair of ends connected by two 1/2"-diameter dowels. Notches cut in the upper back corners hold a T-square (*Figs. 1 and 3*).

■ To hold the rack in place, screw up through the shelf into the ends.

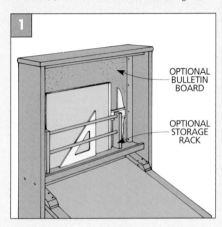

OPTIONAL BULLETIN BOARD

OPTIONAL STORAGE RACK

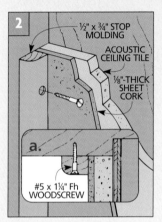

1/2" x 3/4" STOP MOLDING

ACOUSTIC CEILING TILE

1/8"-THICK SHEET CORK

a.

#5 x 1 1/4" Fh WOODSCREW

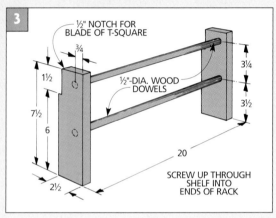

1/2" NOTCH FOR BLADE OF T-SQUARE

3/4

1 1/2

7 1/2

6

2 1/2

3 1/4

1/2"-DIA. WOOD DOWELS

3 1/2

20

SCREW UP THROUGH SHELF INTO ENDS OF RACK

---

## SHOP INFO . . . . . . . . . . . . . . . . . . . . . . . . . . . . . . . . . . . *Shop Drawings*

Every project I build starts with a detailed series of plans. But the drawings don't have to be complicated. The idea is to answer all the woodworking questions — the dimensions of each piece, the size and placement of the joints, and how the hardware is mounted — before beginning.

You don't have to be a draftsman to design projects. A basic set of drafting tools (see photo) can help transfer ideas onto paper. The place to start is with rough sketches, then create a set of shop drawings (a perfect opportunity to use the Drafting Cabinet).

**TO SCALE.** All drawings should show the project to scale. If it's a large project, use a small scale (like one inch equals one foot). For a small project, full-size drawings are usually best. At the minimum, you'll need three separate views of the project.

**FRONT VIEW.** The first drawing to make is a front view. This view shows the height and width of the project. It also shows interior details like shelves, doors, or anything else you'd see looking at it from the front.

**TOP VIEW.** A top view shows the depth of the project. It's made by first extending a pair of lines up from the front view. These indicate the sides of the project. Then, an intersecting pair of lines is drawn to show the front and back edges. The top view should also show the positions of interior pieces.

**SIDE VIEW.** Normally the last drawing that's needed is a view of the project from the side. A side view helps you see the interior pieces and joints from a different angle.

**OTHER DETAILS.** Additional detail drawings help show critical parts of a project, like the joinery or a rounded-over edge. These drawings are best shown actual size, so you can match the details accordingly.

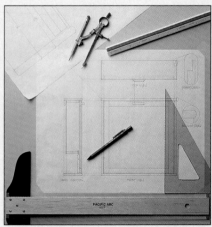

*Shop drawings allow you to make (and correct) mistakes on paper, and refine your design before heading to the shop.*

# Finishing Cabinet

*This cabinet does more than store your finishing supplies. It features a pull-out tray for extra space, a convenient turntable top, pegboard panels, and casters so it can be rolled out of the way.*

When it's time to finish a project, it seems like I hunt for an hour to find all the things I need. Brushes hang in one place while stain and varnish are somewhere else.

Then it's a challenge finding a clean place to set the project while applying finish. I could use my workbench, but I'm usually building another project (making all kinds of dust). And it's easy to spill varnish or stain on the top.

So I decided it was time to organize my finishing "tools." That's what this Finishing Cabinet is designed to do. It stores all the supplies needed to finish a project in one handy location with room on top to hold most projects.

**CABINET.** All my finishing supplies fit in this cabinet that's basically a big box on wheels. The doors and sides have pegboard panels, which provide ventilation inside the cabinet and are also a good place to hang brushes, tape, and other supplies on the outside.

Just above the doors is a tray that pulls out from either side and holds your finishing supplies while you work.

**TURNTABLE.** Another useful feature we built into this project is the turntable top. This is especially handy for small projects — you can sit in one place and still reach all sides of the project.

A complete hardware kit is available for this project (see Sources, page 126).

**SURFACE PREPARATION.** I thought this was a good place to include some tips on preparing a surface for finishing. The Finishing article on pages 72-73 will help you really enjoy this cabinet.

# EXPLODED VIEW

**OVERALL DIMENSIONS:**
24W x 25½D x 29¼H

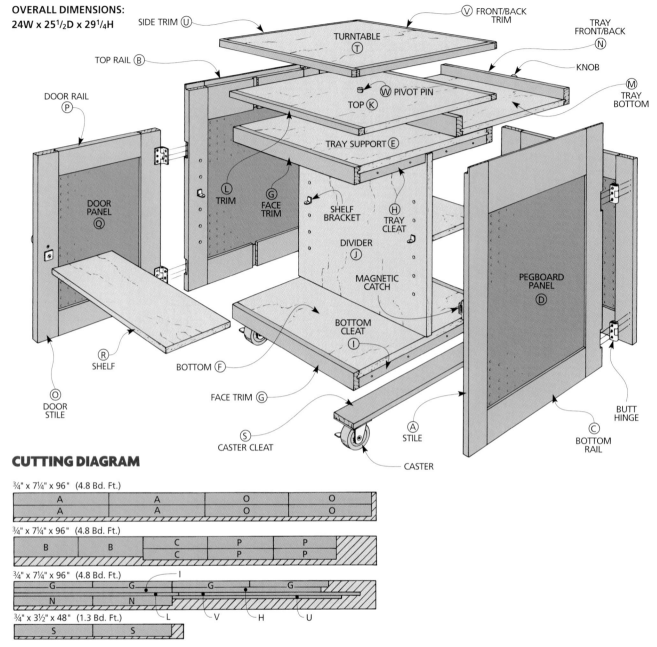

# CUTTING DIAGRAM

¾" x 7¼" x 96" (4.8 Bd. Ft.)

| A | A | O | O |
|---|---|---|---|
| A | A | O | O |

¾" x 7¼" x 96" (4.8 Bd. Ft.)

¾" x 7¼" x 96" (4.8 Bd. Ft.)

¾" x 3½" x 48" (1.3 Bd. Ft.)

**ALSO NEED:** ONE 4' x 8' SHEET ¾" PLYWOOD, ONE 4' x 4' SHEET ¼" PEGBOARD, ¾"-DIA. DOWEL

## MATERIALS LIST

**WOOD**

| | | |
|---|---|---|
| **A** | Stiles (4) | ¾ x 3 - 25¼ |
| **B** | Top Rails (2) | ¾ x 5 - 17 |
| **C** | Bottom Rails (2) | ¾ x 3 - 17 |
| **D** | Pegboard Panels (2) | ¼ pgbd. - 17 x 17¾ |
| **E** | Tray Support (1) | ¾ ply - 21 x 21½ |
| **F** | Bottom (1) | ¾ ply - 21 x 21½ |
| **G** | Face Trim (4) | ¾ x 1¾ - 21 |
| **H** | Tray Cleats (4) | ¾ x 1 - 10⅛ |
| **I** | Bottom Cleats (2) | ¾ x 1 - 21 |
| **J** | Divider (1) | ¾ ply - 21½ x 19½ |
| **K** | Top (1) | ¾ ply - 22 x 21 |

| | | |
|---|---|---|
| **L** | Trim Pieces (2) | ¾ x ¾ - 22 |
| **M** | Tray Bottom (1) | ¾ ply - 20¹⁵⁄₁₆ x 21½ |
| **N** | Tray Front/Back (2) | ¾ x 2³⁄₁₆ - 20¹⁵⁄₁₆ |
| **O** | Door Stiles (4) | ¾ x 3 - 22 |
| **P** | Door Rails (4) | ¾ x 3 - 17 |
| **Q** | Door Panels (2) | ¼ pgbd. - 17 x 16½ |
| **R** | Shelves (2) | ¾ ply - 9½ x 20⅞ |
| **S** | Caster Cleats (2) | ¾ x 3 - 21 |
| **T** | Turntable (1) | ¾ ply - 22½ x 22½ |
| **U** | Side Trim (2) | ¾ x ¾ - 22½ |
| **V** | Front/Back Trim (2) | ¾ x ¾ - 24 |
| **W** | Pivot Pin (1) | ¾ dowel x 1½ |

**HARDWARE SUPPLIES**

(16) No. 6 x ⅝" Fh woodscrews
(18) No. 8 x 1¼" Fh woodscrews
(6) No. 8 x 1½" Fh woodscrews
(14) No. 8 x 2" Fh woodscrews
(16) ¼"-dia. x 1½" lag screws
(4) 1¼"-dia. wood knobs
(12) ⅞"-dia. nylon tack glides
(2 pr.) 2" butt hinges
(2) Magnetic catches
(8) Shelf supports
(4) 3" swivel casters with brakes

I started work on the cabinet by making two identical side assemblies. Each side assembly is made up of two stiles, two rails, and a pegboard panel.

The key to holding these pieces together is a groove on the inside edge of each stile and rail. This groove holds the panel, and forms a mortise for the tenons on the ends of the rails *(Fig. 1a)*.

Since the groove is the same size on all the pieces ($1/4$" wide x $1/4$" deep), I started by cutting all the stiles and rails (A, B, C) to their finished widths and lengths *(Fig. 1)*. Then I cut a centered groove on the inside edge of each piece.

The next step is to cut tenons on the ends of the rails to fit the grooves in the stiles. With the tenons complete, the pegboard panels (D) can be cut to size. Then the entire side assembly can be glued and clamped together.

After the sides are assembled, there are still two more things to do before they're complete. First, a rabbet needs to be cut on the top inside face of each side assembly *(Fig. 1b)*. The rabbet is sized to accept a $3/4$" plywood top that's added later (refer to *Fig. 6*).

Second, a dado is cut down the center of each side assembly *(Figs. 1 and 1c)*. A divider fits in this dado when the cabinet is put together (refer to *Fig. 4*).

**TRAY SUPPORT/BOTTOM.** With the sides done, I started making the tray support (E) and bottom (F) *(Fig. 2)*.

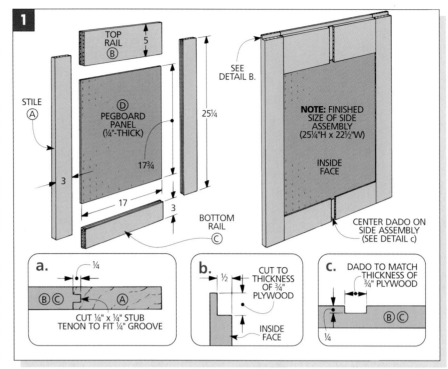

They're made from $3/4$" plywood and connect the two side assemblies. Since they're the same size (21" wide x $21^{1}/2$" long), I cut both at the same time.

But before the support and bottom are attached to the side assemblies, I added face trim (G) to both *(Fig. 2)*. These trim pieces are cut to the same length (21") to hide the plywood edges on the support and bottom. A tongue and groove joint helps hold the trim in position until the glue dries *(Fig. 2a)*.

**CLEATS.** Next, add cleats to the tray support (E) and bottom (F). These pieces of $3/4$" stock attach the tray support and bottom to the side assemblies.

But since you need a $3/4$" gap for the divider, I used four tray cleats (H) on the tray support but only two cleats (I) on the bottom (refer to *Figs. 2b and 4*).

**ASSEMBLY.** When the cleats are glued in place, the cabinet can be assembled. To do this, glue and screw the bottom to the side assemblies *(Fig. 3)*.

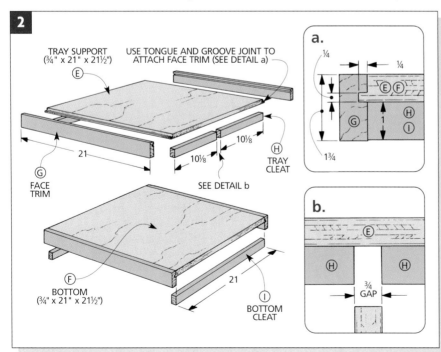

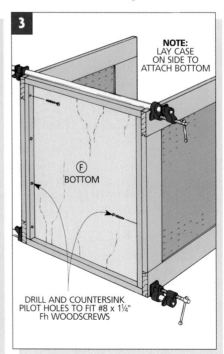

## DIVIDERS & TOP

Now measure between the dadoes in the side panels and cut the divider (J) to fit (21½" wide x 19½" long) *(Fig. 4)*. Then slip the divider into the dadoes and glue and screw it to the bottom.

Set the tray support on the divider so the cleats straddle the divider *(Fig. 4)*. Then align the bottom of the cleats with the bottom edge of the top rails, and screw the tray support to the side assemblies and divider *(Fig. 4a)*.

**TOP.** To make the ³/₄" plywood top, first measure from shoulder to shoulder between the two rabbets on the sides for the width (22"). For the length, measure the width of the sides and subtract 1½" for trim pieces added later. Cut the top (K) to size (22" wide x 21" long) *(Fig. 5)*.

I glued trim pieces (L) to the front and back edges *(Fig. 5)*. Then glue and screw the top to the cabinet *(Fig. 6)*.

## TRAY

The next step is to make a tray to fit between the top (K) and tray support (E).

**TRAY.** The tray is a piece of ³/₄"-thick plywood with identical front and back pieces installed on the ends. These pieces have plastic glides mounted on top to help the tray slide easily and keep it from sagging when it's pulled out.

To determine the size of the tray bottom (M), measure the width of the opening and subtract ¹/₁₆" for clearance *(Fig. 7)*. (Mine was 20¹⁵/₁₆" wide.)

Finding the length is trickier (you need to consider the joinery and the thickness of the front/back pieces). So I took the depth of the cabinet, subtracted 1", and cut the bottom to length (21½"). Then to complete the bottom, cut ¹/₄" tongues on two edges *(Fig. 7)*.

The next step is to cut the front/back (N) pieces to size. The length of the pieces is the same as the width of the tray bottom (20¹⁵/₁₆"). But to find the height (width), measure the opening in the cabinet and subtract ⁵/₁₆" — for the thickness of the glides (¹/₄") plus ¹/₁₆" clearance *(Fig. 7a)*. (In my case 2³/₁₆".)

Now a ¹/₄"-wide groove can be cut on one face of each piece to fit the tongues cut on the tray bottom *(Fig. 7a)*.

After gluing the front/back pieces to the bottom, I screwed a knob on each. Then to complete the tray, I added plastic glides to the top edge of the front/back pieces *(Figs. 7 and 7a)*.

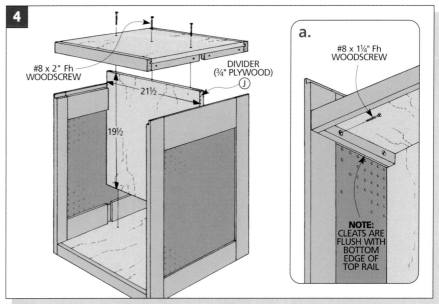

**4**

#8 x 2" Fh WOODSCREW

21½

19½

DIVIDER (¾" PLYWOOD) Ⓙ

**a.**

#8 x 1¼" Fh WOODSCREW

**NOTE:** CLEATS ARE FLUSH WITH BOTTOM EDGE OF TOP RAIL

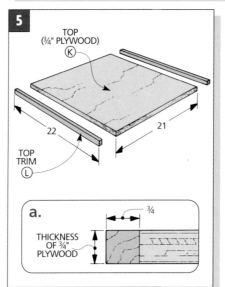

**5**

TOP (¾" PLYWOOD) Ⓚ

22

21

TOP TRIM Ⓛ

**a.**

¾

THICKNESS OF ¾" PLYWOOD

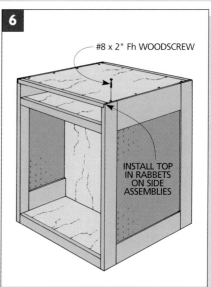

**6**

#8 x 2" Fh WOODSCREW

INSTALL TOP IN RABBETS ON SIDE ASSEMBLIES

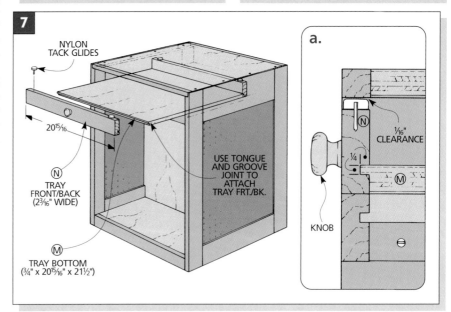

**7**

NYLON TACK GLIDES

20¹⁵/₁₆

Ⓝ

TRAY FRONT/BACK (2³/₁₆" WIDE)

Ⓜ

TRAY BOTTOM (¾" x 20¹⁵/₁₆" x 21½")

USE TONGUE AND GROOVE JOINT TO ATTACH TRAY FRT./BK.

**a.**

Ⓝ

¹/₁₆" CLEARANCE

¼

Ⓜ

KNOB

## DOORS

Next, I started on the two doors (for the front and back). They're built like the sides — frame and panel construction.

**FRAME AND PANEL.** To build the frames, cut the stiles (O) to match the distance from the bottom of the cabinet to the top of the tray support (22") *(Fig. 8)*. Then to match the width of the door to the cabinet, cut the rails (P) 17" long.

After cutting grooves in the edges of all the pieces and tenons on the ends of the rails, the door panels (Q) can be cut to size *(Figs. 8 and 8a)*. Now glue and clamp all the door pieces together.

**HARDWARE.** The next step is to hang the doors. Butt hinges mortised into the front edges of the stiles hold the doors on the cabinet *(Fig. 8)*. Then I installed the catches and knobs on both doors.

**SHELF.** After the doors are mounted, two shelves are added inside. They sit on shelf supports spaced 2" apart *(Fig. 9)*.

Normally you'd drill shelf support holes in the sides of a cabinet. But that won't work on hardboard panels. Instead, I drilled one set of holes on the side rails (A) and the other set in the divider (D). Then install the supports in the holes and cut the shelves (R) to fit.

**CASTERS.** Next, install casters. To do this, glue and screw two cleats (S) to the bottom of the cabinet *(Fig. 9)*. Then use ¼"-dia. lag screws to attach the casters.

**TURNTABLE.** Finally, add a turntable (see the Shop Tip below). ∎

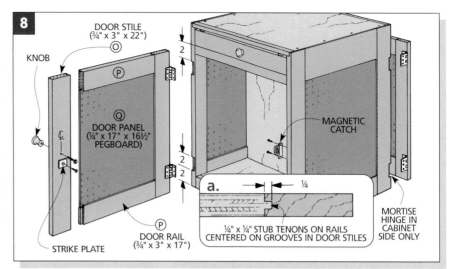

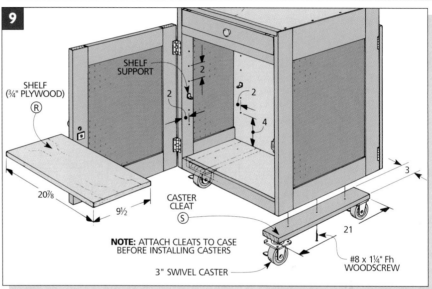

## SHOP TIP . . . . . . . . . . . . . . . . . . . . . . . . . . . . . . . . . . *Turntable*

To make a turntable, cut a plywood square to match the cabinet top (22½" x 22½"). Hide the edges with trim (U, V) *(Fig. 1)*.

Next, trim the glide nails and drill pilot holes in the plywood. Then install the glides in a circle *(Fig. 1a)*.

I used a Forstner bit to drill a ¾"-dia. hole ½" deep in the turntable and a hole through the cabinet top *(Figs. 1 and 2)*.

Finally, cut a pivot pin (W) and glue it in *(Fig. 2)*.

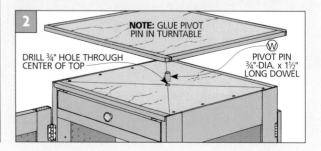

Applying a finish is like a "Catch-22." Although it normally adds to the overall beauty of a project by emphasizing the color and grain of the wood, it also tends to put a magnifying glass on even the tiniest flaws.

Once you apply the finish, any tool marks, nicks, or glue spots will stand out like a chrome bumper on a hay wagon. Fortunately, you can prevent this by carefully preparing the surface of the wood.

As a rule, I usually get as many workpieces as possible ready for the finish before beginning assembly. Take an ordinary table, for instance. It's easier to sand the legs and apron separately than when they're already joined together at right angles.

**Note:** To ensure a tight fit, just be sure not to sand around the areas where the pieces will be joined together until *after* you have assembled the project. That way you'll still have clean edges and corners to work with (which make for better glue surfaces).

## REMOVE TOOL MARKS

Working on the pieces individually also makes it easy to see the "ridges" that often get left behind by the cutters on a jointer, planer, or router. It is easy to see flaws if you shine a light across the work at a low angle (see photo above right). To remove these ridges effectively, I use an ordinary hand scraper skewed at an angle *(Step 1)*.

But you're not finished preparing the workpiece yet. A scraper will leave a surface that looks different than the surrounding area when you apply a finish. So you'll need to create a smooth, uniform surface. This is accomplished through proper sanding.

## SANDING

Although it's not the most exciting job in the world, sanding doesn't have to be a time-consuming chore either, if you follow a few helpful guidelines. The whole key to good sanding is to work

**Scraper.** *Use a sharp scraper to remove any leftover tool marks or ridges from your workpiece. Skew the scraper at an angle for the best cut.*

**Power Sanding.** *A power sander is convenient because it makes quick work of removing material from large, flat surfaces (like the face of your workpiece).*

**Hand Sanding.** *But on a narrow workpiece, a power sander won't work well. A sanding block ensures a crisp corner and a flat surface.*

more efficiently — not harder.

**POWER AND HAND.** It goes without saying that a power sander speeds up the sanding process *(Step 2)*. But while this works fine on large, flat surfaces (like the face of a workpiece), the "give" in the foam pad has a tendency to round over the edges. To maintain a crisp edge (especially on narrow pieces), I switch to a sanding block *(Step 3)*.

**Note:** Check that sandpaper is tight on power sander or sanding block.

**GRIT.** Another thing to consider is the sandpaper grit. If it's too coarse, the sandpaper will leave deep scratches in your workpiece that take a long time to sand out. So unless the surface is extremely rough, I start with 120-grit sandpaper on most projects.

Even so, don't waste time with 120-grit sandpaper if you run across a particularly deep scratch. Switch to a coarser grit to remove the scratch. Then, to ensure that the area takes the finish (or stain) evenly, go back over it with 120-grit sandpaper.

**CHANGE PAPER.** As you're sanding, remember to change the sandpaper frequently. The abrasive particles on the paper only cut fast for the first few minutes. So it just doesn't pay to massage the surface with sandpaper after it's worn out.

**DIRECTION.** The direction you sand is also important. The old rule of thumb holds true here — sand *with* the grain in a back and forth motion. The noticeable scratches left behind if you sand across the grain require a lot of re-sanding to remove.

**CHECK PROGRESS.** The fine dust that builds up as you sand the workpiece will eventually make the surface *feel* smooth. But the real test is how it looks. The goal here is to get a consistent pattern of scratches.

But in order to check, you'll need to clean off the dust *(Step 4)*. This process will also pick up any loose pieces of abrasive which can leave tell-tale scratches of their own when you sand with a finer grit.

**FINE GRIT.** Basically, the fine grit sandpaper creates a series of small scratches that replace the ones made by the previous grit. While it may be tempting to "jump" a few grits to save some time, you'll actually end up sanding even longer with very fine grits. So I always follow up with the next finest grit (150).

The final grit you work up to actually depends on the finish you're planning to use. For a thin, oil finish where the feel of the wood is important, I sand with 180 and 220 grits to create an extra-smooth surface. But with a built-up finish like varnish or lacquer, 150-grit is plenty smooth.

**END GRAIN.** One exception to all this is end grain. Because it's porous and soaks up more finish (or stain), the color will be darker than on the surface grain. To get around this problem, an old trick that works well is to sand the end grain one grit finer.

## GLUE

Although it's convenient to sand pieces in advance, there's a "catch" that comes up when you assemble the project. Any glue squeeze-out that's left on the wood will show up as a light spot when you apply a stain or finish.

The best way to remove glue is to wait until it "skins over" and then simply scrape off the excess *(Step 5)*. Or you can just keep the glue from getting on the wood in the first place (see the Shop Tip below).

**MINERAL SPIRITS.** No matter how careful you are, there's a chance that a stray "glueprint" will go unnoticed. To make these smudges reappear, I wipe down the project with mineral spirits *(Step 6)*. Then, remove the excess glue.

### SHOP TIP

## Keeping Glue off Wood

Instead of scraping off excess glue, there's an easy way to keep it from getting on the surface of the wood.

I use strips of masking tape. It's simple to remove, and there's no damage to the wood (see drawing).

**Vacuum.** *Before assembly, remove sanding dust and bits of abrasive that have fallen off the sandpaper using a shop vacuum and brush.*

**Removing Glue.** *After you've assembled your project, scrape off the "skinned over" glue with a chisel (see the Shop Tip above for an alternative).*

**Mineral Spirits.** *Finally, before applying finish, wipe down the surface of your workpiece with a rag soaked in mineral spirits to reveal any stray glue smudges.*

# TOOL STANDS

**Y**ou can build a box or table, set a tool on it, and call it a tool stand. But by adding mobility, providing extra storage, or making a tool more stable, these stands also make the most of your shop's floor space.

# Flip-Top Tool Stand

*It's a very simple idea — maximize your shop's floor space by mounting two tools in one stand. And by putting the stand on wheels, you can roll it out of the way when the job is done.*

Benchtop tools are great space savers, but they can still fill a small shop in a hurry. That became clear to me one day when I realized I had more tools than I had bench tops to put them on. So after clearing a small space to do some drawing, I came up with this tool stand. It does double-duty by flipping its lid.

What makes this stand different from most others is that you can mount tools on *both* sides of the top. Then when you want to use a different tool, all you have to do is flip the top 180°.

I used my stand to hold two tools I was tired of hoisting on and off my bench. My planer is fastened to one side and my power miter saw is on the other. But this stand would also be a great home for a grinder, benchtop jointer, sanding station, or even a dovetail jig.

**LOCKING KNOBS.** Once you've got the top flipped to the right tool, you want to make sure it stays put. So there's a built-in locking system made from readily-available hardware. Simply tighten a plastic threaded knob at each corner to secure the platform in place against the sides. That keeps it from rotating while you're using a tool.

**ROTATING THE STAND.** One thing to keep in mind as you use the stand is that the tools mounted to it aren't likely to balance each other perfectly. So when you release the locking system, the top will probably want to rotate. For this reason, always keep a firm grip on the tool before releasing the last lock.

**PLYWOOD.** The stand is built almost entirely out of plywood. And it's sized so that you can cut all the pieces out of a single 4' x 8' sheet. You'll also need just a few strips of hardwood, and a couple short lengths of dowel to use as the pivot pins for the top. Since there's no fancy joinery (just a couple of dadoes and some screws), you can probably build this stand in about a day.

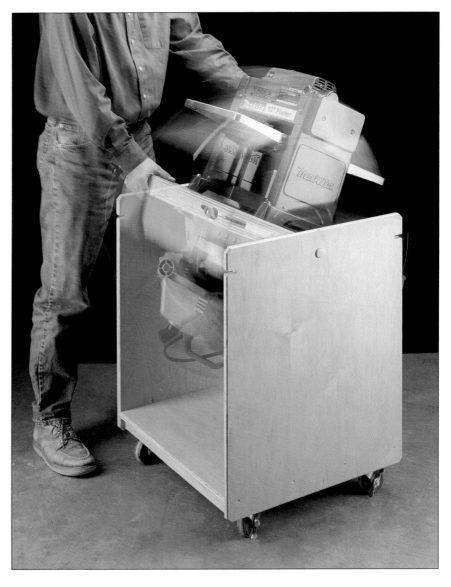

**CASTERS.** In a small shop, mobile tools help you maximize space. But putting two tools on one stand can make for a heavy unit. So to make the stand easy to move, I mounted it on heavy-duty casters. Once you've rolled the stand to where you need it, just step on a lever on each caster to lock it in place. *Woodsmith Project Supplies* offers a set of casters for this project (see page 126 for information).

**HARDWARE.** The rest of the hardware should be easy to find at most hardware stores or home centers. However, the plastic threaded knobs may not be carried by some stores. If you have trouble finding them, a number of mail order sources are listed on page 126.

## EXPLODED VIEW

**OVERALL DIMENSIONS:**
**25¼W x 23¾D x 31⅝H**

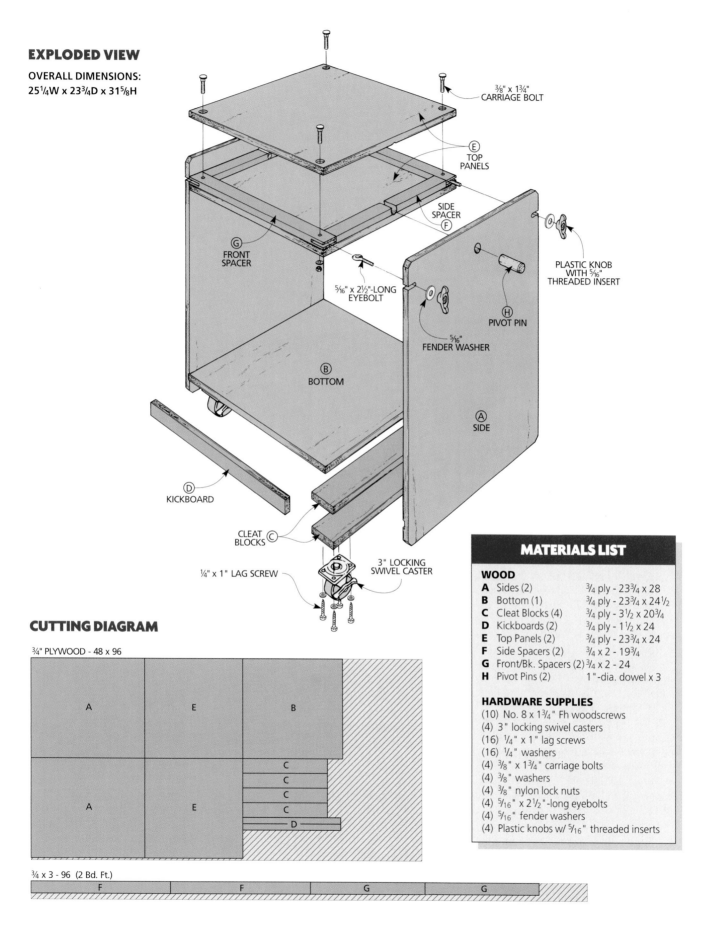

⅜" x 1¾"
CARRIAGE BOLT

E
TOP
PANELS

SIDE
SPACER

F

G
FRONT
SPACER

PLASTIC KNOB
WITH ⁵⁄₁₆"
THREADED INSERT

⁵⁄₁₆" x 2½"-LONG
EYEBOLT

H
PIVOT PIN

⁵⁄₁₆"
FENDER WASHER

B
BOTTOM

A
SIDE

D
KICKBOARD

CLEAT
BLOCKS C

3" LOCKING
SWIVEL CASTER

¼" x 1" LAG SCREW

## CUTTING DIAGRAM

¾" PLYWOOD - 48 x 96

| A | E | B |
| A | E | C |
| | | C |
| | | C |
| | | C |
| | | D |

¾ x 3 - 96 (2 Bd. Ft.)

| F | F | G | G |

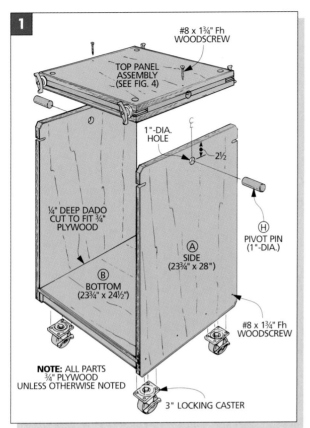

**1**

#8 x 1¾" Fh WOODSCREW

TOP PANEL ASSEMBLY (SEE FIG. 4)

1"-DIA. HOLE

2½

¼" DEEP DADO CUT TO FIT ¾" PLYWOOD

SIDE (A) (23¾" x 28")

BOTTOM (B) (23¾" x 24½")

PIVOT PIN (H) (1"-DIA.)

#8 x 1¾" Fh WOODSCREW

**NOTE:** ALL PARTS ¾" PLYWOOD UNLESS OTHERWISE NOTED

3" LOCKING CASTER

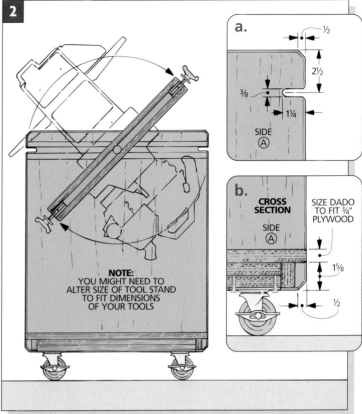

**2**

**NOTE:** YOU MIGHT NEED TO ALTER SIZE OF TOOL STAND TO FIT DIMENSIONS OF YOUR TOOLS

**a.**

½

2½

⅜

1¼

SIDE (A)

**b.**

**CROSS SECTION**

SIDE (A)

SIZE DADO TO FIT ¾" PLYWOOD

1⅝

½

## BASE

The base of the stand is nothing more than a couple of ¾"-thick plywood sides (A) joined by a bottom (B) *(Fig. 1)*. Then cleats are added to the bottom, and casters are fastened to the cleats.

**Note:** Before starting construction, measure the bases and the heights of the tools you plan to mount to the stand. You may have to alter the stand's dimensions to accommodate your tools.

After the sides (A) and bottom (B) are cut to size, the sides can be notched and drilled for the locking hardware and top pivot pins *(Figs. 1 and 2a)*. To cut each slot, I drilled a ⅜"-dia. hole to mark the end, then removed the waste with a jig saw.

A ¼"-deep dado cut on the inside face of each side (A) holds the bottom (B) in place. But before assembling the three case pieces, small chamfers are routed all around the sides pieces and on the front and back edges of the bottom *(Fig. 2b)*. I also knocked off the sharp corners of each side panel by cutting a ½" chamfer on each corner. Once this is done, the sides can be glued and screwed to the bottom.

**CLEATS AND KICKBOARDS.** In order to strengthen the bottom of the base and

make it more rigid, cleat blocks and kickboards are added. The cleat blocks also provide extra thickness for the lag screws that hold the casters.

The cleats (C) are glued up from two pieces of ¾" plywood *(Fig. 3)*. These are glued in place against the sides and bottom. Then plywood kickboards (D) are glued to the ends of the cleats at the front and back of the base.

**CASTERS.** To allow the tool stand to

be moved around easily but locked in place when in use, a locking swivel caster is added to each corner. (See page 126 for sources.)

To mark the positions for the pilot holes for each caster, simply hold the caster in place and mark through the holes in the caster's plate. After drilling ⁵⁄₃₂"-dia. pilot holes, the casters can be attached to the cleat blocks with ¼" x 1" lag screws *(Fig. 3)*.

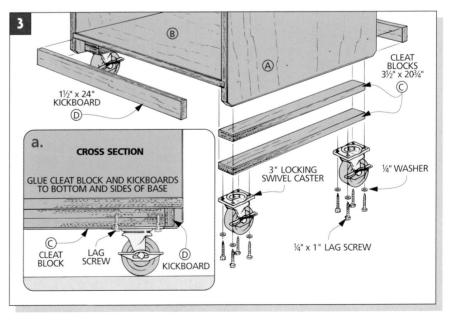

**3**

B

A

CLEAT BLOCKS 3½" x 20¾" (C)

1½" x 24" KICKBOARD (D)

3" LOCKING SWIVEL CASTER

¼" WASHER

¼" x 1" LAG SCREW

**a.**

**CROSS SECTION**

GLUE CLEAT BLOCK AND KICKBOARDS TO BOTTOM AND SIDES OF BASE

CLEAT BLOCK (C)

LAG SCREW

KICKBOARD (D)

Once the base is finished, all that's left is to build the top for the tool stand. The top is made out of two layers of plywood with hardwood spacers sandwiched in between (*Fig. 4*). This extra thickness helps keep the base from racking when the locking knobs are tightened.

Cut the two plywood top pieces (E) to size first. Then the side spacers (F) and front and back spacers (G) are cut to size from ³⁄₄"-thick hardwood.

In addition to separating the plywood layers, the front and back spacers serve another purpose. Notches cut in the ends of these pieces house the eyebolts that lock the top in place (*Figs. 4 and 5*). These notches can be cut on the table saw. Sneak up on their width until the eyebolts fit smoothly in the notches without being forced in place.

Once these notches are cut, the plywood top pieces and the spacers can be glued up. Then holes for the locking hardware can be drilled (*Fig. 5*). To keep the hardware below the surface of the plywood, drill a counterbore for the head of each carriage bolt and for each washer and lock nut (*Fig. 5*).

**LOCK-DOWNS.** With the exception of the large plastic wing nuts, the lockdowns at each corner of the top use common hardware. An eyebolt fits into the slot cut in each corner of the top and is held in place by a carriage bolt, washer, and nylon lock nut (*Fig. 5*).

A large fender washer and plastic wing nut are threaded onto the eyebolt (*Fig. 5*). The wing nuts are then tightened down against the sides to lock the top in place (see photos above).

**PIVOT PINS.** All that's left to complete the stand is to attach the top to the base. The top rests on a pair of pivot pins (H)

*To lock the top in place, tighten the knob at each corner against the side.*

*To flip the top, loosen the knobs and swing the eyebolts out of the notches.*

that pass through the sides of the base and into holes drilled in the edge of the top (*Fig. 6*). To locate the pivot pin holes in the edge of the top, just place the top between the sides of the base and secure it in place with the locking hardware. Now, using the hole in each side of the base as a guide, drill holes into the edge of the top.

The pivot pins are nothing more than short sections of 1"-dia. hardwood dowel. After chamfering the ends, the

pins can be slipped through the sides and into the top. Then each one is secured by a single screw (*Fig. 6a*).

To use the stand, simply mount a tool on each side of the top using lag screws. Then to flip the top around, just loosen the wing nuts in each corner, swing the eyebolts out of the notches in the base sides, and carefully rotate the top. Then before using the tool, make sure to slide the eyebolts back in place and firmly tighten down the wing nuts. ∎

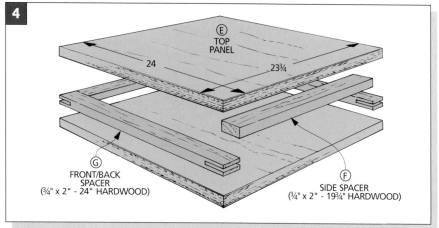

**4**

TOP PANEL (E)

24    23¾

Ⓖ FRONT/BACK SPACER (¾" x 2" - 24" HARDWOOD)

Ⓕ SIDE SPACER (¾" x 2" - 19¾" HARDWOOD)

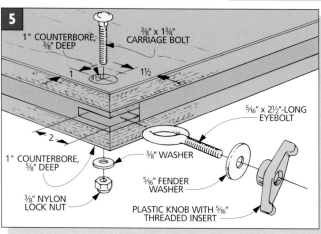

**5**

1" COUNTERBORE, ³⁄₈" DEEP

³⁄₈" x 1¾" CARRIAGE BOLT

1    1½

2

1" COUNTERBORE, ⁵⁄₈" DEEP

³⁄₈" WASHER

⁵⁄₁₆" x 2½"-LONG EYEBOLT

⁵⁄₁₆" FENDER WASHER

³⁄₈" NYLON LOCK NUT

PLASTIC KNOB WITH ⁵⁄₁₆" THREADED INSERT

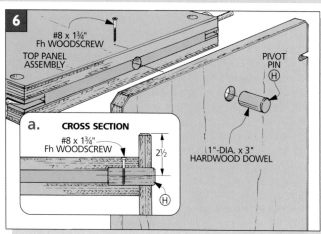

**6**

#8 x 1¾" Fh WOODSCREW

TOP PANEL ASSEMBLY

PIVOT PIN Ⓗ

**a.   CROSS SECTION**

#8 x 1¾" Fh WOODSCREW

2½

Ⓗ

1"-DIA. x 3" HARDWOOD DOWEL

# Lathe Stand

*The mass built into this stand helps your lathe run vibration-free. You can customize the drawers to meet your needs and add an optional swing-out rack to keep your turning tools close while you work.*

With my new bench-top lathe all set up, I had visions of a quiet evening turning a project. But after going down to the shop to try it out, I was disappointed. Unlike the smooth, full-size lathes I had seen, it rumbled and shook as I was turning.

Fortunately, the problem wasn't the lathe at all — it was the stand the lathe was mounted on. Even though the stand was fairly rigid, it was still too lightweight to damp the vibration set up by the spinning workpiece.

**WEIGHT.** To improve the performance of the lathe (and hopefully the quality of my turnings), I decided to build a heavy stand — one that would work like a big sponge to absorb vibration. The trick was to add enough weight to keep the lathe from rattling around without making the stand look like a wood boxcar.

After looking around for a heavy, dense material, I found just what I needed — ¾"-thick particleboard. Two layers of this particleboard are built into the legs and the top of the stand.

**BEAM.** To add even more weight, a hollow "beam" runs between the legs of the stand. But how can a *hollow* beam add weight? The secret is filling it with sand. This provides almost 60 pounds of additional ballast to further damp vibration (see the Shop Tip on page 82).

**KNOCKS DOWN.** But all this weight can be a mixed blessing if it comes time to move things around in the shop. To keep it from becoming a "permanent" fixture, the stand is bolted together so it can be knocked down easily.

**OTHER FEATURES.** While I was at it, I added a pair of drawers with full-extension slides to store my lathe accessories. I also designed an optional pivoting tool rack that positions your lathe tools within easy reach while you're turning. (For more on this, see the Designer's Notebook on page 84.)

# EXPLODED VIEW

**OVERALL DIMENSIONS:**
**60W x 16D x 32H**

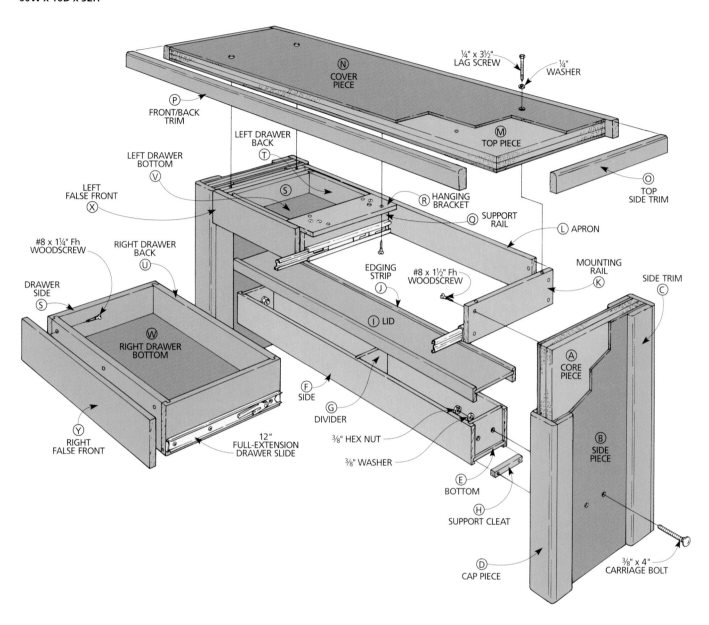

Labels within the exploded view:

- ¼" x 3½" LAG SCREW
- ¼" WASHER
- N COVER PIECE
- M TOP PIECE
- P FRONT/BACK TRIM
- LEFT DRAWER BACK T
- LEFT DRAWER BOTTOM V
- LEFT FALSE FRONT X
- S
- R HANGING BRACKET
- Q SUPPORT RAIL
- L APRON
- O TOP SIDE TRIM
- #8 x 1¼" Fh WOODSCREW
- RIGHT DRAWER BACK U
- DRAWER SIDE S
- EDGING STRIP J
- #8 x 1½" Fh WOODSCREW
- MOUNTING RAIL K
- SIDE TRIM C
- W RIGHT DRAWER BOTTOM
- F SIDE
- G DIVIDER
- I LID
- A CORE PIECE
- Y RIGHT FALSE FRONT
- 12" FULL-EXTENSION DRAWER SLIDE
- ⅜" HEX NUT
- ⅜" WASHER
- E BOTTOM
- H SUPPORT CLEAT
- B SIDE PIECE
- D CAP PIECE
- ⅜" x 4" CARRIAGE BOLT

## MATERIALS LIST

**LEGS**

| | | |
|---|---|---|
| **A** | Core Pieces (4) | ¾ ptbd. - 13 x 30 |
| **B** | Side Pieces (4) | ¼ hdbd. - 13 x 30 |
| **C** | Side Trim (8) | ¾ x 2¾ - 30 |
| **D** | Cap Pieces (4) | ¾ x 3½ - 30 |

**BEAM**

| | | |
|---|---|---|
| **E** | Bottom (1) | ¾ x 4¾ - 42½ |
| **F** | Sides (2) | ¾ x 6 - 42½ |
| **G** | Dividers (3) | ¾ x 4¾ - 4½ |
| **H** | Support Cleats (2) | ¾ x ¾ - 4 |
| **I** | Lid (1) | ¾ x 6½ - 42¼ |
| **J** | Edging Strips (2) | ¾ x 1¾ - 42¼ |
| **K** | Mounting Rails (2) | ¾ x 5 - 12 |
| **L** | Apron (1) | ¾ x 5 - 41 |

**TOP**

| | | |
|---|---|---|
| **M** | Top Pieces (2) | ¾ ptbd. - 14½ x 58½ |
| **N** | Cover Pieces (2) | ¼ hdbd. - 14½ x 58½ |
| **O** | Top Side Trim (2) | ¾ x 2 - 14½ |
| **P** | Front/Back Trim (2) | ¾ x 2 - 60 |

**DRAWERS**

| | | |
|---|---|---|
| **Q** | Support Rail (2) | ¾ x 4¼ - 12 |
| **R** | Hanging Bracket (1) | ¾ x 4½ - 12 |
| **S** | Drawer Sides (4) | ¾ x 4 - 12 |
| **T** | Left Drwr. Fr./Bk. (2) | ¾ x 4 - 12¾ |
| **U** | Rt. Drwr. Fr./Bk. (2) | ¾ x 4 - 21¾ |
| **V** | Left Drwr. Btm. (1) | ¼ hdbd. - 11¼ x 12¾ |
| **W** | Right Drwr. Btm. (1) | ¼ hdbd. - 11¼ x 21¾ |
| **X** | Left False Front (1) | ¾ x 4⅞ - 15¹³⁄₁₆ |

**Y** Right False Front (1)  ¾ x 4⅞ - 24¹³⁄₁₆

**HARDWARE SUPPLIES**

(10) No. 8 x 1¼" Fh woodscrews
(34) No. 8 x 1½" Fh woodscrews
(32) No. 8 x ½" Ph screws
(4) ⅜" x 4" carriage bolts
(4) ⅜" washers
(4) ⅜" hex nuts
(4) ¼" x 3½" lag screws
(4) ¼" washers
(2 pr.) 12" full-extension drawer slides

## CUTTING DIAGRAM

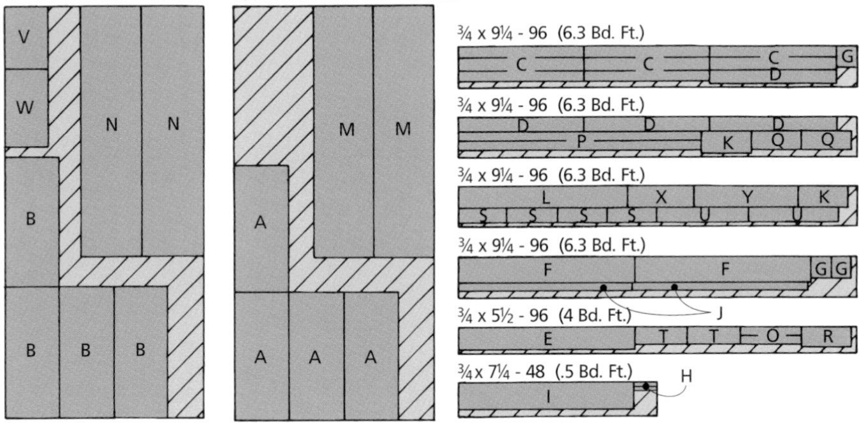

¼" HARDBOARD - 48 x 96    ¾" PARTICLEBOARD - 48 x 96

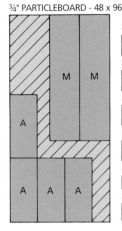

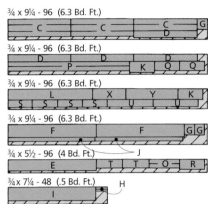

¾ x 9¼ - 96  (6.3 Bd. Ft.)
¾ x 9¼ - 96  (6.3 Bd. Ft.)
¾ x 9¼ - 96  (6.3 Bd. Ft.)
¾ x 9¼ - 96  (6.3 Bd. Ft.)
¾ x 5½ - 96  (4 Bd. Ft.)
¾ x 7¼ - 48  (.5 Bd. Ft.)

## LEGS

I started work on the lathe stand by building the legs. The unusual thing about the legs is they're not your ordinary square posts fastened to each corner. Instead, they're solid "slabs" that are designed to damp the vibration set up by the lathe.

**SLAB.** Using one slab at each end of the stand provides a stiffer support than two separate legs. To make the slabs as heavy as possible, they're built up from two core pieces (A) of ¾"-thick particleboard *(Fig. 1)*. Then each face of the built-up core is covered with a ¼"-thick hardboard side piece (B).

**Note:** The finished height of the stand is the height (length) of the legs, plus 2" for the thickness of the top. To position the center of a workpiece about even with my elbow, I made the legs 30" long (high). You may want to alter this dimension to find the most comfortable working height for you.

**CONTACT CEMENT.** When gluing up the slabs, I used contact cement to create an instant bond. The problem is getting the edges aligned. To do this, I cut one core piece to exact size. Then I built up each layer by attaching an oversized piece and trimming the edges flush with a flush trim bit. (Refer to the Shop Tip on page 13.)

**TRIM PIECES.** To provide more attractive, finished edges on the front and back of each leg, I added ¾"-thick hardwood (maple) trim pieces. After routing a ⅜" roundover on one edge of each side trim piece (C), they're glued in place, flush with the edge of the hardboard *(Fig. 1a)*. Then the cap pieces (D) are ripped to width to cover the edges of the particleboard and the side trim. Once the cap pieces are glued on, their outside edges are rounded over to match the side trim.

## BEAM

Now that the trim is installed, the next step is to build the beam. This is just a box that connects the legs, but it also serves another purpose. I filled mine with sand to add more mass to the stand and help absorb vibration. (See the Shop Tip below.)

The beam consists of a hardwood bottom (E), sides (F), and dividers (G). I cut the sides to size first *(Fig. 2)*.

The bottom fits in a groove cut in each beam side (F) *(Fig. 2b)*. The grooves are positioned ¾" from the bottom edges of the sides.

Before assembling the beam, three dadoes need to be cut in each side piece. Each dado will accept a divider (G) that is also screwed to the bottom (E) *(Figs. 2a and 2b)*. The dado for

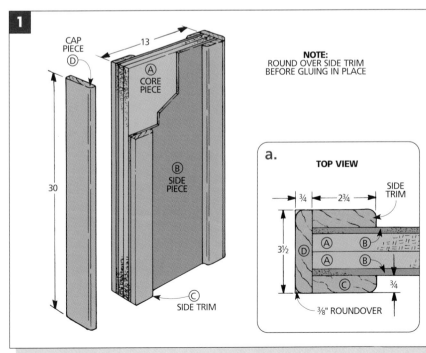

**1**

CAP PIECE (D)

13

(A) CORE PIECE

30

(B) SIDE PIECE

SIDE TRIM (C)

**NOTE:** ROUND OVER SIDE TRIM BEFORE GLUING IN PLACE

**a.**  TOP VIEW

¾    2¾    SIDE TRIM

3½

(D)  (A)  (B)
     (A)  (B)
     (C)

¾

⅜" ROUNDOVER

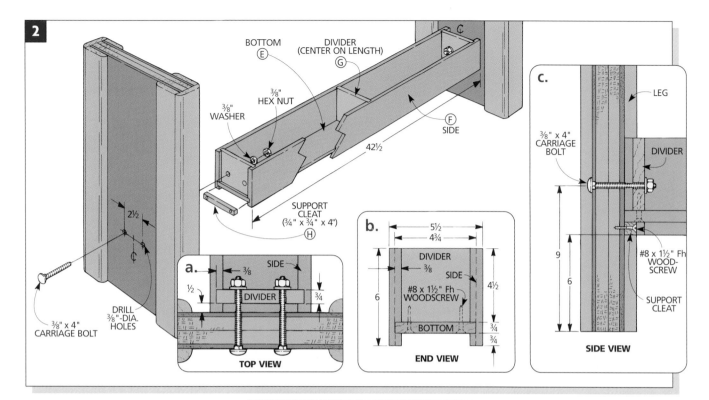

**2**

BOTTOM (E)

DIVIDER (CENTER ON LENGTH) (G)

³⁄₈" HEX NUT

³⁄₈" WASHER

2½

DRILL ³⁄₈"-DIA. HOLES

³⁄₈" x 4" CARRIAGE BOLT

SIDE (F)

42½

SUPPORT CLEAT (³⁄₄" x ³⁄₄" x 4") (H)

**c.**

LEG

³⁄₈" x 4" CARRIAGE BOLT

DIVIDER

9

6

#8 x 1½" Fh WOOD-SCREW

SUPPORT CLEAT

**SIDE VIEW**

**a.**

SIDE

³⁄₈

½

DIVIDER

³⁄₄

**TOP VIEW**

**b.**

5½

4¾

DIVIDER

³⁄₈

SIDE

#8 x 1½" Fh WOODSCREW

6

4½

³⁄₄

³⁄₄

BOTTOM

**END VIEW**

each end divider (G) is ½" from each end of the sides (F) *(Fig. 2a)*. The dado for the third divider is centered on the beam's length *(Fig. 2)*.

Since the bottom and dividers are the same width, once I had the table saw set up, I ripped them all to size.

**ATTACH BEAM.** After assembling the beam, you're ready to attach it to the legs. The ends of the beam fit over two support cleats (H) screwed to the inside of the legs *(Figs. 2 and 2c)*. To hold the stand together (and to make it easy to knock down), holes are drilled through the legs and the end dividers (G) before bolting the beam in place.

To make sure everything would line up, I clamped the beam between the legs while drilling these holes.

**LID.** Next, I cut a lid (I) from ³⁄₄"-thick hardwood. It fits between the legs with ¼" of clearance so it's easy to remove *(Fig. 3)*. To hold the lid in place, it's glued into grooves in a pair of edging strips (J) *(Fig. 3a)*. When the lid sits on the beam, this creates a lipped shelf for temporary storage of lathe accessories.

**MOUNTING RAILS.** With the beam complete, there are only two things left to do. Two mounting rails (K) are screwed to the side trim pieces (C) so you can attach the top later *(Fig. 4)*. And to support the back edge of the top, an apron (L) is screwed to the ends of these rails *(Figs. 4 and 4a)*.

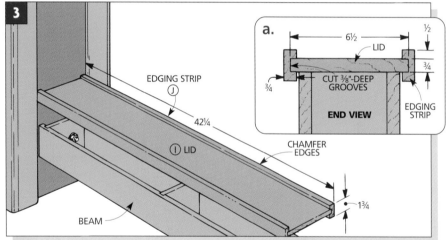

**3**

EDGING STRIP (J)

42¼

(I) LID

BEAM

CHAMFER EDGES

1¾

**a.**

6½

½

LID

³⁄₄

³⁄₄

CUT ³⁄₈"-DEEP GROOVES

**END VIEW**

EDGING STRIP

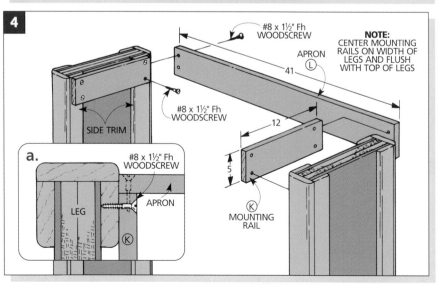

**4**

#8 x 1½" Fh WOODSCREW

APRON (L)

41

**NOTE:** CENTER MOUNTING RAILS ON WIDTH OF LEGS AND FLUSH WITH TOP OF LEGS

#8 x 1½" Fh WOODSCREW

SIDE TRIM

12

5

(K) MOUNTING RAIL

**a.**

#8 x 1½" Fh WOODSCREW

LEG

APRON

(K)

## TOP

Like the legs, the top is built up from two layers of particleboard top pieces (M) "sandwiched" between two hardboard cover pieces (N) *(Fig. 5)*.

**TRIM.** To cover the exposed edges of the particleboard and hardboard, I "wrapped" the top with ³⁄₄"-thick hardwood trim pieces. After ripping the pieces to width to match the thickness of the top (2"), the side trim (O) and

front/back trim pieces (P) are glued on. Then complete the top by chamfering the top edges and corners of the trim.

**ATTACH TOP.** Now it's just a matter of attaching the top to the base. To do this, center the top from side-to-side and

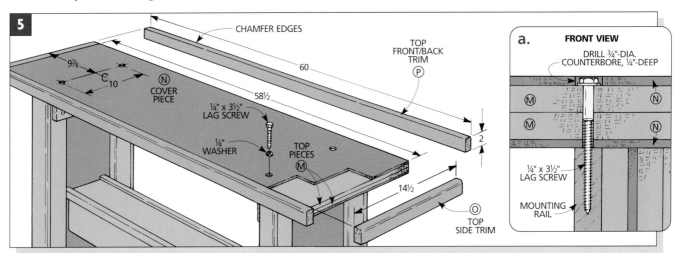

## DESIGNER'S NOTEBOOK

*Put your tools at your fingertips while you work, then swing them out of the way when you're done.*

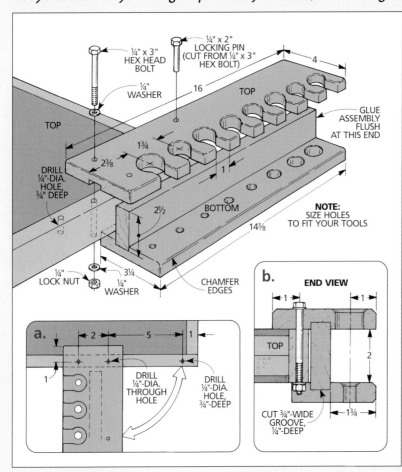

### PIVOTING TOOL RACK

■ This optional tool rack is a three-part I-shaped assembly that fits over the edge of the lathe stand (see drawing). It can be mounted to either the left or right side of the stand.

■ To keep the tools in place, cut a row of open-ended holes in the top that are slightly smaller than the thick part of the handles (see photo). The holes in the bottom of the rack are slightly larger than the diameters of the tool blades.

■ The rack pivots on a hex bolt that passes through a hole drilled through the top of the rack and the front trim piece of the lathe stand (see detail 'b'). Two other holes accept a steel pin (a hex bolt with the threads cut off) that "locks" the rack in either the open or closed position (see detail 'a').

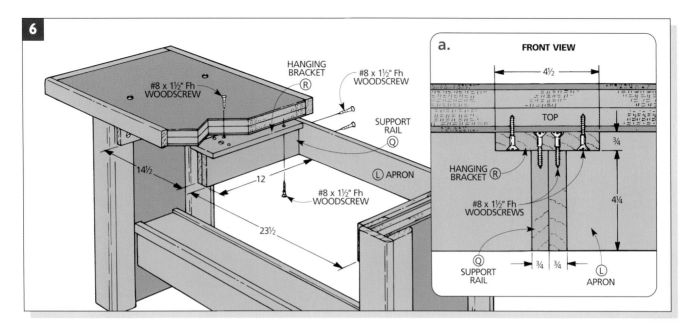

**6**

HANGING BRACKET (R)

#8 x 1½" Fh WOODSCREW

#8 x 1½" Fh WOODSCREW

SUPPORT RAIL (Q)

(L) APRON

14½

12

#8 x 1½" Fh WOODSCREW

23½

**a.** **FRONT VIEW**

4½

TOP

¾

HANGING BRACKET (R)

#8 x 1½" Fh WOODSCREWS

4¼

(Q) SUPPORT RAIL

¾  ¾

(L) APRON

---

front-to-back. After drilling counterbored shank holes, secure the top to the rails with lag screws *(Fig. 5a)*. (Don't use glue. This allows the stand to be taken apart if you need to move it.)

**Note:** If the motor on your lathe hangs below the headstock, you'll need to cut an opening in the top for the belt to fit through.

## DRAWERS

Once the top was in place, I started work on the two drawers that fit under the top. These drawers are mounted on full-extension slides. (For more on these slides, refer to page 86.)

The drawer openings are created by screwing a simple T-shaped piece to the

top *(Figs. 6 and 6a)*. It consists of a support rail (Q) glued up from two ¾"-thick pieces, and a hanging bracket (R) which is screwed to the top edge of the support rail.

**Note:** The end of the support rail is also screwed to the apron (L) *(Fig. 6)*.

**DRAWERS.** After establishing the openings, work can begin on the drawers. They're held together with a locking rabbet joint *(Fig. 7b)*. Before cutting the joints though, you'll need to figure out the size of the drawer pieces.

**DETERMINE SIZE.** This is easy for the drawer sides (S). They're all the same length (12"). The tricky part is determining the length of the front/back pieces (T, U) for each drawer.

To do this, start by measuring the width of the opening. (In my case, this was 23½" for the right-hand drawer.) Then subtract the amount of clearance you'll need for the drawer slides. (The slides I used required ½" clearance on each side for a total of 1".)

The last thing to take into account is the locking rabbet joints. After subtracting ¾" (⅜" on each side), I ended up with front/back pieces for the right-hand drawer that were 21¾" long.

**LOCKING RABBETS.** Now you can cut the joints. This is just a matter of rabbeting the front/back pieces to form a tongue *(Fig. 7b)*. Then cut dadoes in the side pieces to accept the tongues.

Before assembling the drawers, each piece is grooved to accept a drawer bottom (V, W) *(Fig. 7a)*. Then I drilled holes in the drawer fronts for two false fronts (added later) *(Fig. 7)*.

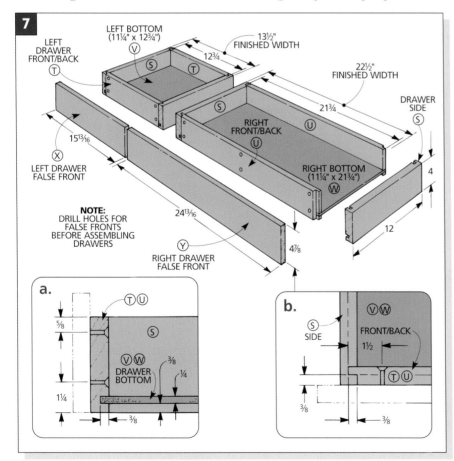

**7**

LEFT BOTTOM (11¼" x 12¾") (V)

13½" FINISHED WIDTH

12¾

LEFT DRAWER FRONT/BACK (T)

(S)  (T)

22½" FINISHED WIDTH

21¾

DRAWER SIDE (S)

(S)

RIGHT FRONT/BACK (U)

RIGHT BOTTOM (11¼" x 21¾") (W)

4

15¹³⁄₁₆

(X)

LEFT DRAWER FALSE FRONT

12

**NOTE:** DRILL HOLES FOR FALSE FRONTS BEFORE ASSEMBLING DRAWERS

24¹³⁄₁₆

(Y)

RIGHT DRAWER FALSE FRONT

4⅞

**a.**

(T)(U)

⅝

(S)

(V)(W)  ⅜

DRAWER BOTTOM  ¼

1¼

⅜

**b.**

(S) SIDE

(V)(W)

FRONT/BACK

1½

(T)(U)

⅜

⅜

**INSTALLING SLIDES.** With the drawers assembled, the slides can be installed (*Figs. 8a and 8b*). I used a pair of heavy-duty 12" slides for each drawer. (See page 126 for sources.)

**FALSE FRONTS.** Next, to cover the gap between the drawer and the slides and to provide a uniform look across the front, I added false fronts (X, Y) to the drawers (refer to *Fig. 7*). I cut the fronts to allow $\frac{1}{8}$" clearance around the edges and ends. This lets you open and close the drawers without them hitting each other. To complete the lathe stand, the false fronts are screwed in place. Since I can easily hook my fingers underneath the drawers to pull them open, I didn't add knobs or pulls. This gave the stand a clean appearance across the front. ■

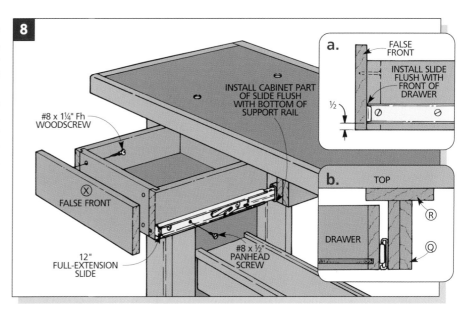

**8**

#8 x 1¼" Fh WOODSCREW

INSTALL CABINET PART OF SLIDE FLUSH WITH BOTTOM OF SUPPORT RAIL

FALSE FRONT

12" FULL-EXTENSION SLIDE

#8 x ½" PANHEAD SCREW

a.
FALSE FRONT
INSTALL SLIDE FLUSH WITH FRONT OF DRAWER
½

b.
TOP
DRAWER
R
Q

# HARDWARE ........................ *Full-Extension Slides*

One way to increase the usable space in a drawer is to install full-extension drawer slides. These slides let you pull the drawer all the way out of a cabinet, giving you easy access to what's inside — even the stuff that tends to "migrate" to the back corners.

The secret is a system of telescoping "channels." As the drawer is opened, these channels cantilever the drawer out in front of the cabinet.

With the channels fully extended, you'd think the drawers would tend to sag. But that's not the case. They're designed to carry loads that range from 75 to 150 pounds — strong enough for a whole drawer full of tools.

**BEARINGS.** Even with that much weight, the operation is smooth. And the slides are about as quiet as a caterpillar crawling across a pool table. That's because the channels ride on a line of steel (or nylon) ball bearings.

**INSTALLATION.** Although full-extension slides are precision-made, you don't have to be a jeweler to install them. Just press a quick-release lever to separate the slide's two parts *(Fig. 1)*.

Then attach one part to the cabinet and the other to the drawer.

**Note:** Face-frame cabinets require a slightly different installation *(Fig. 2)*. And since the clearance requirements vary depending on the slide, it's best to have the slides in hand before you start building the project.

**ADJUSTMENT.** Once the slides are installed, the horizontal slots in the cabinet part of the slides allow you to adjust the drawer in or out *(Fig. 1)*. And the vertical slots in the drawer part let you adjust it up or down.

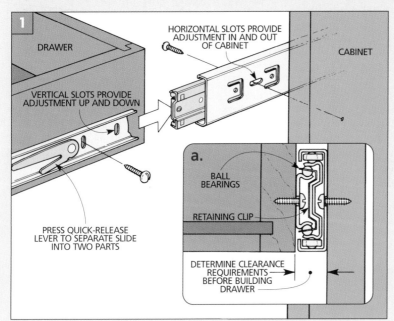

**1**

DRAWER

HORIZONTAL SLOTS PROVIDE ADJUSTMENT IN AND OUT OF CABINET

CABINET

VERTICAL SLOTS PROVIDE ADJUSTMENT UP AND DOWN

PRESS QUICK-RELEASE LEVER TO SEPARATE SLIDE INTO TWO PARTS

a.
BALL BEARINGS
RETAINING CLIP
DETERMINE CLEARANCE REQUIREMENTS BEFORE BUILDING DRAWER

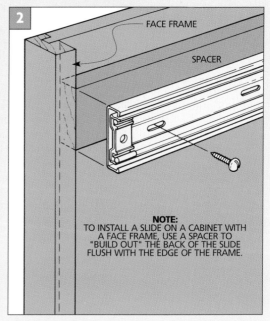

**2**

FACE FRAME

SPACER

**NOTE:** TO INSTALL A SLIDE ON A CABINET WITH A FACE FRAME, USE A SPACER TO "BUILD OUT" THE BACK OF THE SLIDE FLUSH WITH THE EDGE OF THE FRAME.

# Benchtop Jointer Stand

*Increase the performance and convenience of your benchtop jointer with this enclosed stand.*
*Shop-built extension tables let you joint longer stock and built-in chip collection keeps things clean.*

It's amazing what a few strips of aluminum and a can of paint can do. Take this benchtop jointer stand, for instance. At a glance, it appears to be a store-bought accessory for the jointer. But it's really just a simple, shop-made box with some very practical features.

Actually, there's more to this jointer stand than a nice paint job and some shiny metal strips.

**STABLE BASE.** For one thing, the stand provides a stable base that holds the jointer at a more comfortable working height than a bench.

The stand also ensures the jointer stays put during a cut. It's made of medium-density fiberboard (MDF) so it provides a solid base. And to keep that solid base from rocking on an uneven shop floor, I added a leveler at each corner along the bottom edge. When you combine that with a pair of shop-made extension tables, it's like having a full-size, stationary tool.

**EXTENSION TABLES.** One of the drawbacks of a benchtop jointer is that it won't do a very good job jointing longer stock. By adding a shop-made extension table to each end of the jointer, I increased the length of the bed to 50". And the extensions are simple to make with most of the same materials used for the jointer stand. They're just some aluminum angle and MDF, with plastic laminate covering the top and bottom. (For step-by-step plans on building the extension tables, refer to the Designer's Notebook on page 92.)

**CHIP COLLECTION.** But perhaps one of the handiest features on this jointer stand is something you don't even see until you open the door. The chips produced by the jointer fall into a plastic trash can that slides in and out of the stand (refer to the photo on page 91). When it's full, you simply open the door, pull the trash can out of the stand and throw the chips away.

# EXPLODED VIEW

**OVERALL DIMENSIONS:**
30W x 16D x 30¼H

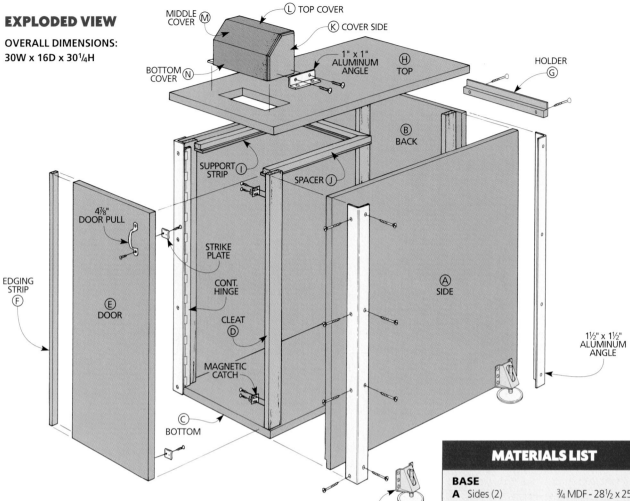

MIDDLE COVER Ⓜ
Ⓛ TOP COVER
Ⓚ COVER SIDE
1" x 1" ALUMINUM ANGLE
Ⓗ TOP
HOLDER Ⓖ
BOTTOM COVER Ⓝ
Ⓑ BACK
SUPPORT STRIP Ⓘ
SPACER Ⓙ
4⅞" DOOR PULL
STRIKE PLATE
CONT. HINGE
Ⓐ SIDE
EDGING STRIP Ⓕ
Ⓔ DOOR
CLEAT Ⓓ
MAGNETIC CATCH
1½" x 1½" ALUMINUM ANGLE
Ⓒ BOTTOM
LEG LEVELER

# CUTTING DIAGRAM

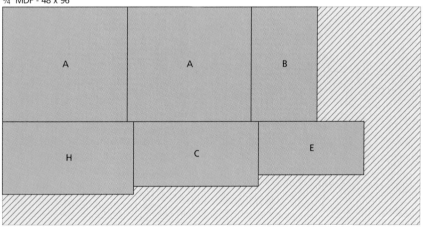

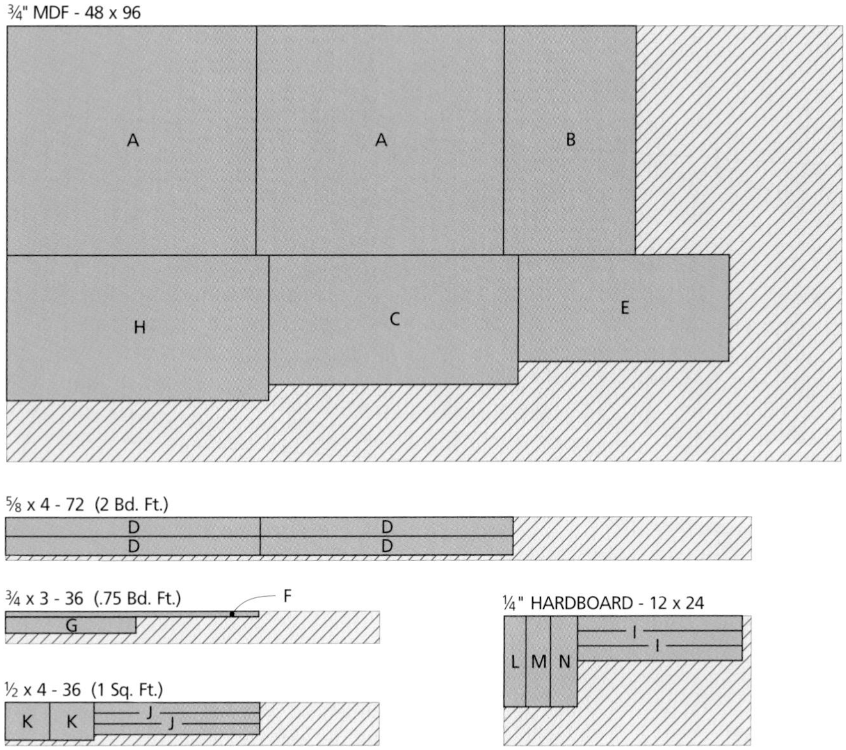

¾" MDF - 48 x 96

A | A | B
H | C | E

⅝ x 4 - 72 (2 Bd. Ft.)

D | D
D | D

¾ x 3 - 36 (.75 Bd. Ft.)
G    F

¼" HARDBOARD - 12 x 24
L M N
I
I

½ x 4 - 36 (1 Sq. Ft.)
K | K | J
J

---

## MATERIALS LIST

### BASE
| | | |
|---|---|---|
| **A** | Sides (2) | ¾ MDF - 28½ x 25¼ |
| **B** | Back (1) | ¾ MDF - 15¼ x 25¼ |
| **C** | Bottom (1) | ¾ MDF - 14¼ x 28¾ |
| **D** | Cleats (4) | ⅝ x 1¾ - 24½ |
| **E** | Door (1) | ¾ MDF - 11¾ x 24⅜ |
| **F** | Edging Strip (1) | ¾ x ½ - 24⅜ |
| **G** | Holder (1) | ¾ x 1½ - 12½ |

### TOP
| | | |
|---|---|---|
| **H** | Top (1) | ¾ MDF - 16 x 30 |
| **I** | Support Strip (3) | ¼ hdbd. - 1⅜ x custom length |
| **J** | Spacer (1) | ½ x 1 - cust. length |

### COVER
| | | |
|---|---|---|
| **K** | Cover Sides (2) | ½ x 3½ - 4 |
| **L** | Top Cover (1) | ¼ hdbd. - 2¹/₁₆ x 8⅜ |
| **M** | Middle Cover (1) | ¼ hdbd. - 2⁵/₁₆ x 8⅜ |
| **N** | Bottom Cover (1) | ¼ hdbd. - 2⁹/₁₆ x 8⅜ |

### HARDWARE SUPPLIES
(8) No. 8 x ½" Fh sheet metal screws
(40) No. 8 x 1¼" Fh sheet metal screws
(6) No. 8 x 2" Fh sheet metal screws
(2) 1" x 1" - 3⅝" aluminum angle
(4) 1½" x 1½" - 25¼" aluminum angle
(4) Leg levelers w/ screws
(1) 1¹/₁₆" x 24⅜" continuous hinge
(1) 4⅞" door pull
(2) Magnetic catches w/ strikes
(4) ¼" x 1½" hex bolts
(4) ¼" T-nuts
(4) ¼" washers
(1) 36-quart trash can

# BASE

The stand starts out as a tall base that's open on the top and one end *(Fig. 1)*. I used $3/4$"-thick medium-density fiberboard (MDF) because it's an inexpensive source of large, flat panels. Plus, MDF accepts paint well. (To learn more about working with MDF, refer to the Woodworker's Notebook on page 95.)

The base is made up of two sides (A) and a back (B) that are rabbeted to accept a bottom (C) *(Fig. 1a)*. To strengthen the corners, I glued a couple of hardwood cleats (D) to each side piece *(Figs. 1 and 1b)*. The cleats in back provide a large glue surface when the base is assembled. The front cleats provide mounting surfaces for a hinge and some magnetic catches added later.

**ALUMINUM ANGLE.** After gluing and clamping the base together, the next step is to add a piece of aluminum angle to each corner. (You can find aluminum angle at most home centers.)

The pieces of aluminum cover the exposed edges of the base, protecting the corners from getting chipped. They also add extra rigidity to the stand.

The aluminum angle is held in place with screws. But before installing it, you may want to shine it up. (To find out how to do this, along with other tips on working with aluminum, refer to the Technique article on page 94.)

**LEG LEVELERS.** To prevent the stand

from wobbling if the floor is uneven, I added four sturdy leg levelers *(Fig. 2)*. These levelers wrap around the bottom edge of each side and are secured to the side panels with screws.

The levelers each have a large, metal "foot" that serves as a stable platform. The foot is attached to a threaded rod and can be adjusted higher or lower with an ordinary Allen wrench (see the photo on page 91). (*Woodsmith Project*

*Supplies* is offering these levelers. See page 126 for more information and for other sources.)

**DOOR.** With the levelers in place, I added a door (E) to enclose the front of the stand *(Fig. 2)*. When determining the size of the door, there are several things to keep in mind.

First, to provide a mounting surface for the hinge, a $1/2$"-wide wood strip will be attached to the door *(Fig. 2a)*. You'll also need to account for the thickness of the hinge itself. And remember to allow for a $1/16$" gap between the other three edges of the door and the stand.

**EDGING STRIP.** After cutting the door to size, you can add the edging strip (F) to the edge of the door *(Fig. 2)*.

**Note:** The edge of the MDF will "drink up" a good amount of glue. Cover the edge of the MDF with glue, let it absorb for a minute and then apply more glue to any areas that need it.

When the glue dries, just hinge the door to the cleat (D) *(Fig. 2a)*.

**CATCHES.** To hold the door closed, the cleat on the opposite side of the hinge provides a mounting surface for a pair of magnetic catches. After installing the catches, I screwed the strike plates to the back of the door and fastened a small door pull to the front of the door *(Fig. 2)*.

Once the base was done, I decided to add a push block holder (see the Designer's Notebook on the next page).

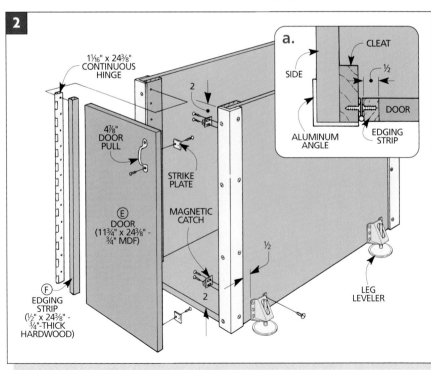

*Keep your push blocks close at hand with this simple bracket that attaches to the jointer stand.*

## PUSH BLOCK HOLDER

■ The holder (G) is simply a strip of hardwood that fits between the pieces of aluminum angle on the corners of the stand (see drawing). To prevent the push blocks from falling out, there's a lip that's formed by rabbeting the top edge of the holder (detail 'a').

■ To attach the holder to the stand, secure it with a couple of screws.

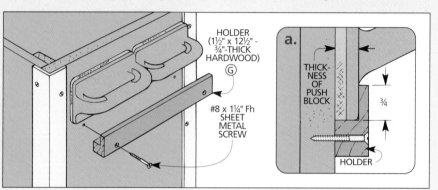

## TOP

With the base complete, I added a top. It provides a solid mounting platform for the jointer *(Fig. 3)*. In addition, the top holds a cover that encloses the chip chute on the jointer.

**TOP.** The top (H) is a large MDF panel that's sized to overhang all four edges of the base slightly. To ease the sharp corners of the panel, I routed slight ($^1/_{16}$") chamfers on the top and bottom edges *(Fig. 4a)*.

**CUT OPENING.** To allow chips to fall into the trash can, there's a rectangular opening in the top *(Fig. 4)*.

**Note:** The size and location of this opening may vary from what is pictured, depending on your jointer.

An easy way to determine the location is to center your jointer on the width of the top. But to end up with an opening directly over the trash can, the jointer is offset toward one end *(Fig. 3)*.

Now just lay out the opening right below the chip chute on the jointer. Make your opening as wide as the chip chute on the tool. Then extend the layout lines $3^1/_2$" from the base *(Fig. 4)*. After drilling a starter hole near each corner of the layout, remove the rest of the waste with a jig saw.

**MOUNTING HOLES.** Once the chip opening is completed, it's a good time to locate the mounting holes for the jointer. The idea here is to set the jointer in place so the chip chute aligns with the edge of the opening. This allows chips to fall into the trash can without piling up on the top.

Now you can mark and drill the mounting holes. The holes are sized to accept the barrel of a T-nut that's installed from underneath *(Fig. 3a)*. Later, the T-nuts make it easy to bolt the jointer to the top of the stand.

**SUPPORT BRACKET.** There's one last thing to do before attaching the top to the stand. That's to add a U-shaped support bracket under the top *(Fig. 3)*. The support bracket suspends the trash can against the top and underneath the chip opening. It also guides the trash can as you slide it in and out of the stand.

**Note:** I used a plastic 36-quart trash can. Adjust the size of the brackets to fit whatever size trash can you use.

The support bracket consists of three sections that form the U-shape. Each section is made up of two pieces: a $^1/_4$" hardboard support strip (I) and a

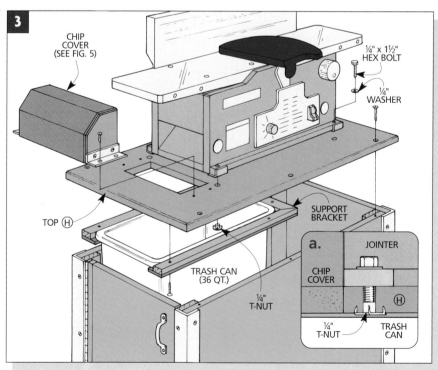

# WOODWORKER'S NOTEBOOK

*Think of medium-density fiberboard as particleboard with better manners. Since it's smooth, stable, heavy, and machines beautifully, it's a good material for jigs, shop cabinets, and furniture.*

## MDF

Medium-density fiberboard (MDF) is an engineered (man-made) product that's been around since the 1960s.

MDF is in the same family as particleboard. But unlike particleboard (which is a mixture of shavings and wood chunks held together with resin), MDF is much more refined (see photo below).

This finer material can be more tightly compressed to form a denser, stronger panel. For example, it takes approximately 23" of fiber/resin mix to make a $3/4$"-thick sheet of MDF. It only takes about 4" to 6" of wood chips and sawdust to form a $3/4$"-thick sheet of particleboard.

**ADVANTAGES.** Breaking down wood into a fibrous material has a number of

advantages. First, there's no grain to it. This means changes in humidity have little effect on MDF — it's extremely stable. A piece of red oak, for example, will expand or contract approximately 1% in width (about $1/8$" per 12"). MDF, on the other hand, will move as little as 0.1% (less than $1/64$" per 12").

And second, the finer material results in a smooth, flat, uniform surface. This makes it the perfect base for wood veneer and plastic laminate.

You'll also find that it holds an edge very well (see photos above and below left). And you won't run into voids, like you might with plywood.

**MACHINING.** Since it's denser than regular wood, MDF can be a bit harder

on tools. But it can be worked like any other wood product — as long as carbide cutters are used. About the only thing you shouldn't do to MDF is run it through a thickness planer or over an edge jointer.

**Safety Note:** Whenever you work with MDF, treat it like any wood product. Use a dust collector if you have one, and always wear a dust mask — especially when you're sanding. Since the fibers are so fine to begin with, sanding MDF kicks up a lot of fine dust that can hang in the air.

**FASTENERS.** Regular wood glues or contact cement work well for joining MDF face-to-face with other pieces. For edge joints, screws help reinforce the glue joint. See the photos below for tips on this.

**FINISH.** MDF isn't usually stained or finished naturally (although it can be). It's most commonly covered with a wood veneer or plastic laminate — or it's simply painted. (Whenever I use MDF for shop jigs, I simply protect it with a couple coats of varnish.)

**AVAILABILITY.** Like particleboard, a standard sheet of MDF is 49" by 97" (the extra is for trimming). And it's available as thin as $5/32$", and as thick as $1^5/8$" (see photo above).

Although it's gaining in popularity, not all lumberyards carry MDF. It's best to call around first to find a retailer in your area.

**MDF Starts This Way.** *Finely processed wood fibers are mixed with resin to form medium-density fiberboard.*

**Machines Well.** *Since there's no grain to deal with, MDF machines very well in any direction with no chipout.*

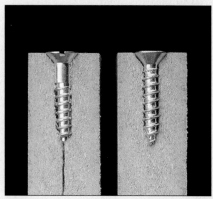

**Pilot Holes.** *To avoid splitting when screwing into an edge, drill pilot holes and use straight-shanked screws (right).*

**Clamp.** *After drilling a pilot hole, clamp a handscrew across the workpiece to help prevent splitting.*

# Portable Planer Stand

*Getting your planer where you want it is much easier when it's mounted to this roll-around stand. And by adding an optional drawer, your planer accessories are always close at hand.*

Put a handle on the top and call it portable. That seems to be the idea with "portable" benchtop planers. But weighing in at 58 pounds, my portable planer is a chore to lift and carry around. So I decided to make it *truly* portable by building a simple roll-around stand for it.

**ACCESSIBLE AND MOBILE.** There are a number of advantages to mounting a planer to a stand. First, it's always accessible. I don't have to drag the planer out and look for a place to clamp it down. Instead, it's always set up and ready to use on its own benchtop.

Second, adding a pair of wheels to the stand allows you to roll it around wherever you need it. For instance, when planing long boards, you might move it over near an open door — or even outside onto the driveway.

**OUTFEED EXTENSION.** To make it even easier to plane long boards, I added an outfeed extension. The extension provides additional support to your workpiece as it comes out of the planer.

There's also an adjustment system built into the outfeed table so you can set it to exactly the right height.

And when it's not being used, the outfeed extension "knocks down." The table lifts off and can be stored on one of the shelves. Then the support wings fold flat against the sides, giving the stand a smaller "footprint" for storage.

**OPTIONAL DRAWER.** Finally, the stand can be fitted with an optional drawer under the planer platform to hold all your planer accessories (see the Designer's Notebook on page 101).

**MATERIALS.** The stand is designed so you can cut all the pieces (including the drawer) from one 4' x 8' sheet of plywood. You'll also need a small piece of hardboard for the outfeed support, and for the drawer bottom if you add the drawer. All the hardware should be easy to find at your local hardware store.

## EXPLODED VIEW

**OVERALL DIMENSIONS:**
27W x 34½D x 32H

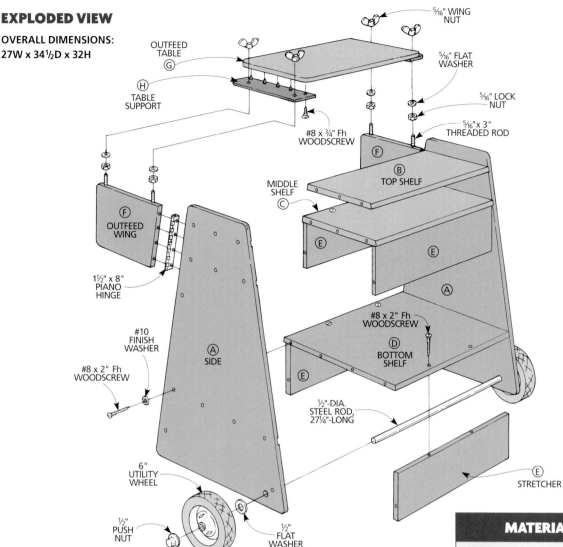

5⁄16" WING NUT

OUTFEED TABLE
Ⓖ

5⁄16" FLAT WASHER

Ⓗ
TABLE SUPPORT

5⁄16" LOCK NUT

5⁄16" x 3" THREADED ROD

#8 x ¾" Fh WOODSCREW

Ⓕ

Ⓑ
TOP SHELF

MIDDLE SHELF
Ⓒ

Ⓕ
OUTFEED WING

Ⓔ

Ⓔ

1½" x 8" PIANO HINGE

Ⓐ

#8 x 2" Fh WOODSCREW

#10 FINISH WASHER

Ⓐ
SIDE

Ⓓ
BOTTOM SHELF

#8 x 2" Fh WOODSCREW

Ⓔ

½"-DIA. STEEL ROD, 27¼"-LONG

6" UTILITY WHEEL

½" PUSH NUT

½" FLAT WASHER

Ⓔ
STRETCHER

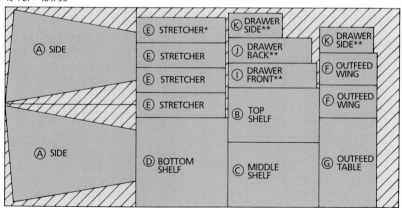

### MATERIALS LIST

**WOOD**

| | | |
|---|---|---|
| **A** | Sides (2) | ¾ ply - 23½ x 32 |
| **B** | Top Shelf (1) | ¾ ply - 13¼ x 22¼ |
| **C** | Middle Shelf (1) | ¾ ply - 15¼ x 22¼ |
| **D** | Bottom Shelf (1) | ¾ ply - 21¼ x 22¼ |
| **E** | Stretchers (4) | ¾ ply - 6 x 22 |
| **F** | Outfeed Wings (2) | ¾ ply - 8 x 14 |
| **G** | Outfeed Table (1) | ¾ ply - 21¼ x 14 |
| **H** | Table Supports (2) | ¼ hdbd. - 3 x 14 |

**HARDWARE SUPPLIES**

(16) No. 5 x 1¼" Fh woodscrews
(10) No. 8 x ¾" Fh woodscrews
(36) No. 8 x 2" Fh woodscrews
(28) No. 10 finish washers
(2) 1½" x 8" piano hinges
(1) ½"-dia. steel rod, 27¼" long
(2) 6"-dia. utility wheels*
(2) ½" push nuts
(2) ½" flat washers
(4) T-nuts and bolts**
(4) 5⁄16"-18 threaded rods, 3" long
(4) 5⁄16" lock nuts
(4) 5⁄16" flat washers
(4) 5⁄16"-18 wing nuts
*Actual diameter slightly less than 6".
**Size to fit your planer.

## CUTTING DIAGRAM

¾" PLY - 48 x 96

| | |
|---|---|
| Ⓐ SIDE | Ⓔ STRETCHER*    Ⓚ DRAWER SIDE** |
| | Ⓔ STRETCHER    Ⓙ DRAWER BACK**    Ⓚ DRAWER SIDE** |
| | Ⓔ STRETCHER    Ⓘ DRAWER FRONT**    Ⓕ OUTFEED WING |
| | Ⓔ STRETCHER    Ⓑ TOP SHELF    Ⓕ OUTFEED WING |
| Ⓐ SIDE | Ⓓ BOTTOM SHELF    Ⓒ MIDDLE SHELF    Ⓖ OUTFEED TABLE |

*NOT NEEDED IF DRAWER IS USED.
**DRAWER IS OPTIONAL (SEE PAGE 101).

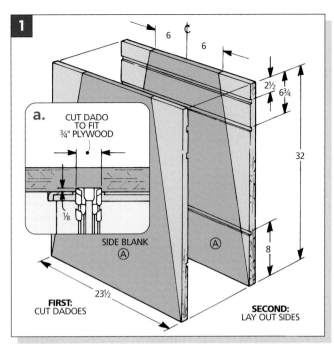

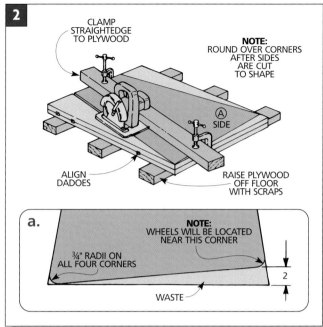

## SIDES

The planer stand is a simple plywood case: two sides dadoed to accept three shelves. I began work on the case by making the tapered sides *(Fig. 1)*.

The sides (A) are narrow at the top, and wide at the bottom for stability. Since it would be awkward to cut dadoes in triangular pieces, I started with rectangular blanks *(Fig. 1)*. Then I located and cut the shallow (1/8"-deep) dadoes for the three shelves.

**ANGLED CUTS.** Once the dadoes have been cut, the next step is to cut the sides to shape. The important thing here is to make sure the pieces are the same shape and the dadoes align.

To do this, use carpet tape to fasten the two blanks together with the dadoes aligned *(Fig. 2)*. Then mark the angled cuts. Using a circular saw and a straightedge, cut the sides to shape.

Once the sides are tapered, use this same procedure to taper the bottom edges of the sides *(Fig. 2a)*. (This pro-

vides clearance for the wheels that will be added later to the front of the stand.)

Finally, before separating the sides, I rounded over all four corners.

## SHELVES

With the sides complete, work can begin on the top (B), middle (C), and bottom (D) shelves *(Fig. 3)*. The top provides a solid platform for your planer. The middle shelf under the top is a handy place to set boards in between passes through the planer. And the bottom can be used for additional storage.

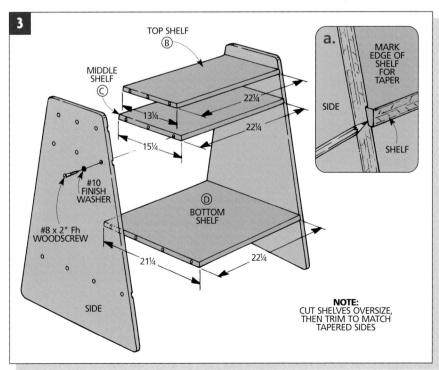

## SHOP TIP

### Finish Washers

Finish washers prevent woodscrews from digging too deep into the plywood. And, as their name says, they provide a nice, finished look.

All three shelves are the same length (22¼"). The only difference is their width *(Fig. 3)*. The tricky part is getting each one to the correct width so its edges match the tapers of the sides.

**BEVEL RIP.** The easiest way to do this is to start by cutting the pieces slightly oversize. Then simply set each piece in its corresponding dado and mark the taper *(Fig. 3a)*. Now adjust the blade on your table saw to match this angle and rip each piece to width.

**ASSEMBLY.** After the shelves have been cut, the stand can be glued and screwed together *(Fig. 3)*. But before doing that, dry-assemble the sides and shelves, and drill shank and pilot holes to prevent splitting the plywood. I then used finish washers under the screw heads as I assembled the stand (see the Shop Tip on the opposite page).

## STRETCHERS

Once the sides and shelves were assembled, I added stretchers (E) under the bottom and middle shelves *(Fig. 4)*. These strengthen the stand and prevent it from racking.

**Note:** If you're going to add the optional drawer shown on page 101, you'll only need three of these.

The stretchers (E) are all 6" tall (wide) and are cut to fit in between the sides. Then they're glued and screwed in place flush with the bottom edge of each shelf *(Figs. 4 and 4a)*.

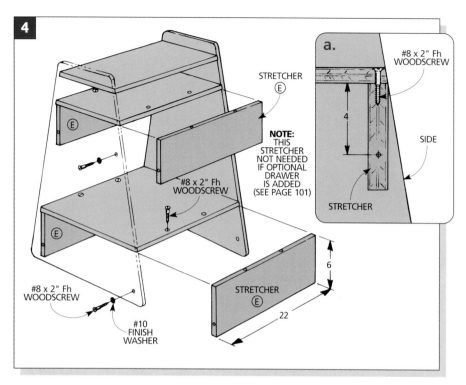

## WHEELS

To make the planer stand easy to move around, I added a pair of 6" rubber utility wheels *(Figs. 5 and 5a)*.

The wheels slip onto a ½"-dia. steel rod that passes through holes drilled in the sides. They're held in place with push nuts. (A push nut is a small metal "cap" that press fits onto a metal rod — no threads required.)

**Note:** To prevent the wheels from rubbing against the sides, I installed washers between the wheels and the sides to serve as spacers *(Fig. 5b)*.

**ATTACH PLANER.** The final step is to attach your planer to the stand now that the wheels are in place *(Fig. 6)*. With the planer centered on the top shelf, mark and drill mounting holes.

**Note:** Drill the mounting holes to match the diameter of the barrels of the T-nuts, not the bolt diameter *(Fig. 6a)*.

Then bolt your planer to the stand.

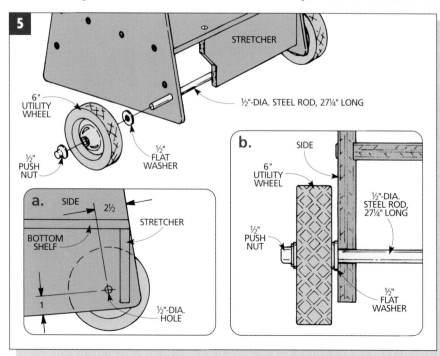

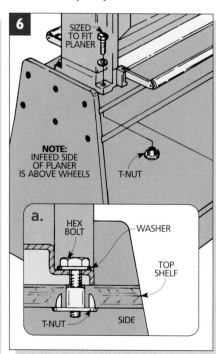

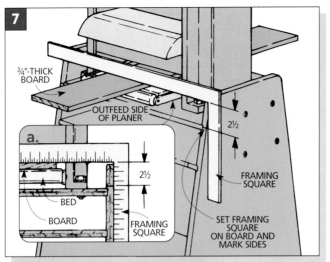

**7**

¾"-THICK BOARD

OUTFEED SIDE OF PLANER

2½

FRAMING SQUARE

SET FRAMING SQUARE ON BOARD AND MARK SIDES

**a.**

2½

BED

BOARD

FRAMING SQUARE

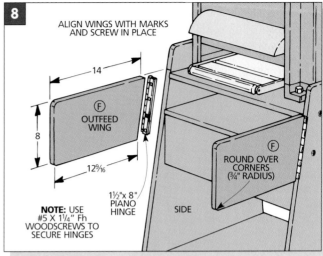

**8**

ALIGN WINGS WITH MARKS AND SCREW IN PLACE

14

8

F

OUTFEED WING

12⁹⁄₁₆

1½"x 8" PIANO HINGE

**NOTE:** USE #5 X 1¼" Fh WOODSCREWS TO SECURE HINGES

F

ROUND OVER CORNERS (¾" RADIUS)

SIDE

## WINGS

With the planer in place, the next step is to add the outfeed extension. It consists of a table fastened to two "wings". The table supports a workpiece as it exits the planer (see photo).

**Note:** This extension is designed for planers where the bed stays stationary.

I started on the outfeed extension by making the outfeed wings (F) *(Fig. 8)*. They're two rectangular pieces of plywood with one end tapered to match the angle of the stand. The two outside corners of each wing are rounded over.

**MOUNT THE WINGS.** The wings are attached to the sides with a pair of piano hinges cut to match the length of the wing's tapered edge. This allows you to fold them against the sides when you're not using the stand.

The tricky part is locating the wings so the outfeed table ends up flush with the planer bed. The problem is the tapered sides prevent you from measuring down from the bed of the planer.

To solve this problem, I used a flat board and a framing square *(Fig. 7)*. The board extends the bed of the planer. And the square allows you to transfer the wing locations to the sides.

Start by unplugging your planer. Then insert a ¾"-thick board and lower the cutterhead to "clamp" the board in place. Now set your square on the board and make a mark 2½" down on each side of the stand.

Finally, line up each wing with a mark and screw them to the sides.

**Note:** Use extra-long (1¼") screws instead of the screws that come with the piano hinge. Drill pilot holes to prevent splitting the plywood.

## OUTFEED TABLE

Once the wings are in place, the next step is to add the adjustment system and outfeed table.

**ADJUSTMENT SYSTEM.** The adjustment system holds the outfeed table in place and allows you to adjust it to the correct height for your planer.

The system consists of four pieces of threaded rod. Two pieces are glued with epoxy into the top edge of each wing *(Figs. 9 and 9b)*. Then, to adjust the height of the table, I threaded lock nuts and washers on each rod.

**OUTFEED TABLE.** With the nuts and washers in place, the next step is to make the outfeed table (G). It's just a piece of ¾" plywood with the corners rounded off *(Fig. 9)*.

To recess the wing nuts that secure the table to the wings, I screwed table supports (H) to the bottom of the outfeed table *(Fig. 9b)*.

Next, holes are drilled in the table supports to fit over the threaded rods *(Figs. 9 and 9a)*. Finally, adjust the table flush with the bed of your planer and secure it with wing nuts. ∎

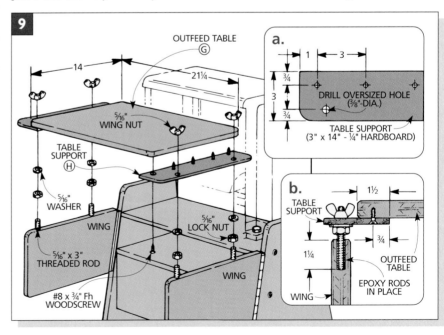

**9**

OUTFEED TABLE
G

14

21¼

⁵⁄₁₆" WING NUT

TABLE SUPPORT
H

⁵⁄₁₆" WASHER

WING

⁵⁄₁₆" x 3" THREADED ROD

#8 x ¾" Fh WOODSCREW

⁵⁄₁₆" LOCK NUT

WING

**a.**

1   3

¾

3

¾

DRILL OVERSIZED HOLE (³⁄₈"-DIA.)

TABLE SUPPORT (3" x 14" - ¼" HARDBOARD)

**b.**

1½

TABLE SUPPORT

¾

1¼

OUTFEED TABLE

WING

EPOXY RODS IN PLACE

# DESIGNER'S NOTEBOOK

*By adding a drawer under the planer, your accessories will always be right at hand no matter where you roll the stand. And you won't have to dig through a pile of shavings to find them.*

## CONSTRUCTION NOTES:

■ All the drawer parts are the same height ($5^7/8$"), but their lengths are different. To determine the length of the drawer front (I), measure between the sides and subtract $1/8$" for clearance ($21^7/8$"). Then, cut the front to size and rabbet the ends to accept the drawer sides *(Fig. 1a)*.

■ The drawer sides (K) are $13^1/4$" long and are grooved for slides that are added later *(Fig. 1b)*. The drawer back (J) fits *between* the sides *(Fig. 1)*.

■ Before assembling the drawer, a groove is cut on the inside face of each piece to accept the $1/4$"-thick hardboard bottom (L) *(Fig. 1b)*. This creates a lip under the drawer front which is used like a handle to pull the drawer open.

■ The drawer rides on a set of hardwood slides (M) cut to fit the grooves in the drawer sides (K) *(Fig. 2)*.

■ Finally, to keep the drawer closed when the stand is moved, I added bullet catches and strike plates *(Fig. 2)*.

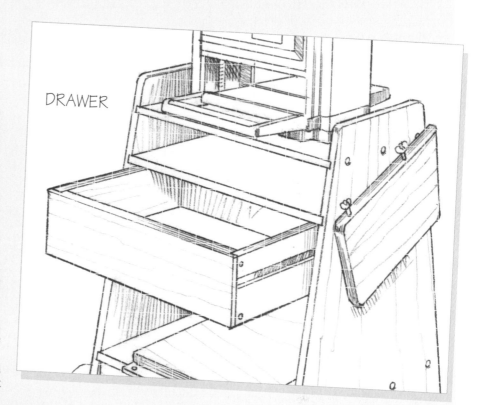

DRAWER

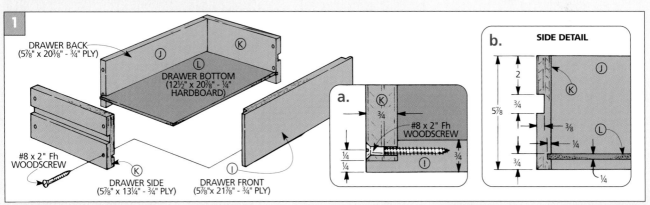

**1**

DRAWER BACK
($5^7/8$" x $20^3/8$" - $3/4$" PLY)

DRAWER BOTTOM
($12^1/2$" x $20^7/8$" - $1/4$"
HARDBOARD)

#8 x 2" Fh
WOODSCREW

DRAWER SIDE
($5^7/8$" x $13^1/4$" - $3/4$" PLY)

DRAWER FRONT
($5^7/8$"x $21^7/8$" - $3/4$" PLY)

**a.**

$3/4$
#8 x 2"
WOODSCREW
$1/4$
$1/4$
$3/4$

**b.** SIDE DETAIL

2
$3/4$
$5^7/8$
$3/8$
$1/4$
$3/4$
$1/4$

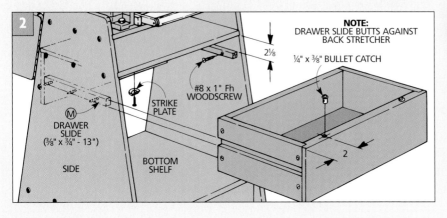

**2**

$2^1/8$

NOTE:
DRAWER SLIDE BUTTS AGAINST
BACK STRETCHER

$1/4$" x $3/8$" BULLET CATCH

#8 x 1" Fh
WOODSCREW

STRIKE
PLATE

DRAWER
SLIDE
($3/8$" x $3/4$" - 13")

SIDE

BOTTOM
SHELF

2

## MATERIALS LIST

### WOOD

| | | |
|---|---|---|
| **I** | Drawer Front (1) | $3/4$ ply - $5^7/8$ x $21^7/8$ |
| **J** | Drawer Back (1) | $3/4$ ply - $5^7/8$ x $20^3/8$ |
| **K** | Drawer Sides (2) | $3/4$ ply - $5^7/8$ x $13^1/4$ |
| **L** | Drawer Bottom (1) | $1/4$ hdbd - $12^1/2$ x $20^7/8$ |
| **M** | Drawer Slides (2) | $3/4$ x $3/8$ - 13 |

### HARDWARE SUPPLIES

(6) No. 8 x 1" Fh woodscrews
(8) No. 8 x 2" Fh woodscrews
(2) $1/4$" x $3/8$" bullet catches w/ strike plates

# Drill Press Storage Cart

*Combining storage and work supports, this cart makes use of the unused space below your drill press. The locking casters keep it exactly where you want it or let you roll it out of the way when necessary.*

Whenever anyone visits my shop, I always look forward to showing them around for a couple of reasons. First, I enjoy talking to fellow woodworkers. But second, I never know when I might come away from the visit with a new woodworking tip or shop idea.

That's just what happened last summer when a friend of mine stopped by. As he was looking around my shop, he paused at the drill press. While casually moving the controls up and down as if he were actually drilling a hole, he asked if I had ever considered building a mobile storage cart that would roll right up against the drill press column.

I had to admit that the idea had never occurred to me, and it seemed like a good one. So I put pencil to paper and started working out a design.

**WORK SURFACE.** There are several features that make this drill press cart a real pleasure to use in the shop. It has a large, sturdy top, which provides a convenient place to set drill bits or other tools when you're working on a project. By swinging the drill press's metal table out of the way, I've got a broad surface for supporting taller workpieces.

**STORAGE.** The deep drawer and shelf below offer plenty of storage space. An adjustable outfeed support on each side of the cart can be raised or lowered to support long workpieces.

**MOBILE.** And on the rare occasion when you need to utilize the full height of your drill press, the cart can easily be rolled out of the way.

**MATERIALS.** I built this cart using about a sheet and a half of Baltic birch plywood, a half sheet of hardboard, plus some poplar for the drawer. *Woodsmith Project Supplies* offers a hardware kit with the hardware you'll need from woodscrews to drawer slides. All you'll need to add is the casters. See page 126 for more about this kit and other sources of hardware and casters.

# EXPLODED VIEW

**OVERALL DIMENSIONS:**
28W x 20D x 34H

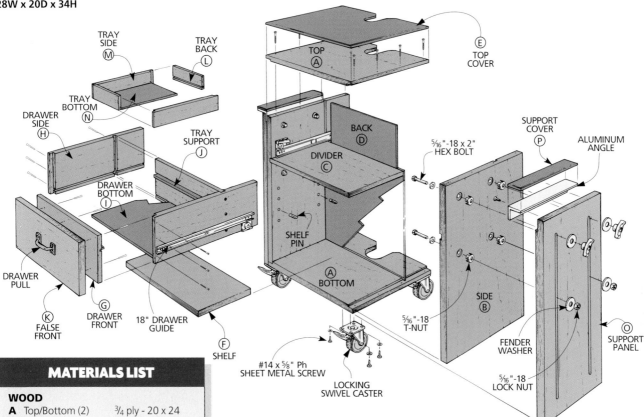

TRAY SIDE (M)
TRAY BACK (L)
TOP (A)
TOP COVER (E)
TRAY BOTTOM (N)
DRAWER SIDE (H)
TRAY SUPPORT (J)
BACK (D)
SUPPORT COVER (P)
ALUMINUM ANGLE
DRAWER BOTTOM (I)
DIVIDER (C)
5/16"-18 x 2" HEX BOLT
DRAWER PULL
SHELF PIN
BOTTOM (A)
SIDE (B)
5/16"-18 T-NUT
5/16"-18 LOCK NUT
FENDER WASHER
SUPPORT PANEL (O)
FALSE FRONT (K)
DRAWER FRONT (G)
18" DRAWER GUIDE
SHELF (F)

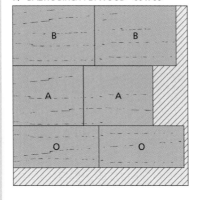

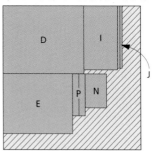

#14 x 5/8" Ph SHEET METAL SCREW
LOCKING SWIVEL CASTER

## MATERIALS LIST

### WOOD

| | | |
|---|---|---|
| **A** | Top/Bottom (2) | ¾ ply - 20 x 24 |
| **B** | Sides (2) | ¾ ply - 20 x 27¾ |
| **C** | Divider (1) | ¾ ply - 13¾ x 23 |
| **D** | Back (1) | ¼ hdbd. - 23 x 27¾ |
| **E** | Top Cover (1) | ¼ hdbd. - 20 x 24 |
| **F** | Shelf (1) | ¾ ply - 13¾ x 22⅜ |
| **G** | Drawer Fr./Bk. (2) | ½ x 7½ - 21 |
| **H** | Drawer Sides (2) | ½ x 7½ - 18 |
| **I** | Drawer Bottom (1) | ¼ hdbd. - 12¼ x 21 |
| **J** | Tray Supports (2) | ¼ hdbd. - ½ x 20½ |
| **K** | False Front (1) | ¾ ply - 7¾ x 22⅜ |
| **L** | Tray Fr./Bk. (2) | ½ x 2½ - 7½ |
| **M** | Tray Sides (2) | ½ x 2½ - 11¹¹⁄₁₆ |
| **N** | Tray Bottom (1) | ¼ hdbd. - 7½ x 11³⁄₁₆ |
| **O** | Support Panels (2) | ¾ ply - 14 x 28⅝ |
| **P** | Support Covers (2) | ¼ hdbd. - 2 x 14 |

### HARDWARE SUPPLIES

(12) No. 6 x 1" Fh woodscrews
(10) No. 8 x 1" Fh woodscrews
(16) No. 8 x 2" Fh woodscrews
(6) No. 8 x ½" Fh sheet metal screws
(16) No. 14 x ⅝" Ph sheet metal screws
(4) ¼"-dia. brass spoon-style shelf pins
(4) 4"-dia. locking swivel casters
(16) ¼" flat washers
(2) 18" drawer guides w/ screws
(1) Drawer pull w/ screws
(2) ⅛" x 2" x 2" aluminum angle (14" long)
(8) ⁵⁄₁₆"-18 long prong T-nuts
(8) ⁵⁄₁₆"-18 x 2" hex bolts
(8) ⁵⁄₁₆" flat washers
(8) ⁵⁄₁₆"-i.d. x 1½"-o.d. fender washers
(4) ⁵⁄₁₆"-18 through-hole wing nuts
(4) ⁵⁄₁₆"-18 lock nuts w/ nylon insert

## CUTTING DIAGRAM

¾" BALTIC BIRCH PLYWOOD - 60 x 60

B   B
A   A
O   O

¾" BALTIC BIRCH PLYWOOD - 30 x 60

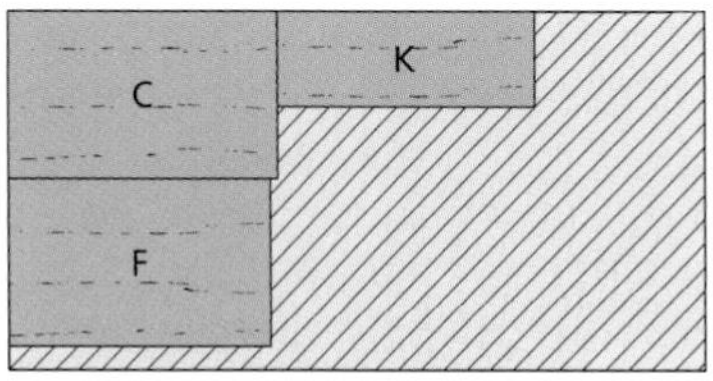

C   K
F

¼" TEMPERED HARDBOARD - 48 x 48

D   I
E   P   N   J

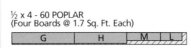

½ x 4 - 60 POPLAR
(Four Boards @ 1.7 Sq. Ft. Each)

G   H   M L

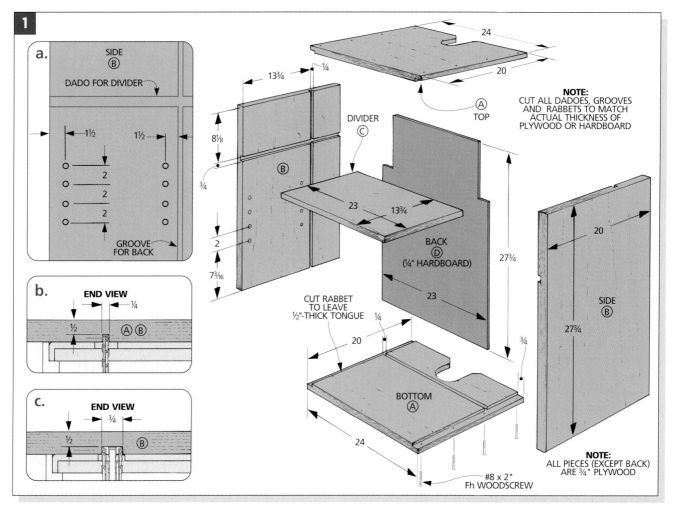

**1**

**a.** SIDE B
DADO FOR DIVIDER
$1\frac{1}{2}$   $1\frac{1}{2}$
2
2
2
GROOVE FOR BACK

**b.** END VIEW
$\frac{1}{4}$
$\frac{1}{2}$   A B

**c.** END VIEW
$\frac{3}{4}$
$\frac{1}{2}$   B

$13\frac{3}{4}$   $\frac{1}{4}$
$8\frac{1}{8}$
$\frac{3}{4}$
2
$7\frac{3}{16}$

DIVIDER C

24
20
A TOP

**NOTE:**
CUT ALL DADOES, GROOVES AND RABBETS TO MATCH ACTUAL THICKNESS OF PLYWOOD OR HARDBOARD

23   $13\frac{3}{4}$

BACK D ($\frac{1}{4}$" HARDBOARD)

$27\frac{3}{4}$

23

CUT RABBET TO LEAVE $\frac{1}{2}$"-THICK TONGUE

20   $\frac{1}{4}$
BOTTOM A
24

#8 x 2" Fh WOODSCREW

SIDE B
20
$27\frac{3}{4}$
$\frac{3}{4}$

**NOTE:**
ALL PIECES (EXCEPT BACK) ARE $\frac{3}{4}$" PLYWOOD

## CASE

I started designing the cart by figuring an overall size. The cart shouldn't interfere with drill press operations. At the same time, it needed to be at a convenient working height and wide enough to provide outfeed support on the sides.

**Note:** The U-shaped notches at the back of the cart were sized to fit around the base and column of my drill press. You may need to alter their sizes and adjust the position of the back panel to fit your drill press.

**JOINERY.** The cart is really just a plywood case on wheels. (I used Baltic

birch plywood.) But the interesting thing is that all the case pieces interlock with dadoes, grooves, and rabbets — almost like a Chinese puzzle box. The result is a strong case that resists racking and can stand up to abuse.

**TOP/BOTTOM.** The case is made up of a top panel (A) and bottom panel (A)

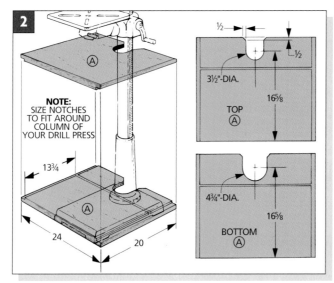

**2**

A

**NOTE:**
SIZE NOTCHES TO FIT AROUND COLUMN OF YOUR DRILL PRESS

$13\frac{3}{4}$
A
24   20

$\frac{1}{2}$
$\frac{1}{2}$
$3\frac{1}{2}$"-DIA.
$16\frac{5}{8}$
TOP A

$4\frac{3}{4}$"-DIA.
$16\frac{5}{8}$
BOTTOM A

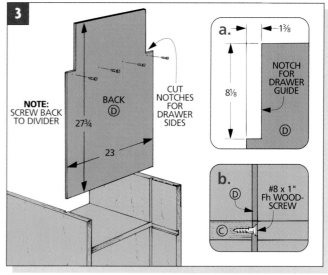

**3**

**NOTE:**
SCREW BACK TO DIVIDER

BACK D
$27\frac{3}{4}$
23

CUT NOTCHES FOR DRAWER SIDES

**a.**   $1\frac{3}{8}$
NOTCH FOR DRAWER GUIDE
$8\frac{1}{8}$
D

**b.**
D
#8 x 1" Fh WOODSCREW
C

that are rabbeted to hold the sides (B) *(Fig. 1)*. The trick when making these rabbets is to size them to match the exact thickness of the plywood sides. This thickness can vary from sheet to sheet, so it pays to test-fit each piece.

**SIDES.** The sides of the case each receive a shallow dado to hold a plywood divider (C). Before you can determine the size of this divider, however, you'll have to dry-assemble the sides to the top and bottom and measure across the cart from dado to dado.

**BACK.** There are a couple of unusual things about the back of this cart. To start with, the back (D) is set in to allow clearance for the column of the drill press. A groove is positioned on the inside face of each piece to hold the back *(Figs. 1a and 1b)*.

The second thing about the back worth noting is that the top corners are notched out. This allows the sides of the drawer to pass through. (I'll talk more about this when we build the drawer.) For now, simply notch the corners of the completed back *(Figs. 3 and 3a)*.

**HOLES AND NOTCHES.** Before assembling the case, there are a couple of details to take care of. First, holes are drilled on the inside faces of the sides for shelf pins. It's easier to drill these holes on the drill press now rather than trying to reach inside the case with a hand drill afterwards.

Second, U-shaped notches are made on the top and bottom panels to fit around the column and base of the drill press. I used a jig saw to make these notches and then a drum sander to sand them smooth *(Fig. 2)*.

**ASSEMBLY.** Because all of the pieces interlock, it's a good idea to have a plan before you start gluing everything. I began by gluing and screwing the bottom panel to the two sides. Then I glued in the divider and slipped the back in place. The back is held secure by screwing it to the edge of the divider *(Figs. 3 and 3b)*. Finally, the top panel can be glued and screwed in place.

**TOP COVER.** A hardboard top cover (E) creates a durable work surface on top of the case. To get the edges of the cover flush with the top of the case, I cut the cover slightly oversize. After gluing it down with contact cement, I trimmed it using a flush trim bit in the router. Then ⅛" roundovers can be routed on the cover's edges *(Fig. 4a)*.

**SHELF AND CASTERS**. Next, I made a

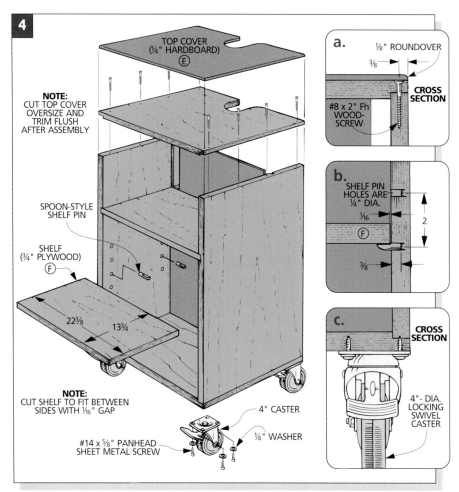

**4**

TOP COVER
(¼" HARDBOARD)
Ⓔ

NOTE:
CUT TOP COVER
OVERSIZE AND
TRIM FLUSH
AFTER ASSEMBLY

SPOON-STYLE
SHELF PIN

SHELF
(¾" PLYWOOD)
Ⓕ

22⅜    13¾

NOTE:
CUT SHELF TO FIT BETWEEN
SIDES WITH 1/16" GAP

#14 x ⅝" PANHEAD
SHEET METAL SCREW

4" CASTER

¼" WASHER

**a.**
⅛" ROUNDOVER
⅜

CROSS
SECTION

#8 x 2" Fh
WOOD-
SCREW

**b.**
SHELF PIN
HOLES ARE
¼" DIA.

1/16
Ⓕ
2
⅜

**c.**
CROSS
SECTION

4"- DIA.
LOCKING
SWIVEL
CASTER

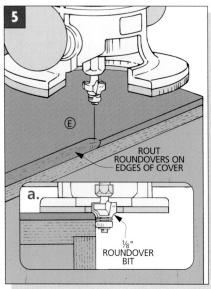

**5**

ROUT
ROUNDOVERS ON
EDGES OF COVER

Ⓔ

**a.**
⅛"
ROUNDOVER
BIT

plywood shelf (F) to fit inside the cart with a ¹/₁₆" gap at each end *(Fig. 4)*. The shelf rests on spoon-style shelf pins that are inserted into the holes in the sides of the case *(Fig. 4b)*.

To complete the case, I added a 4" locking swivel caster to each corner (see the Shop Tip at right).

**SHOP TIP**
*Locking Wheels*

Stepping on the lever on one of these locking casters not only prevents the wheel from rolling, it also keeps the caster from swiveling. So once the base is in position, lock it in place for a steady, stay-put work surface.

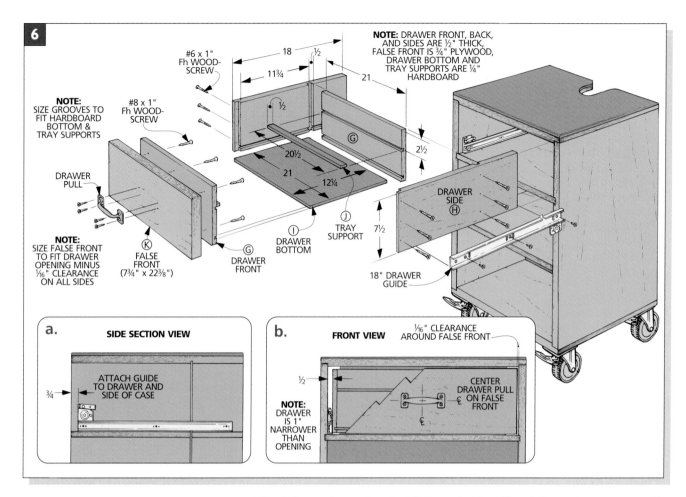

**6**

NOTE: DRAWER FRONT, BACK, AND SIDES ARE ½" THICK, FALSE FRONT IS ¾" PLYWOOD, DRAWER BOTTOM AND TRAY SUPPORTS ARE ¼" HARDBOARD

#6 x 1" Fh WOOD-SCREW

#8 x 1" Fh WOOD-SCREW

NOTE: SIZE GROOVES TO FIT HARDBOARD BOTTOM & TRAY SUPPORTS

18

11¾

½

21

½

20½

21

12¼

2½

(G)

DRAWER PULL

NOTE: SIZE FALSE FRONT TO FIT DRAWER OPENING MINUS 1/16" CLEARANCE ON ALL SIDES

(K) FALSE FRONT (7¾" x 22⅜")

(G) DRAWER FRONT

DRAWER BOTTOM

(I)

(J) TRAY SUPPORT

DRAWER SIDE (H)

7½

18" DRAWER GUIDE

**a.** SIDE SECTION VIEW

ATTACH GUIDE TO DRAWER AND SIDE OF CASE

¾

**b.** FRONT VIEW

1/16" CLEARANCE AROUND FALSE FRONT

½

NOTE: DRAWER IS 1" NARROWER THAN OPENING

CENTER DRAWER PULL ON FALSE FRONT

## DRAWER & SLIDING TRAY

Once the case is complete, you can begin working on the drawer and tray.

I started by gluing up enough ½"-thick poplar stock to make the drawer front and back (G) and the two drawer sides (H). After cutting these pieces to size, I started to work on the joinery.

The joinery is pretty straightforward. A rabbet on the front end of each drawer side holds the drawer front. And a dado on the inside face of each side holds the drawer back.

**GROOVES.** Before assembling the drawer, you need to make grooves in the pieces to hold a bottom and a couple of tray supports. Both the drawer

bottom (I) and the two tray supports (J) are made out of ¼" hardboard.

**ASSEMBLY.** Once the grooves are completed, the drawer can be glued and screwed together. Then the tray supports can be glued into their grooves.

**DRAWER GUIDES.** Whenever you have a drawer for storing small items (like drill bits), you want to have full access to the inside of the drawer. Usually, this means using rather expensive, full-extension drawer guides. But I was able to use less expensive guides. These guides extend beyond the drawer back (G) through the notches in the back of the case *(Fig. 6a)*. This gives you the benefit of a "full-extension" drawer without the added cost.

**FALSE FRONT.** Once the drawer is mounted on the guides, a plywood false front (K) is screwed to the drawer, and a pull is added *(Fig. 6b)*.

**SLIDING TRAY.** There's not much to the sliding tray. The front and back (L) and sides (M) are made from ½"-thick poplar *(Fig. 7)*. These pieces are held together with rabbet joints *(Fig. 7b)*. And a groove in each piece holds a hardboard bottom (N) *(Fig. 7a)*.

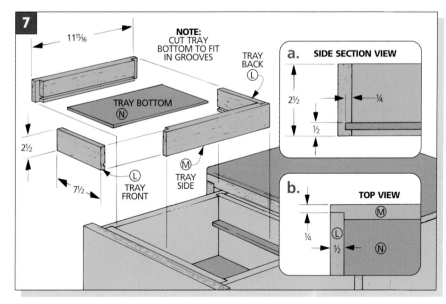

**7**

11¹¹/₁₆

NOTE: CUT TRAY BOTTOM TO FIT IN GROOVES

TRAY BACK (L)

TRAY BOTTOM (N)

2½

7½

(L) TRAY FRONT

(M) TRAY SIDE

**a.** SIDE SECTION VIEW

2½

¼

½

**b.** TOP VIEW

(M)

(L)

(N)

¼

½

## OUTFEED SUPPORTS

With the cart more or less complete, the only things left to add are the outfeed supports *(Fig. 8)*. These are made up of two plywood panels, reinforced along the top edge with a piece of aluminum angle. The supports can be raised or lowered as needed to match the height of the drill press table.

Each outfeed support panel (O) has a shallow rabbet at one end to hold the aluminum angle *(Fig. 9)*. (The aluminum angle is added later.)

In addition to the rabbet, a couple of slots are routed along the length of each panel to allow them to slide up and down. These can be made by drilling a hole at each end of the slot and then routing away the waste between the holes on a router table *(Fig. 10)*.

**ALUMINUM ANGLE.** Before attaching the outfeed supports to the cart, I added the aluminum angle edging. This is simply trimmed to length and then screwed in place. (Tips on working with aluminum can be found on page 94.)

**SUPPORT COVERS.** Like the top of the cart, I also added hardboard covers (P) to the top surface of the outfeed supports. The procedure here is similar — the only differences are that I used epoxy instead of contact adhesive and I sanded the covers flush instead of routing them. (This is because the aluminum doesn't provide enough of a bearing surface to use a flush trim bit.)

**MOUNTING HARDWARE.** The outfeed supports are attached to the cart with T-nuts, bolts, and washers. A large pair of plastic wing nuts allows you to lock the supports in any position. And the T-nuts prevent the bolts from turning when you are loosening or tightening down the wing nuts.

To mount the hardware, start by drilling shallow counterbores in the sides of the cart for the T-nuts. I laid out the positions of the upper counterbores by clamping the support panels to the sides of the cart so they were flush with the top and front edges. Then I used a drill bit to mark the tops of the slots on the sides of the case (see the Shop Tip below). To locate the lower counterbores, I simply measured down 9" from the upper ones.

In the center of each counterbore, a hole is drilled for the bolt. Then install the T-nuts and add the bolts, washers, lock nuts, and wing nuts *(Fig. 8a)*. Now you can roll the cart right up to your drill press and start loading it up with drill bits and accessories. ■

8

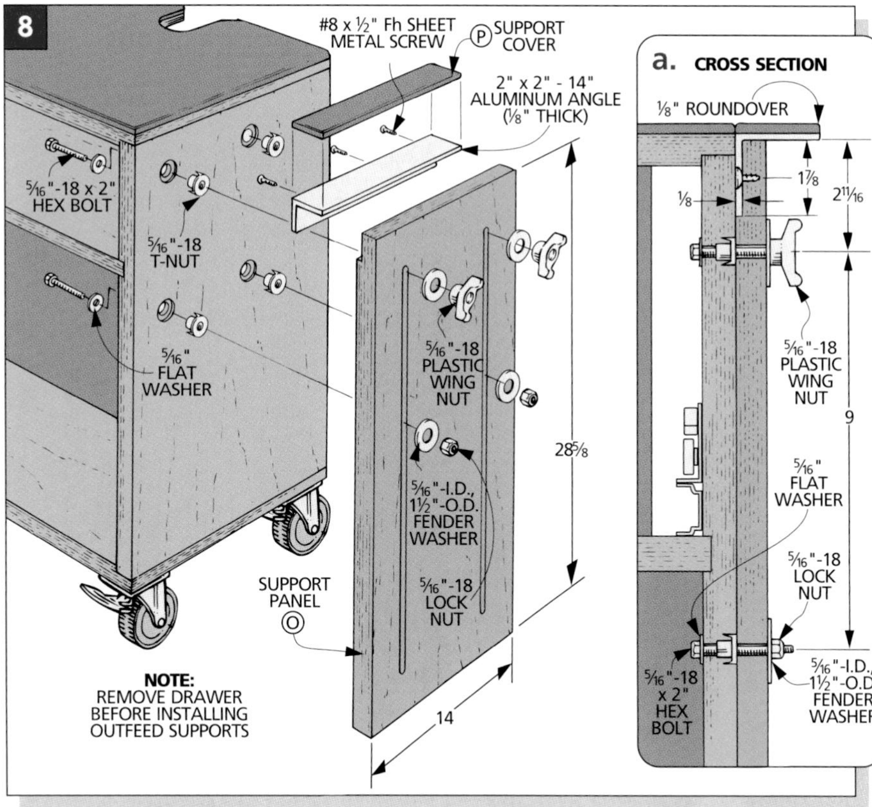

#8 x 1/2" Fh SHEET METAL SCREW
P SUPPORT COVER
2" x 2" - 14" ALUMINUM ANGLE (1/8" THICK)
5/16"-18 x 2" HEX BOLT
5/16"-18 T-NUT
5/16" FLAT WASHER
5/16"-18 PLASTIC WING NUT
5/16"-I.D., 1 1/2"-O.D. FENDER WASHER
5/16"-18 LOCK NUT
28 5/8
14
SUPPORT PANEL O
NOTE: REMOVE DRAWER BEFORE INSTALLING OUTFEED SUPPORTS
a. CROSS SECTION
1/8" ROUNDOVER
1/8
1 7/8
2 11/16
5/16"-18 PLASTIC WING NUT
9
5/16" FLAT WASHER
5/16"-18 LOCK NUT
5/16"-18 x 2" HEX BOLT
5/16"-I.D., 1 1/2"-O.D. FENDER WASHER


9

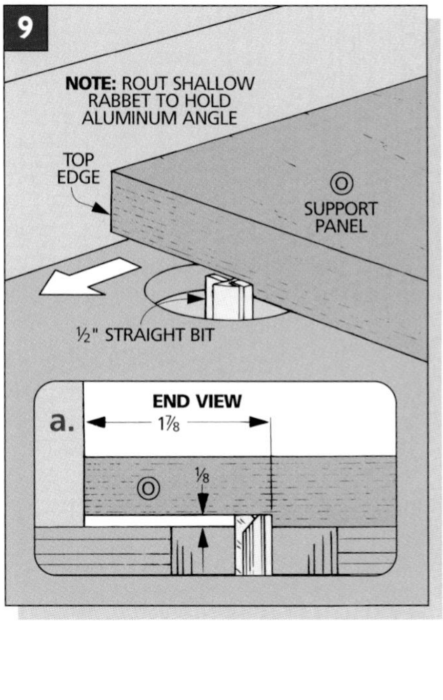

NOTE: ROUT SHALLOW RABBET TO HOLD ALUMINUM ANGLE
TOP EDGE
O SUPPORT PANEL
1/2" STRAIGHT BIT
a. END VIEW
1 7/8
O
1/8


10

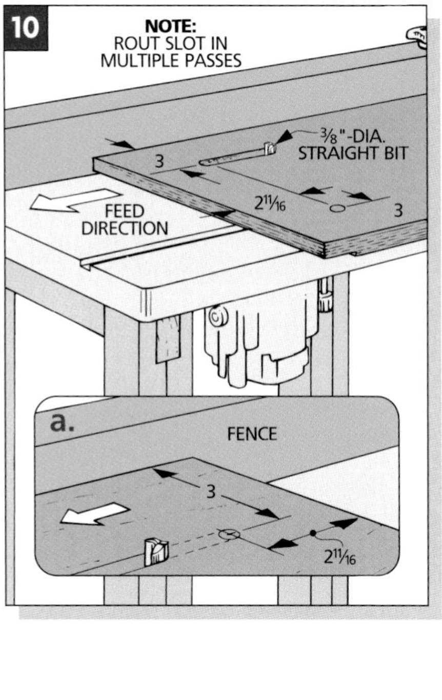

NOTE: ROUT SLOT IN MULTIPLE PASSES
3/8"-DIA. STRAIGHT BIT
3
FEED DIRECTION
2 11/16
3
a.
FENCE
3
2 11/16


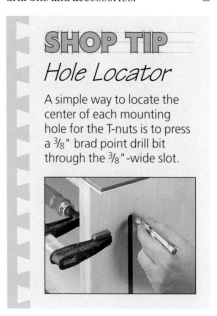

## SHOP TIP

### *Hole Locator*

A simple way to locate the center of each mounting hole for the T-nuts is to press a 3/8" brad point drill bit through the 3/8"-wide slot.

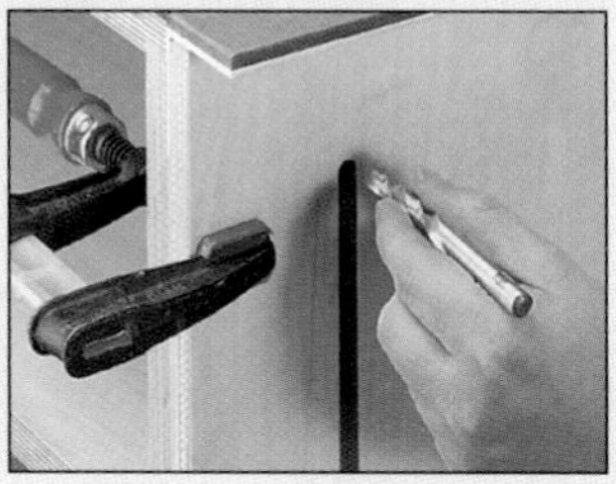

# Radial Arm Saw Stand

*Here's a solid, level base for your saw that also organizes storage space for accessories, cutoff lumber, and sheet goods. You can easily customize any of the components to best suit your space and needs.*

When I first set up my radial arm saw, it didn't take long for me to realize I'd have to do some work before I could make it as useful as I wanted it to be.

For one thing, the saw's metal stand didn't provide the solid foundation I was hoping for. Plus the short table on the saw made it impossible to cut long stock without outfeed supports. And the more I used the saw, the bigger the pile of cutoffs below it grew.

So I came up with this project that's really as much a system as it is a stand. The unique thing about this system is it can be tailored to fit your shop.

**BASE.** I started by replacing the metal stand with a sturdy base. The base features a lift-out bin for scraps that are too small to use. And there's a handy drawer for storing wrenches, extra blades, and accessories. If you're tight on space, you can build just the base.

**STORAGE UNITS.** Since I also needed a way to organize my cutoffs, I added a storage unit on each side of the base. Then, to provide bins for different sizes (or types) of stock, one storage unit has adjustable shelves. The other is open for storing sheet goods.

**TOP.** To complete the work station, I added a table top between the two bins.

This provides support for long workpieces. You can alter the length of this table top to best fit your space.

The table top features a replaceable insert. When it gets rough from use, simply slide the old one out and a new one in. (The Woodworker's Notebook on page 115 shows how to build this.) There's also a long fence to help position workpieces square to the blade.

**MATERIALS.** All the materials are available at your lumber yard. The base and storage units are made of ³/₄" plywood and hardwood. The surface of the table top and fence and the bottoms for the bin and drawer are ¹/₄" hardboard.

# EXPLODED VIEW

**OVERALL DIMENSIONS:**
**96W x 30D x 41H**

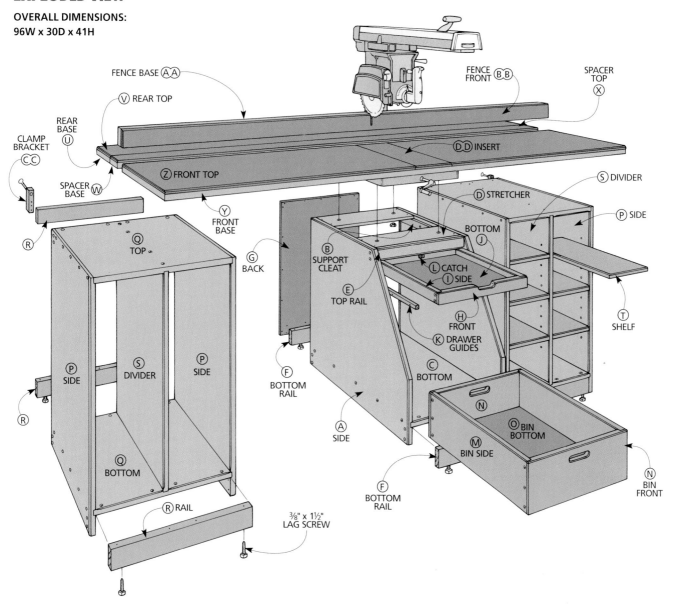

FENCE BASE (AA)

(V) REAR TOP

REAR BASE (U)

CLAMP BRACKET (CC)

SPACER BASE (W)

(Z) FRONT TOP

(R)

(Y) FRONT BASE

(Q) TOP

(G) BACK

(B) SUPPORT CLEAT

(E) TOP RAIL

(F) BOTTOM RAIL

(A) SIDE

(P) SIDE

(S) DIVIDER

(P) SIDE

(Q) BOTTOM

(R) RAIL

(R)

⅜" x 1½" LAG SCREW

FENCE FRONT (BB)

SPACER TOP (X)

(DD) INSERT

(D) STRETCHER

(S) DIVIDER

(P) SIDE

BOTTOM (J)

(L) CATCH
(I) SIDE

(H) FRONT

(K) DRAWER GUIDES

(C) BOTTOM

(T) SHELF

(N)

(O) BIN BOTTOM

(M) BIN SIDE

(N) BIN FRONT

(F) BOTTOM RAIL

---

## MATERIALS LIST

### STAND

| | | |
|---|---|---|
| **A** | Sides (2) | ¾ ply - 30 x 32 |
| **B** | Support Cleats (2) | ¾ ply - 1¾ - 21 |
| **C** | Bottom (1) | ¾ ply - 29¾ x 23 |
| **D** | Stretchers (2) | ¾ ply - 6 x 22½ |
| **E** | Top Rail (1) | ¾ ply - 2½ - 22½ |
| **F** | Bottom Rails (2) | ¾ ply - 3 - 22½ |
| **G** | Back (1) | ¼ hdbd. - 23½ x 32 |
| **H** | Drawer Fr./Bk. (2) | ¾ ply - 2½ x 22⁷⁄₁₆ |
| **I** | Drawer Sides (2) | ¾ ply - 2½ x 21¼ |
| **J** | Drawer Bottom (1) | ¼ hdbd. - 21⅜ x 20¹¹⁄₁₆ |
| **K** | Drawer Guides (2) | ¾ x ½ - 21¾ |
| **L** | Drawer Catch (1) | ¼ hdbd. - ¾ x 1½ |
| **M** | Bin Sides (2) | ¾ ply - 8 x 29¼ |
| **N** | Bin Fr./ Bk. (2) | ¾ ply - 8 x 22⁷⁄₁₆ |
| **O** | Bin Bottom (1) | ¼ hdbd. - 21⅜ x 28¹¹⁄₁₆ |

### STORAGE UNITS

| | | |
|---|---|---|
| **P** | Sides (4) | ¾ ply - 23⅞ x 37⅝ |
| **Q** | Tops/Bottoms (4) | ¾ ply - 23⅞ x 23 |
| **R** | Rails (6) | ¾ x 3 - 22½ |
| **S** | Dividers (2) | ¾ ply - 23⅞ x 33⅝ |
| **T** | Shelves (6) | ¾ ply - 23⅞ x 10¹¹⁄₁₆ |

### TABLE TOP

| | | |
|---|---|---|
| **U** | Rear Base (1) | ¾ ply - var.* x 96 |
| **V** | Rear Top (1) | ¼ hdbd. - var.* x 96 |
| **W** | Spacer Base (1) | ¾ ply - var.* x 96 |
| **X** | Spacer Top (1) | ¼ hdbd. - var.* x 96 |
| **Y** | Front Base (1) | ¾ ply - var.* x 96 |
| **Z** | Front Top (1) | ¼ hdbd. - var.* x 96 |
| **AA** | Fence Base (1) | ¾ ply - 3¼ x 96 |
| **BB** | Fence Front (1) | ¼ hdbd. - 3¼ x 96 |
| **CC** | Clamp Brackets (2) | ¾ x ¾ - 4¾ |
| **DD** | Insert (1) | ¼ hdbd. - 6 x var.* |

### HARDWARE SUPPLIES

(25) No. 4 x ¾" Fh woodscrews
(12) No. 6 x ½" Rh woodscrews
(2) No. 8 x ½" Fh woodscrews
(1) No. 8 x ¾" Fh woodscrew
(6) No. 8 x 1" Fh woodscrews
(18) No. 8 x 1¼" Fh woodscrews
(200) No. 8 x 1½" Fh woodscrews
(12) ⅜" x 1½" lag screws
(2) ¼" threaded inserts
(2) ¼" x 1½" thumbscrews
(2) ¼" lock nuts
(24) ¼" shelf supports

* Cut to fit width of your saw's table.

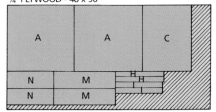

¾" PLYWOOD - 48 x 96

¾" PLYWOOD - 48 x 96

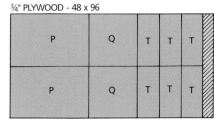

¾" PLYWOOD - 48 x 96

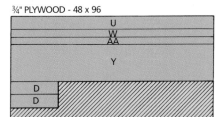

¾" PLYWOOD - 48 x 96

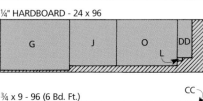

¼" HARDBOARD - 48 x 96

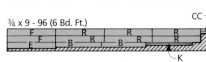

¼" HARDBOARD - 24 x 96

¾ x 9 - 96 (6 Bd. Ft.)

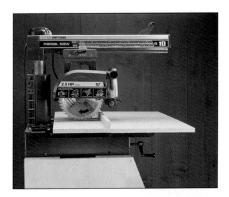

For a saw with a short frame, you'll need to angle the sides to provide clearance for the blade adjustment handle (top photo). If your saw has a wider base, the stand can be left square (bottom photo).

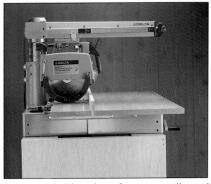

## BASE

I started by building a base to support the saw. It's simply a plywood case that's open in the front (*Fig. 1*). On top there's a set of stretchers that provide a convenient way to mount the saw.

**CASE.** The first step is to make a U-shaped case that consists of two sides and a bottom. Depending on the frame

of your saw, you may need to cut the sides (A) at an angle to provide clearance for the handle that adjusts the blade height (see the photos above).

**SIDES.** To determine how much you'll need to angle your sides, first measure the depth of your saw frame (front to back). Then add ⅛" (this allows room for a chamfer that's routed later).

To lay out the angle, first transfer

this measurement to the top edge of each side piece (*Fig. 1*). Then measure up 11¾" from the bottom of the sides and connect the two marks. Now you can cut along the line with a jig saw.

Next, cut a dado and a rabbet in each side piece to accept the bottom (C) and back (G) (*Figs. 1a and 1b*). (These pieces are added later.)

The sides are held together by the

bottom and a pair of stretchers (D) on top *(Fig. 1)*. The stretchers rest on two hardwood support cleats that are attached to the sides *(Figs. 1 and 1a)*.

**CLEATS.** To determine the length of these support cleats (B), first measure the width of your side panels (at the top). Then subtract 1" from this measurement. This allows $\frac{1}{4}$" for the rabbet along the back edge, and $\frac{3}{4}$" for the thickness of a rail that's added later.

Once they're cut to size, the cleats can be glued and screwed to the sides. Position them $\frac{3}{4}$" down from the top edge, and flush with the rabbet in the back edge *(Figs. 1 and 1a)*.

After the cleats are in place, form the "U" by gluing and screwing the sides (A) to the bottom (C) *(Fig. 1)*.

## TOP

Instead of a solid top for the base, I used a pair of plywood stretchers (D) that allowed me to reach up into the bottom of the saw frame when installing the mounting bolts (refer to *Fig. 3*).

But before attaching the stretchers (D), I did two things. First, I glued a hardwood top rail (E) to the front stretcher to add some stiffness *(Fig. 2)*.

Then to soften the sharp edges, I routed $\frac{1}{8}$" chamfers along the front edges of the rail *(Fig. 2a)*.

To install the stretchers, position the rail on the front stretcher against the front of the cleats *(Fig. 2a)*.

Then position the rear stretcher flush with the rabbet *(Fig. 2b)*.

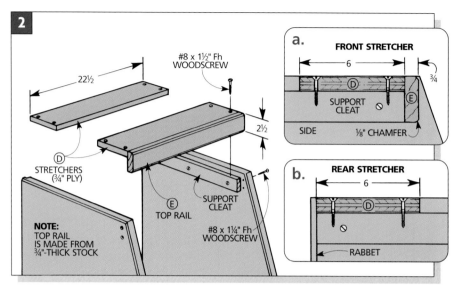

After the stretchers (D) are screwed in place, the next step is to add a pair of bottom rails (F) *(Fig. 3)*.

**BACK.** To strengthen the base, I added a back (G). It's just a piece of $\frac{1}{4}$" hardboard cut to fit the rabbet in each side piece *(Fig. 3)*.

Once the back is glued and screwed in place, chamfer all the exposed edges of the case. To do this, I used a $\frac{1}{8}$" chamfer bit mounted in a handheld router. (A sanding block will also work.)

**LEVELERS.** Finally, to compensate for an uneven floor, I added lag screws to the bottom rails to serve as levelers *(Fig. 3 and the Shop Tip at right)*.

**Note:** To prevent the rails from splitting, predrill holes for the lag screws.

With the base complete, you can bolt your saw to the stretchers *(Fig. 3a)*.

## SHOP TIP
### Levelers

By screwing a lag screw in or out at each corner, you can level the stand's components and provide a solid base.

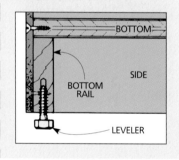

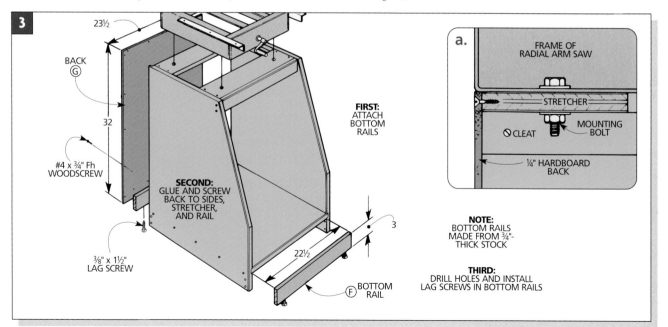

All that's left to complete the base is to add a drawer at the top to hold accessories, and a lift-out bin at the bottom to catch discarded scraps.

**DRAWER.** I started by building the drawer. Determining the length of the drawer front and back (H) is easy. Just measure across the opening of the base and then subtract $^1/_{16}$" for clearance *(Fig. 4)*. (In my case, the front and back are $22^7/_{16}$" long.)

Next, to determine the length of the sides (I), first measure from the front of the top rail (E) to the back of the stand. Then subtract $^1/_2$" from this measurement to allow for the rabbets that join the pieces together *(Figs. 4a and 5)*.

**Note:** When you set up to cut the rabbets on the ends of the drawer front and back, make sure the rabbet is the same width as the thickness of the plywood. Typically, $^3/_4$" plywood is just a bit under $^3/_4$" in thickness.

To complete the drawer, there are three things left to do. First, cut grooves in each piece for a bottom (J) made of $^1/_4$" hardboard *(Fig. 5b)*. Then to make it easy to pull open the drawer, a notch is cut in the drawer front, centered on its length *(Fig. 5a)*. Once these cuts are made, the drawer is glued and screwed together *(Fig. 4a)*. Finally, the top and bottom edges are chamfered *(Fig. 5b)*.

**GUIDES.** The drawer slides on a pair of $^3/_4$"-thick hardwood drawer guides (K) that are screwed to the sides of the base *(Fig. 4b)*. These guides are cut to match the depth (length) of the drawer and are positioned to create a $^1/_{16}$" gap

between the drawer and the top rail.

Then to prevent a drawer full of saw blades from falling on your toes, cut a hardboard catch (L) *(Fig. 4)*. Screw it to the back of the drawer so it extends $^3/_4$" above the drawer's top edge *(Fig. 4b)*.

**BIN.** The construction of the lift-out bin is identical to the drawer. Rabbet joints are used to hold the sides (M) to the front and back (N) *(Figs. 4a and 6)*.

And grooves hold the $^1/_4$" hardboard bottom (O) in place *(Fig. 6b)*.

The only differences between the two are that the bin is taller than the drawer and it's cut to fit the full depth of the base *(Figs. 4 and 6)*.

To make it easy to lift out, I used a jig saw to cut handle holes in both the front and the back (N) pieces before assembling the bin *(Fig. 6a)*.

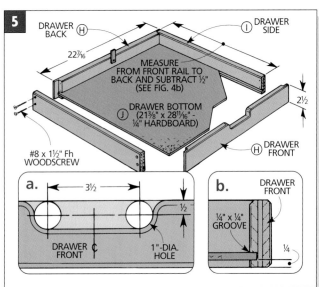

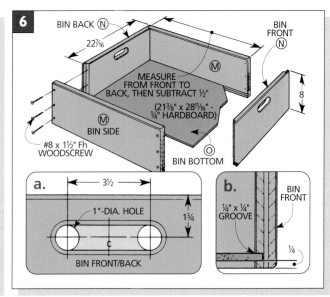

With the base complete, you can turn your attention to the storage units. They both start as identical plywood boxes that are open in the front and back.

The only difference between them is one has adjustable shelves for lumber, and the other is open from top to bottom to hold sheet stock.

**SIDES.** In addition to holding lumber, both units support the ends of the table top when it's added.

So when cutting the sides (P) of the storage units to length, cut them so their length equals the height of your saw frame plus the height of the base of your stand *(Fig. 7).*

Next, rabbets are cut along the top edges of each side piece (P) to accept a plywood top (Q). And dadoes are cut toward the opposite ends to accept a plywood bottom (Q) *(Fig. 8).*

After the tops and bottoms (Q) are cut to size, a $\frac{1}{4}$"-deep dado is cut in each one for a divider that's added later *(Figs. 8 and 10).* Center each dado on the width of the top and bottom. Now the storage units can be glued and screwed together.

**SUPPORT.** To allow longer pieces of lumber to extend out the back, I left both units open in the back. But without a back, each unit could rack. To prevent this from happening, I screwed a top rail and two bottom rails (R) (one in front

and one in back) between the sides of each bin *(Fig. 9).*

**DIVIDERS.** Next, a divider (S) can be cut to fit between the dadoes in the top and bottom of each unit *(Fig. 10).* But for it to fit flush with the front of the case, you'll need to notch each divider to fit around the top rail *(Fig. 10).*

Before screwing the dividers in place, I found it easiest to drill holes in the sides and divider for the shelf supports that hold the shelves added next.

**ADJUSTABLE SHELVES.** After chamfering the exposed edges on both units, install the lag screw levelers (refer to the Shop Tip on page 111). Finally, I added six shelves to one of the storage units (refer to *Fig. 7*). I found it was easier to install and move the shelves after routing slight chamfers on the edges *(Fig. 7a).* To keep the shelves from sliding out the back as scraps were thrown on them, I secured them with a screw through each front shelf support.

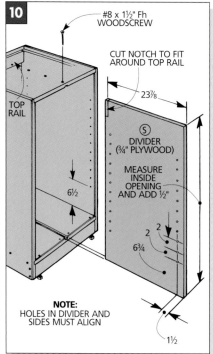

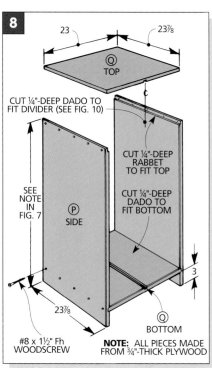

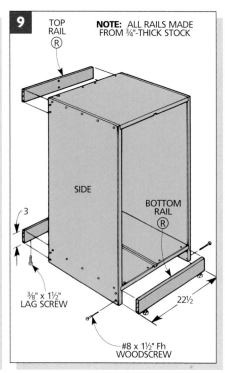

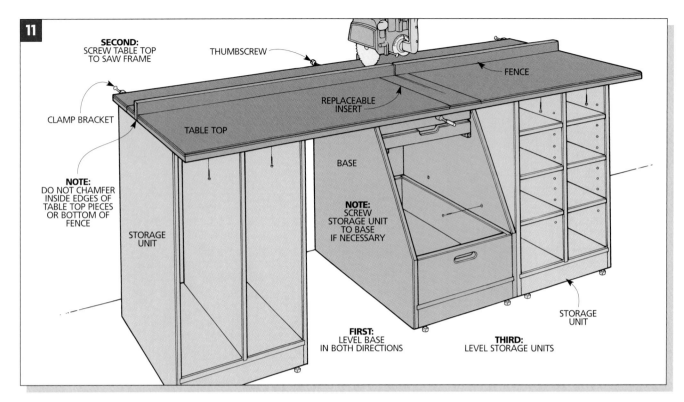

**11**

SECOND:
SCREW TABLE TOP
TO SAW FRAME

THUMBSCREW

FENCE

REPLACEABLE
INSERT

CLAMP BRACKET

TABLE TOP

BASE

**NOTE:**
DO NOT CHAMFER
INSIDE EDGES OF
TABLE TOP PIECES
OR BOTTOM OF
FENCE

**NOTE:**
SCREW
STORAGE UNIT
TO BASE
IF NECESSARY

STORAGE
UNIT

STORAGE
UNIT

**FIRST:**
LEVEL BASE
IN BOTH DIRECTIONS

**THIRD:**
LEVEL STORAGE UNITS

## TABLE TOP

After completing the storage units, it's time to build the table top *(Fig. 11)*.

Just like my old table top, this top is made up of a front piece, a fence, and a "split" rear section *(Fig. 12)*.

**DIMENSIONS.** Determining the width of each piece was easy. I just made them the same width as the pieces of my original table top. But the length takes a little more planning.

The first thing to do is arrange the base and storage units where you want them in your shop. Then, measure across the total width and add 2" for a 1" overhang at each end (refer to *Fig. 13*). (In my case, the top is 8 feet long.)

**LAMINATE PIECES.** After cutting the base pieces (U, W, Y) and the fence base (AA) to size, I laminated each piece with a $1/4$" hardboard top (V, X, Z) and fence front (BB) *(Fig. 12)*. This helps protect the top and provides a smooth surface for ripping.

To do this, I used contact cement to attach a slightly oversize piece of hardboard to each piece.

**Note:** If you're planning on adding a replaceable insert, the Woodworker's Notebook on the opposite page has details on gluing down the hardboard.

Then, using a flush trim bit in a hand-held router, trim the hardboard to match the plywood.

**EDGES.** Finally, I softened the sharp edges by routing $1/8$" chamfers along the edges of the hardboard.

**Note:** Don't chamfer the inside edges of the table top pieces or the bottom edges of the fence *(Fig. 11)*.

**ASSEMBLY.** Once the table top is com-

**12**

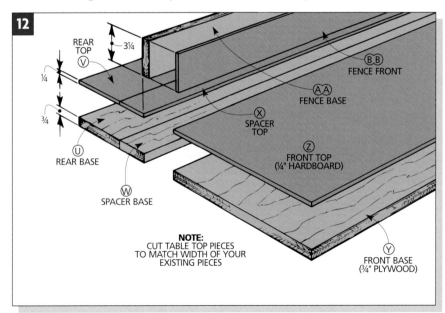

REAR
TOP
V

$3\frac{1}{4}$

$\frac{1}{4}$

$\frac{3}{4}$

U
REAR BASE

W
SPACER BASE

BB
FENCE FRONT

AA
FENCE BASE

X
SPACER
TOP

Z
FRONT TOP
($1/4$" HARDBOARD)

Y
FRONT BASE
($3/4$" PLYWOOD)

**NOTE:**
CUT TABLE TOP PIECES
TO MATCH WIDTH OF YOUR
EXISTING PIECES

**SHOP TIP**

*Label Cutoffs*

Even in a stack of cutoffs, it's easy to find the right piece if you mark the dimensions on the ends of the stock.

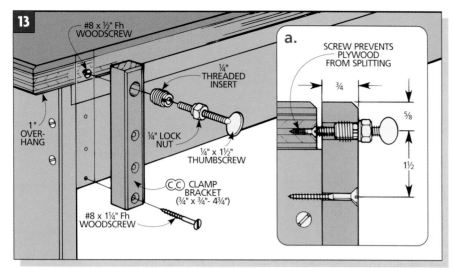

**13**

#8 x ½" Fh
WOODSCREW

¼"
THREADED
INSERT

1"
OVER-
HANG

¼" LOCK
NUT

¼" x 1½"
THUMBSCREW

CC CLAMP
BRACKET
(¾" x ¾"- 4¾")

#8 x 1¼" Fh
WOODSCREW

**a.**

SCREW PREVENTS
PLYWOOD
FROM SPLITTING

¾

⅝

1½

plete, the stand is ready to be assembled. With the base and storage units positioned where you want them, adjust the levelers on the bottom of the base until it's level in both directions.

**MOUNT TOP.** Now the front table top can be mounted to the saw frame. Start by backing out the thumbscrews that pinch the rear section against the fence.

Then place the new table top pieces (and the fence) as they were positioned on your old top.

Next, with the table top pushed against the thumbscrews, use a square to check that the fence and the blade are square to each other. If they're not, adjust one of the thumbscrews.

Finally, attach the front table top by

screwing up through the saw frame into the top. To lock the remaining table top pieces in place, tighten the thumbscrews (finger tight only).

**STORAGE UNITS.** Now you can level the storage units. To do this, first position them so the table top overhangs the ends about 1". Then adjust the levelers so the top is level along its entire length.

Once the top is level, screw the storage units to the base if they're positioned against it *(Fig. 11)*. Then screw the storage units to the bottom of the front table top.

**CLAMP BRACKET.** Because the ends of my table top are quite a ways away from the thumbscrews, I added a simple clamp bracket (CC) to each storage unit to pinch the ends of the top pieces and the fence tight *(Fig. 13)*.

This bracket is nothing more than a block of ¾"-thick hardwood, a threaded insert, and a thumbscrew.

To prevent the thumbscrew from splitting the plywood, it presses against a screw in the top *(Fig. 13a)*. A lock nut then keeps the thumbscrew in place. ■

# WOODWORKER'S NOTEBOOK

*Instead of making a whole new top when the table gets chewed up, just replace this slide-out insert.*

## REPLACEABLE INSERT

■ A hardboard insert fits into a wide, dovetail-shaped opening in the front section of the table top *(Fig. 1)*.
■ By beveling the edges of the insert and the opening, you can slide out the old insert and slide a new one in place.
■ To cut the opening in the top, I used a ½" dovetail bit in a handheld router *(Figs. 2 and 2a)*. Set the depth of the bit to cut through just the hardboard.

■ You could waste out the entire insert area once the top is glued up. But it's easier to first mark the location of the insert on the plywood base (Y) before gluing on the hardboard top (Z). (I used masking tape to mark off the area.)

Just don't apply contact cement to this area so you can cut the opening by making one pass on each side *(Fig. 2)*. Then remove the waste piece.

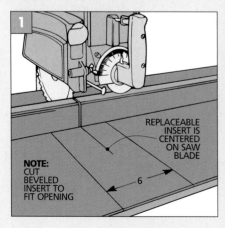

**1**

REPLACEABLE
INSERT IS
CENTERED
ON SAW
BLADE

NOTE:
CUT
BEVELED
INSERT TO
FIT OPENING

6

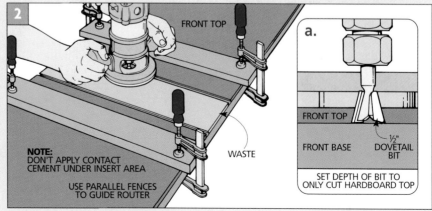

**2**

FRONT TOP

NOTE:
DON'T APPLY CONTACT
CEMENT UNDER INSERT AREA

USE PARALLEL FENCES
TO GUIDE ROUTER

WASTE

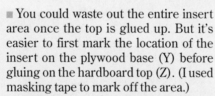

**a.**

FRONT TOP

FRONT BASE

FRONT TOP

FRONT BASE

½"
DOVETAIL
BIT

SET DEPTH OF BIT TO
ONLY CUT HARDBOARD TOP

# Table Saw Stand

*A table saw and all its accessories can take up a lot of space in your shop. Use that space more efficiently with this stand that provides a solid base, storage, and retractable casters for mobility.*

L et's face it. Table saws take up a lot of room. And since shop space is always at a premium, I designed this stand to make the most of the space occupied by a table saw.

First, it's mobile. This way, it can be rolled out of the way when you need some extra floor space (or need to park your car). And second, the stand provides plenty of storage for accessories.

**MOBILITY.** Mobility isn't hard to add to a tool stand — just add casters to the base and away you go.

I added four swivel casters to this stand. These allow it to turn on a dime. You can move the stand front-to-back or

side-to-side easily, and roll it in and out of tight spaces with no problem.

Of course, adding mobility creates another problem — getting the stand *not* to move. The last thing you want when pushing a sheet of plywood through the saw is to wonder if you remembered to lock the casters.

**STABILITY.** Making the saw stable was as easy as making it mobile. I simply built a sturdy frame with four wide corner posts. The thick hard maple and MDF make the frame heavy enough to damp vibration, and half lap joinery holds it together securely.

But how do you get both the stability

and mobility to work together?

The key is retractable casters. To engage the casters, simply step down on a cam bar on each side of the stand. Once the casters are down, the stand can be wheeled around easily. When the saw is in position, just lift the cams to retract the wheels.

**STORAGE.** You'll find lots of room in the stand to store your accessories. The table top keeps your miter gauge or rip fence close at hand. Slide-out pegboard panels let you hang up wrenches and blades. A couple shelves provide space for larger items. And a pull-out sawdust bin makes cleanup easier.

# EXPLODED VIEW

**OVERALL DIMENSIONS:**
$42\frac{1}{2}$W x $24\frac{1}{2}$D x $23\frac{3}{4}$H

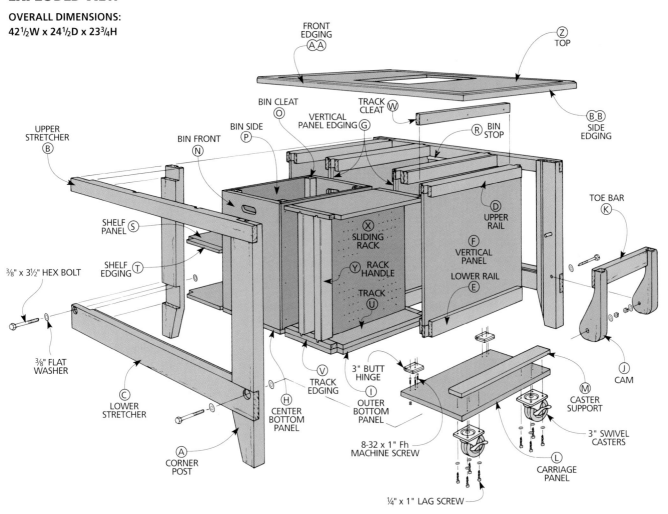

FRONT EDGING — AA
Z TOP
BIN CLEAT — O
TRACK CLEAT — W
VERTICAL PANEL EDGING — G
R BIN STOP
BB SIDE EDGING
BIN SIDE — P
UPPER STRETCHER — B
BIN FRONT — N
TOE BAR — K
UPPER RAIL — D
X SLIDING RACK
F VERTICAL PANEL
SHELF PANEL — S
Y RACK HANDLE
LOWER RAIL — E
SHELF EDGING — T
TRACK — U
$\frac{3}{8}$" x $3\frac{1}{2}$" HEX BOLT
$\frac{3}{8}$" FLAT WASHER
3" BUTT HINGE
J CAM
LOWER STRETCHER — C
TRACK EDGING — V
M CASTER SUPPORT
OUTER BOTTOM PANEL — I
3" SWIVEL CASTERS
CENTER BOTTOM PANEL — H
8-32 x 1" Fh MACHINE SCREW
L CARRIAGE PANEL
A CORNER POST
$\frac{1}{4}$" x 1" LAG SCREW

## MATERIALS LIST

### WOOD

| | | |
|---|---|---|
| **A** | Corner Posts (4) | $1\frac{1}{2}$ x 4 - $23\frac{1}{4}$ |
| **B** | Upper Stretchers (2) | $1\frac{1}{2}$ x $1\frac{1}{2}$ - $40\frac{1}{2}$ |
| **C** | Lower Stretchers (2) | $1\frac{1}{2}$ x $2\frac{1}{2}$ - $40\frac{1}{2}$ |
| **D** | Upper Rails (4) | $1\frac{1}{2}$ x $1\frac{1}{2}$ - $20\frac{1}{2}$ |
| **E** | Lower Rails (4) | $1\frac{1}{2}$ x 2 - $20\frac{1}{2}$ |
| **F** | Vertical Panels (4) | $\frac{1}{2}$ MDF - $15\frac{3}{4}$ x $20\frac{1}{2}$ |
| **G** | Vert. Panel Edg. (4) | $\frac{1}{4}$ x $\frac{1}{2}$ - $14\frac{3}{4}$ |
| **H** | Ctr. Btm. Panel (1) | $\frac{1}{2}$ MDF - $13\frac{3}{4}$ x $20\frac{1}{2}$ |
| **I** | Otr. Btm. Panels (2) | $\frac{1}{2}$ MDF - $9\frac{3}{8}$ x $20\frac{1}{2}$ |
| **J** | Cams (4) | $1\frac{1}{2}$ x $3\frac{3}{4}$ - 9 |
| **K** | Toe Bars (2) | $\frac{3}{4}$ x $2\frac{1}{4}$ - $19\frac{3}{8}$ |
| **L** | Carriage Panels (2) | $\frac{1}{2}$ MDF - $14\frac{5}{8}$ x $19\frac{1}{4}$ |
| **M** | Caster Supports (2) | $\frac{1}{2}$ MDF - $3\frac{1}{8}$ x $19\frac{1}{4}$ |
| **N** | Bin Front/Back (2) | $\frac{1}{2}$ MDF - $13\frac{5}{8}$ x $14\frac{5}{8}$ |
| **O** | Bin Cleats (4) | $\frac{3}{4}$ x $\frac{3}{4}$ - $14\frac{1}{8}$ |
| **P** | Bin Sides (2) | $\frac{1}{4}$ hdbd. - $14\frac{5}{8}$ x $19\frac{3}{4}$ |
| **Q** | Bin Bottom (1) | $\frac{1}{2}$ MDF - $13\frac{1}{8}$ x $19\frac{3}{4}$ |
| **R** | Bin Stop (1) | $\frac{3}{4}$ x $\frac{3}{4}$ - $13\frac{3}{4}$ |
| **S** | Shelf Panel (1) | $\frac{1}{2}$ MDF - $9\frac{1}{4}$ x $19\frac{1}{2}$ |
| **T** | Shelf Edging (2) | $\frac{1}{2}$ x $\frac{3}{4}$ - $8\frac{3}{4}$ |
| **U** | Tracks (2) | $\frac{1}{2}$ MDF - $9\frac{3}{8}$ x $19\frac{1}{2}$ |
| **V** | Track Edging (4) | $\frac{1}{2}$ x $\frac{3}{4}$ - $8\frac{7}{8}$ |
| **W** | Track Cleats (2) | $\frac{3}{4}$ x $1\frac{1}{2}$ - $19\frac{1}{2}$ |
| **X** | Sliding Racks (2) | $\frac{1}{4}$ pgbd. - $14\frac{1}{4}$ x $19\frac{1}{2}$ |
| **Y** | Rack Handles (2) | $\frac{3}{4}$ x $1\frac{1}{2}$ - $13\frac{3}{4}$ |
| **Z** | Top (1) | $\frac{1}{2}$ MDF - $23\frac{3}{4}$ x $41\frac{3}{4}$ |
| **AA** | Fr./Bk. Edging (2) | $\frac{3}{4}$ x $1\frac{1}{2}$ - $42\frac{1}{2}$ |
| **BB** | Side Edging (2) | $\frac{3}{4}$ x $1\frac{1}{2}$ - $24\frac{1}{2}$ |

### HARDWARE SUPPLIES

- (20) No. 6 x $\frac{3}{4}$" Fh woodscrews
- (12) No. 8 x 1" Fh woodscrews
- (8) No. 8 x $1\frac{1}{4}$" Fh woodscrews
- (16) No. 8 x $1\frac{1}{2}$" Fh woodscrews
- (4) $\frac{1}{2}$"-dia. dowels, $1\frac{1}{2}$" long
- (4) 3" swivel casters
- (16) $\frac{1}{4}$" x 1" lag screws
- (16) $\frac{1}{4}$" flat washers
- (4) 3" butt hinges w/ screws
- (12) 8-32 x 1" Fh machine screws
- (12) No. 10 split lock washers
- (12) 8-32 hex nuts
- (4) $\frac{3}{8}$" x $3\frac{1}{2}$" hex bolts
- (12) $\frac{3}{8}$" flat washers
- (4) $\frac{3}{8}$" hex lock nuts
- (4) $\frac{1}{4}$" spoon-style shelf pins

## CUTTING DIAGRAM

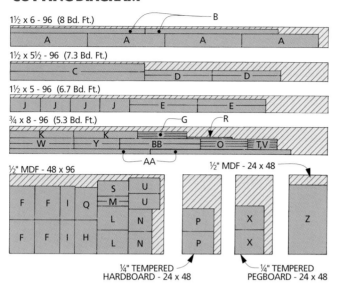

1½ x 6 - 96 (8 Bd. Ft.)

A · · A · A · A

B

1½ x 5½ - 96 (7.3 Bd. Ft.)

C · D · D

1½ x 5 - 96 (6.7 Bd. Ft.)

J J J J · E · E

¾ x 8 - 96 (5.3 Bd. Ft.)

K · K · BB · O · T,V
W · Y · · G · R
AA

½" MDF - 48 x 96

| F | F | I | Q | S / M / L / L | U / U / N / N |
| F | F | I | H | | |

½" MDF - 24 x 48

| P | X | Z |
| P | X | |

¼" TEMPERED HARDBOARD - 24 x 48

¼" TEMPERED PEGBOARD - 24 x 48

## BASE

When designing this stand, I wanted to make sure the base ended up strong and sturdy. To achieve this, I built two frames out of 1½"-thick hard maple. (You could also use "two-by" material.) Then I connected these frames with rails and panels made of ½" medium-density fiberboard (MDF).

I chose MDF for several reasons. It's inexpensive and easy to work with. But it's also heavy, which helps to damp any vibration from the saw. (If you're not familiar with MDF, refer to the Woodworker's Notebook on page 95.)

**FRAMES.** To begin the base, I started with the front and back frames *(Fig. 1)*. Each frame consists of two corner posts connected by an upper stretcher and a lower stretcher. After the frames are built, they will be connected with four panel assemblies.

**FRAME PIECES.** To make the front and back frames, I started by cutting to size the four corner posts (A), the two upper stretchers (B), and the two lower stretchers (C) *(Fig. 1)*.

To join these pieces, I set up a dado blade in the table saw to cut half laps on each. (Check the setup by cutting test joints on scrap before cutting the joints

on the workpieces.) First, the outside face of each corner post gets a narrow half lap at the top and a wider half lap 4½" up from the bottom *(Fig. 1)*.

**Note:** These half laps are different widths to match the widths of the upper and lower stretchers.

Once the half laps are cut in the corner posts, matching half laps are cut on the ends of the stretchers *(Fig. 1c)*.

**DADOES AND GROOVES.** Next, I cut a series of ½" x ½" grooves and dadoes in the frame pieces to hold the panel assemblies that will connect the two frames. These panel assemblies also divide the inside of the stand into three

## SHOP TIP . . . . . . . . . . . . . . . . . . . . . . . . . . . *Mobile Tools*

I don't know too many woodworkers who think their shop is too big. Everyone could use some additional space. One way to more efficiently use the

space you have, is to make your tools mobile so they can be moved out of the way when they're not being used.

The cam-operated caster

assembly on the table saw stand can be adapted to provide a mobile base on other items in your shop.

You could put a jointer, lathe or even your bench

on wheels. Roll them out when needed, then raise the casters, and everything stays put until you're ready to lower the wheels and move them out of the way.

And one thing to keep in mind — make sure that wherever you store your tools provides room on both sides to let you step on the bars and lower the wheels.

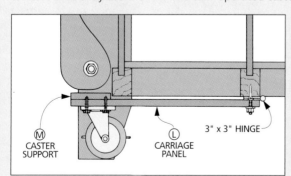

M CASTER SUPPORT

L CARRIAGE PANEL

3" x 3" HINGE

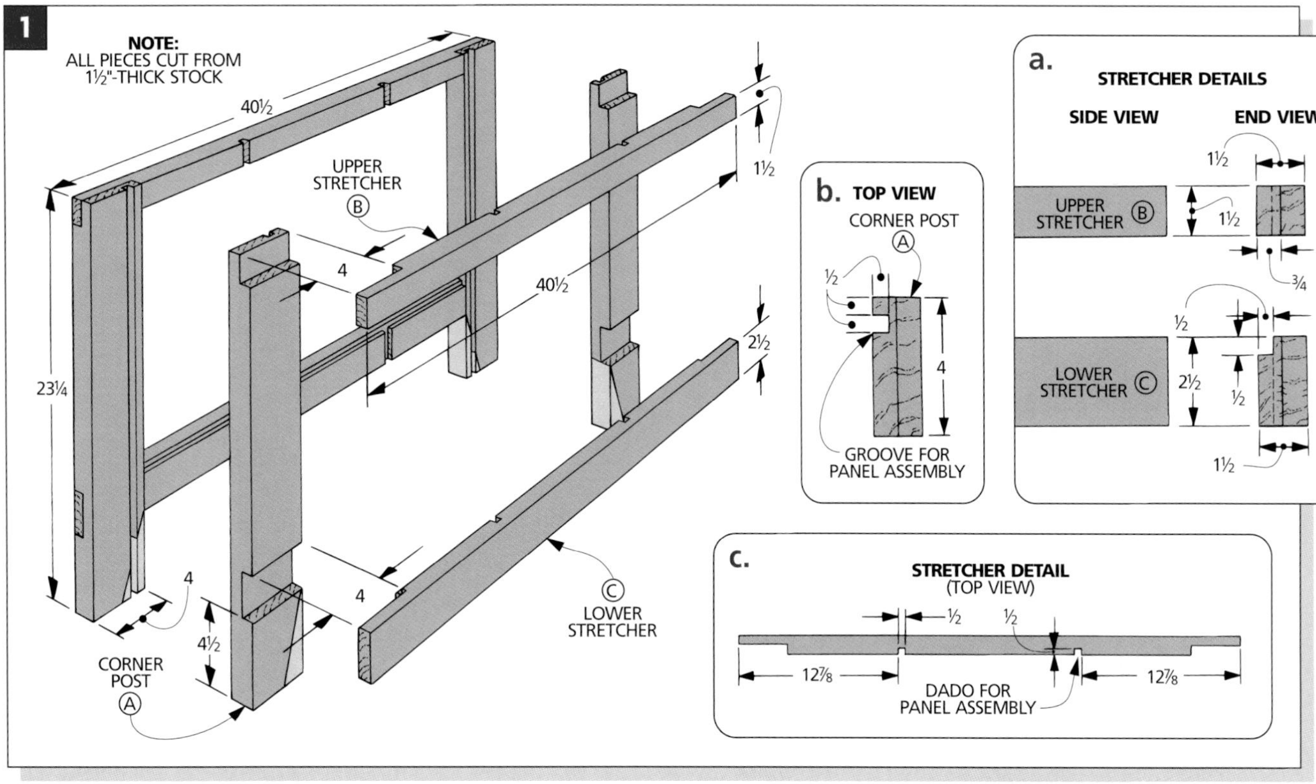
1
NOTE:
ALL PIECES CUT FROM 1½"-THICK STOCK
40½
UPPER STRETCHER
B
4
40½
1½
2½
23¼
4
4
4½
CORNER POST
A
C
LOWER STRETCHER
b. TOP VIEW
CORNER POST
A
½
4
GROOVE FOR PANEL ASSEMBLY
a. STRETCHER DETAILS
SIDE VIEW
END VIEW
1½
UPPER STRETCHER B
1½
¾
½
LOWER STRETCHER C
2½
½
1½
c. STRETCHER DETAIL
(TOP VIEW)
½
½
12⅞
12⅞
DADO FOR PANEL ASSEMBLY

compartments for storage and the dust bin (refer to *Fig. 4* on page 120).

The first cut I made was a groove on the inside face toward the inside edge of each corner post *(Fig. 1b)*. (These grooves will hold the panel assemblies that form the sides of the stand.)

**Note:** Since these corner posts face each other, the grooves should mirror each other. When cutting the grooves, just make sure the inside edge of each post is against the rip fence.

When the grooves in the corner posts are complete, I cut two 1/2" dadoes in each of the stretchers *(Fig. 1c)*. Each dado is cut 12 7/8" from the end. So once you're set up, you can simply flip each piece end for end to cut the second dado. (These dadoes hold panels that divide the interior of the stand.)

In addition to the dadoes, each lower stretcher (C) also needs a 1/2" x 1/2" rabbet. The rabbets will hold three MDF panels that are added later. These panels make up the bottom of the stand (*Fig. 1a* and *Fig. 6* on page 120).

**TAPER.** At this point, all the stretchers are complete, but the corner posts need a little more work. To provide more "toe room" near the corners of the stand, I cut a taper at the bottom of each corner post *(Fig. 3)*. Before making the cut, I cut a plug from scrap and glued it into the groove in the bottom of each corner post *(Fig. 2)*. This plug is positioned flush with the bottom shoulder of the half lap. (The plug doesn't have to be flush with the bottom of the leg since that is the waste area. See the right side of *Fig. 2*.) After the glue is dry, taper the bottom end of each post.

Now the front and back frames can be glued and clamped together. When the glue dries, a counterbored pilot hole needs to be drilled through each lower stretcher (and corner post) *(Fig. 3)*. (These holes are for attaching the cams that will raise and lower the casters.) To do this, first drill the counterbore 3/8" deep. (A Forstner bit or spade bit will work for this.) Then, using the dimple at the center of the counterbore as a guide, drill a 3/8"-diameter shank hole through the assembly.

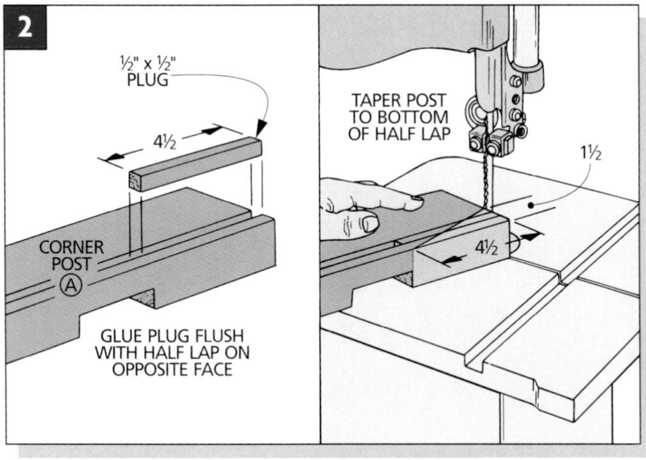
2
½" x ½" PLUG
4½
CORNER POST
A
GLUE PLUG FLUSH WITH HALF LAP ON OPPOSITE FACE
TAPER POST TO BOTTOM OF HALF LAP
1½
4½

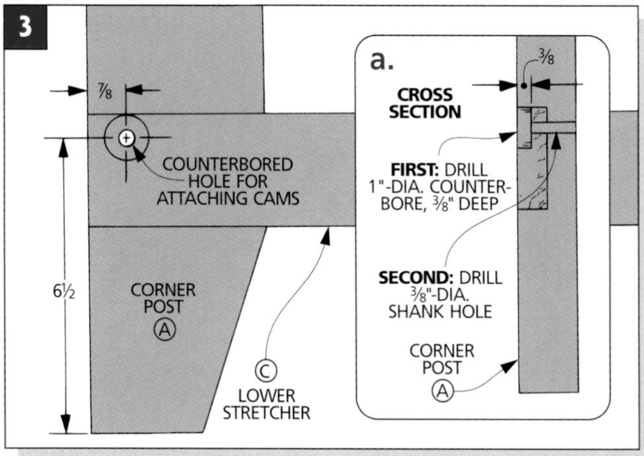
3
⅞
COUNTERBORED HOLE FOR ATTACHING CAMS
6½
CORNER POST
A
C
LOWER STRETCHER
a.
CROSS SECTION
⅜
FIRST: DRILL 1"-DIA. COUNTER-BORE, ⅜" DEEP
SECOND: DRILL ⅜"-DIA. SHANK HOLE
CORNER POST
A

To connect the frames, I built four panel assemblies *(Fig. 4)*. Each consists of a hardwood upper and lower rail and a panel cut from MDF.

**RAILS.** I started by cutting four upper (D) and four lower rails (E) to size. These pieces are identical except for their widths *(Fig. 4a)*.

To hold the panels between the rails, I cut a $^1/_2$" x $^1/_2$" groove centered on the inside edge of each rail *(Fig. 4b)*. Then a $^1/_2$"-long stub tenon can be cut on each end to fit the grooves and dadoes in the frame assemblies.

**PANELS.** The four vertical panels (F) that fit between these rails are cut from $^1/_2$" MDF, and their lengths match the full length of the rails, including the stub tenons. To find their heights, measure between the stretchers on the frames and add 1" to account for the grooves in the rails. (In my case, these measure $15^3/_4$" tall.)

With the panels cut to size, the only thing left is to drill $^1/_4$"-dia. holes for the shelf supports that hold the optional shelves. I drilled three pairs of holes $^3/_8$" deep in one face of each panel *(Fig. 4a)*.

Now the panel assemblies can be glued together. And when the glue was dry, I connected the frames with the four panel assemblies. When positioning the panels, make sure the shelf support holes face each other in the outside sections *(Fig. 5)*.

At this point, there are just a couple things left to do. First, I applied a piece of $^1/_4$"-thick maple panel edging (G) to each exposed edge of the vertical panels *(Fig. 5)*.

Then I cut three MDF panels for the bottom of the base *(Fig. 6)*. The center panel (H) is simply cut to fit the center opening and glued in place. The outer bottom panels (I) must have their outside corners notched to fit around the corner posts *(Fig. 6a)*.

All that's left to complete the base is to rout or sand small chamfers along all the exposed corners (except the top edges, which remain square).

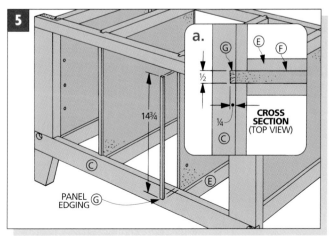

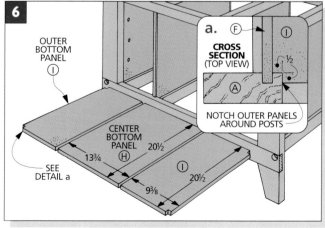

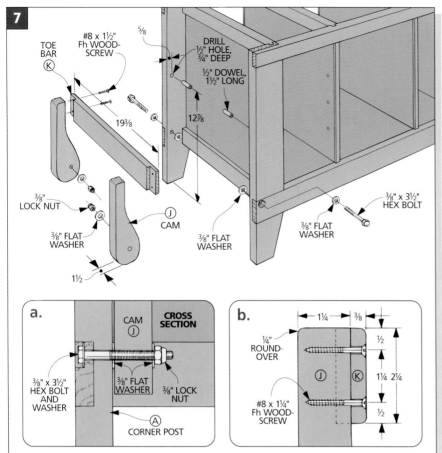

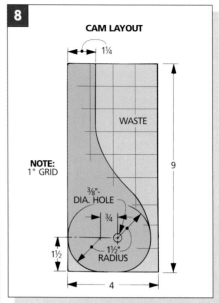

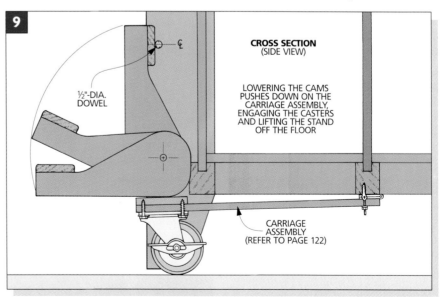

## CAM & TOE BAR

With the base complete, I began work on the cam and carriage system. The idea here is simple. The cams press against and lower the carriage, which engages the casters and lifts the stand off the floor (refer to *Fig. 9*).

**CAMS.** There are four $1\frac{1}{2}$"-thick cams for the cabinet, two on each side *(Fig. 7)*. After laying out the cams (J) on 4" x 9" blanks, I used my band saw to cut within $\frac{1}{16}$" of the lines *(Fig. 8)*. Then after the cams were sanded to final shape, I drilled a $\frac{3}{8}$"-dia. hole in each one to accomodate the hex bolt it will pivot on *(Fig. 8)*.

**TOE BARS.** Next, I made two toe bars (K) out of $\frac{3}{4}$"-thick stock *(Fig. 7)*. Each toe bar simply connects two cams. This lets you raise or lower both cams at once by stepping on (or lifting) the toe bar *(Fig. 9)*. To find their lengths, measure between the corner posts and subtract the thickness of two washers (about $\frac{1}{8}$" total).

With the toe bars cut to size, I cut a half lap on each end to match the thickness of the cams. Then I routed $\frac{1}{4}$"

roundovers on the outside edges of the toe bars and cams *(Fig. 7b)*.

Before assembling the cams and toe bars for good, dry-assemble them and check their fit between the corner posts. You should be able to fit the assembly plus a washer on each end snug between the corner posts.

If the assembly fits properly, each

toe bar can be glued and screwed to a pair of cams. When the glue has dried, soften the remaining sharp edges of the assemblies with sandpaper. Then attach them to the base with $\frac{3}{8}$" hex bolts secured with lock nuts *(Fig. 7a)*. Remember to use a washer between each corner post and cam.

Before going on to the carriage assembly, I added a $\frac{1}{2}$" dowel to the inside of each post. This dowel acts as a simple stop for the cams when they're in the up position *(Fig. 9)*.

To locate the positions for these dowels, raise the cam assembly and mark the centerline of the toe bar onto each corner post *(Fig. 9)*. Then measure in $\frac{5}{8}$" from the edge of each corner post and drill a $\frac{1}{2}$"-dia. hole, $\frac{3}{4}$" deep on each of these marks *(Fig. 7)*.

**CARRIAGE.** Now the carriage can be added *(Fig. 10)*. To begin, cut two carriage panels (L) and two caster supports (M) to size from $1/2$" MDF. The important thing to keep in mind for the caster supports is that they match the base plates on *your* casters.

The caster supports are glued to the tops of the carriage panels. After the glue is dry, the casters can be secured with lag screws (refer to *Fig. 9*).

To mount each carriage, I used a pair of 3" butt hinges. But the screws provided for the hinges won't hold well in MDF, so I used 1"-long machine screws with nuts and lock washers *(Fig. 10a)*.

## DUST BIN

The base of the stand is complete, so next I started work on the dust bin that sits in the center section (see photo).

**FRONT AND BACK.** I started with the bin front and back (N). These pieces are sized to fit the stand's center opening. But to provide clearance all the way around, they're $1/8$" shorter and $1/8$" narrower *(Fig. 11)*.

To keep the weight of the bin down, I decided to use $1/4$"-thick hardboard for the sides. So to hold these pieces, I cut $1/4$"-deep rabbets in the front and back pieces (N) *(Figs. 11 and 11a)*. Then to hold an MDF bottom panel, I cut $1/2$"-wide rabbets along the bottoms of these pieces *(Fig. 11c)*.

Next I cut some handles *(Fig. 11b)*. To do this, simply drill a couple $1\!1/4$"-dia. holes in each of the front and back pieces and then remove the waste between them with a jig saw. To make the handles comfortable, round over the inside and outside edges.

**CLEATS.** With the front and back pieces complete, I added $3/4$" x $3/4$" hardwood cleats (O) to strengthen the corners of the bin *(Figs. 11 and 11a)*. Each cleat extends from the top of the bin to the rabbet for the bottom and is glued flush with the rabbets for the sides.

**SIDES.** Now the $1/4$" hardboard sides (P) can be cut to size. To find their length, measure from the inside edge of the upper rail (B) to the front edge of

the edging strips (H). Then subtract $1/2$" for the rabbets on the front and back (N). (My sides were $19\!3/4$" long.)

At this point, the sides are ready to be glued to the front and back pieces and screwed and glued to the hardwood cleats *(Fig. 11a)*.

**BOTTOM.** The last piece to add is the bottom (Q). This $1/2$" MDF panel is cut to fit the opening in the bottom of the bin. It's glued into the rabbets and screwed through the sides.

Finally, I routed $1/8$" chamfers on the front and back faces.

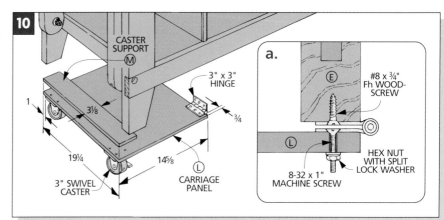

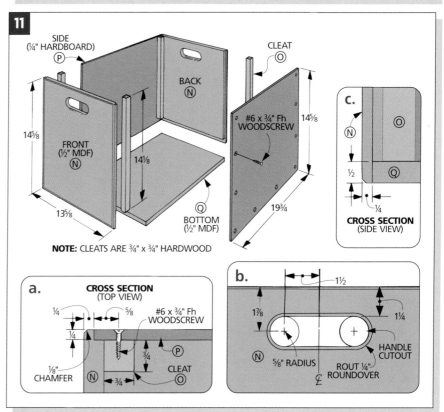

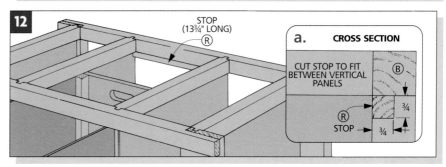

**STOP.** The only problem now is that there's nothing to prevent the bin from sliding out the back. So I added a stop (R) to the stand *(Fig. 12)*. This piece is cut to fit between the vertical panels. Then it's glued to the bottom of the back upper stretcher (B) flush with its inside edge *(Fig. 12a)*.

## ADJUSTABLE SHELF

To add storage, I made a shelf for one of the side openings. It rests on pins that fit into the holes drilled in the vertical panels *(Figs. 13 and 13a)*. (You can make more shelves as needed.)

The shelf panel (S) is cut from $1/2$" MDF to fit snug between the posts. But I allowed a $1/16$" gap on each side so it can be adjusted easily *(Fig. 13a)*.

Next, I added a strip of edging (T) to the shelf. This $3/4$"-wide edging is cut $1/2$" shorter than the width of the shelf panel *(Fig. 13b)*. This automatically creates a notch that will allow the shelf to fit around the corner posts.

## SLIDING RACK ASSEMBLY

There is one last option you can add to the inside of the base. I wanted to have someplace to hang my saw blades, insert plates, and wrenches, so I came up with a pair of vertical sliding racks (see photo).

**TRACKS.** The sliding racks are simply $1/4$" pegboard panels that slide in MDF tracks. These upper and lower tracks (U) are $19^1/2$" long and fit between the vertical panels *(Figs. 14 and 14a)*.

**EDGING.** I added hardwood edging (V) to cover the front edges of the tracks *(Figs. 14 and 14a)*. But this $3/4$"-wide edging doesn't cover the entire edge; it's cut short to create a notch that fits around the post.

With the front edging glued in place, I cut two $1/4$" x $1/4$" grooves through the track and front edging *(Fig. 14a)*. These grooves will guide the racks as they slide in and out.

Then to create a stop for the racks, I added another piece of edging to the back of each track *(Fig. 14a)*.

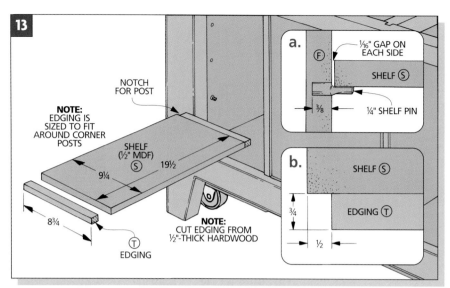

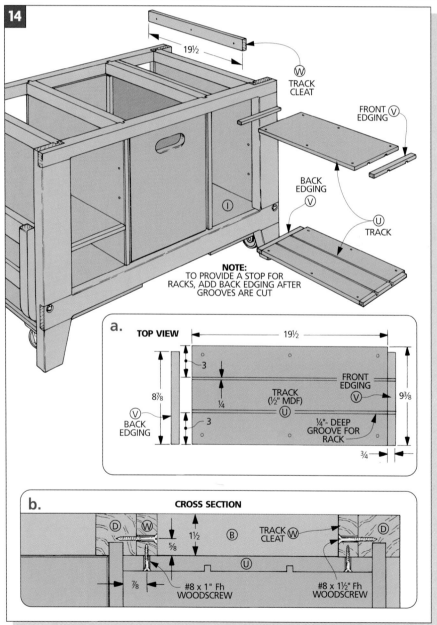

**INSTALLATION.** Now that the tracks are complete, they can be installed in the base. The lower track is easy. It's simply screwed to the outer bottom panel (I) (refer back to *Fig. 14*).

But at this point, there's nothing in the top of the base to screw the upper track to. So I added a pair of track cleats (W) *(Figs. 14 and 14b)*. These are $1\frac{1}{2}$"-wide (tall) hardwood strips cut to fit between the front and rear stretchers (B) and screwed to the rails (D). Then the upper track can be screwed in place.

**SLIDING RACKS.** With work on the tracks complete, I turned my attention to the two sliding racks (X). These are made from $\frac{1}{4}$" pegboard *(Fig. 15)*. They are cut to size so they slide smoothly in the tracks. (Mine were $14\frac{1}{4}$" x $19\frac{1}{2}$".)

**HANDLES.** Then I added a $\frac{3}{4}$"-thick hardwood handle (Y) to the front of each rack *(Figs. 15 and 15a)*.

To attach the handles to the racks, I cut a centered groove $\frac{3}{4}$" deep on each handle *(Fig. 15a)*. Then I glued them to the racks so there was $\frac{1}{4}$" at both the top and bottom so the handle would

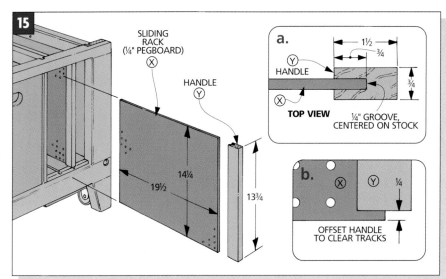

clear the track *(Fig. 15b)*.

Finally, to hold accessories on the racks, I built some hangers. See the Designer's Notebook below for details.

**TOP**

All that's left for this stand is to cut and mount a top *(Fig. 16)*.

**TOP PANEL.** To make the top (Z), the first thing to do is to cut an MDF panel to finished size. Allowing for a $\frac{1}{4}$" overhang on each side, plus $\frac{3}{8}$" on each side for attaching the edging later, my top was $41\frac{3}{4}$" x $23\frac{3}{4}$" *(Fig. 16)*.

Once the top is cut to size, you can lay out and cut the opening over the dust bin *(Fig. 16b)*. To do this, set the

## DESIGNER'S NOTEBOOK

*Regular pegboard hooks can fall off. These heavy-duty hangers hold your accessories and stay put.*

### PEGBOARD HANGERS

■ Each hanger is just a square piece of $\frac{3}{4}$"-thick stock with an angled (15°) hole drilled in the center. (You can cut these squares from scrap.) Then a short length of $\frac{1}{2}$"-dia. dowel is glued into the hole (see drawing).

■ By making two different sizes of hangers, you'll be able to mount the smaller size to one side of the pegboard and still be able to screw a large hanger to the opposite side (see detail 'a').

■ To mount the hangers, simply insert

screws through the holes in the pegboard and drive them into the back of the hanger at each corner. You may need to bore a slight countersink so the screws securing the small hangers sit flush with the pegboard.

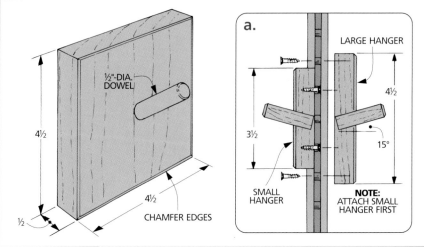

table saw in place. (I positioned my saw so the motor cleared the back edge, and centered the saw side-to-side.) Then trace along the inside of the saw.

Now, remove the table saw and drill holes in each corner of the layout. Then remove the waste with a jig saw.

**EDGING.** To protect the edges of the top, I decided to add ³/₄" hardwood edging (AA, BB). I made this edging 1¹/₂" wide, so it's a little wider than the thickness of the MDF *(Fig. 16a)*.

A ³/₈"-deep rabbet on each piece of edging helps align the edging to the top

*(Fig. 16a)*. Then the edging pieces can be mitered to length.

When the edging was attached, I routed ¹/₈" chamfers around both the top and bottom edges. Then center the completed top on the base and screw it to the upper rails (D). ■

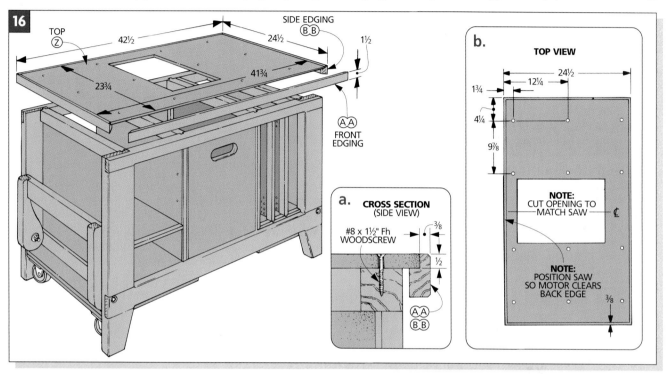

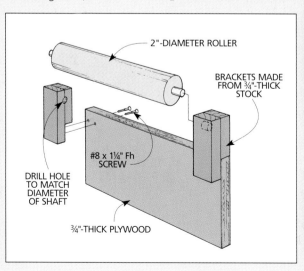

## SHOP TIP .................................. *Outfeed Roller*

This outfeed support roller can be secured in the jaws of a portable workbench (see photo) or clamped to a sawhorse. And when it's not being used, it can

easily be stored in the table saw stand.

The support is simply a roller attached to a piece of plywood by a pair of 1¹/₂"-thick wood brackets

(see drawing). The longer half of each bracket extends down the face of the plywood and serves as a stop to set the height of the support (see photo).

I used the roller from an old copy machine. (Ask a local print shop or copy machine store for discards.) But a typewriter roller would also work.

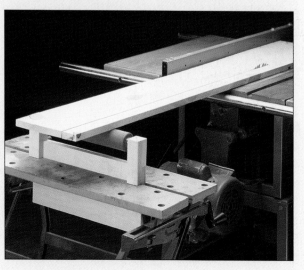

One of the first things we take into consideration when designing projects at *Woodsmith* is whether the hardware is commonly available. Most of the hardware and supplies for the projects in this book can be found at local hardware stores or home centers. Sometimes, though, you may have to order the hardware through the mail. If that's the case, we've tried to find reputable national mail order sources with toll-free phone numbers (see the box at right for more details).

Also, *Woodsmith Project Supplies* offers hardware for some of the projects in this book (see below).

## WOODSMITH PROJECT SUPPLIES

At the time this book was printed, the following project supply kits and hardware were available from *Woodsmith Project Supplies*. The kits include hardware, but you must supply any lumber, plywood, or finish. For current prices and availability, call toll free:

### 1-800-444-7527

**Wall-Hung Tool Cabinet**
(pages 16-27) .............. No. 742200

**Classic Workbench**
(pages 28-39) .............No. 7100100

**Finishing Cabinet**
(pages 67-73) ...............No. 796200

**Flip-Top Tool Stand**
(pages 76-79)
Set of (4) 3" locking casters*
.......................................No. 796250

**Benchtop Jointer Stand**
(pages 87-93)
Set of (2) levelers .......No. 1008306

**Portable Planer Stand**
(pages 96-101) ............No. 6809200

**Drill Press Storage Cart**
(pages 102-107) ..........No. 7127100

*Casters are also suitable for use on the Roll-Around Shop Cart, Hardware Storage Cabinet, Finishing Cabinet, Drill Press Storage Cart, and the Table Saw Stand.

KEY: TL06

## MAIL ORDER SOURCES

Some of the most important "tools" you can have in your shop are mail order catalogs. The ones listed below are filled with special hardware, tools, finishes, lumber, and supplies that can't be found at a local hardware store or home center. You should be able to find many of the supplies for the projects in this book in one or more of these catalogs.

It's amazing what you can learn about woodworking by looking through these catalogs. If they're not currently in your shop, you may want to have them sent to you.

**Note:** The information below was current when this book was printed. Time-Life Books and August Home Publishing do not guarantee these products will be available nor endorse any specific mail order company, catalog, or product.

### THE WOODSMITH STORE

**2625 Beaver Avenue**
**Des Moines, IA 50310**
**800–835–5084**
Our own retail store filled with tools, jigs, hardware, books, and finishing supplies. Though we don't have a catalog, we do send out items mail order. Call for information.

### ROCKLER WOODWORKING & HARDWARE

**4365 Willow Drive**
**Medina, MN 55340**
**800–279–4441**
**www.rockler.com**
A great catalog of general hardware, specialty hardware, plus tool and shop accessories. It's also a good "idea-starter" for projects.

### HIGHLAND HARDWARE

**1045 N. Highland Ave. NE**
**Atlanta, GA 30306-3592**
**800–241–6748**
**www.highlandhardware.com**
A full-line catalog with everything from layout tools to finishing supplies. Find drawer slides, levelers, bench dogs, Wonder Dogs, and vises.

### LEE VALLEY TOOLS LTD.

**12 East River Street**
**P.O. Box 1780**
**Ogdensburg, NY 13669-6780**
**800–871–8158**
**www.leevalley.com**
Several catalogs actually, from the maker of the Wonder Dog bench dog. Find casters, metal countersinks, hinges, drawer slides and more.

### GARRETT WADE

**161 Avenue of the Americas**
**New York, NY 10013**
**800–221–2942**
**www.garrettwade.com**
The "Bible" for hand tools, but also one of the best sources for finishing supplies and high quality accessories. Find bench dogs, hold-downs and a selection of vises.

### TREND-LINES

**135 American Legion Highway**
**Revere, MA 02151**
**800–767–9999**
**www.trend-lines.com**
Another complete source for hardware including hinges, drawer slides, threaded inserts, and shelf pins, plus power tools and accessories.

### WOODCRAFT

**560 Airport Industrial Park**
**P.O. Box 1686**
**Parkersburg, WV 26102-1686**
**800–225–1153**
**www.woodcraft.com**
This catalog has all kinds of hardware, including threaded knobs, label holders, and metal countersinks. You'll also find pre-made bench tops.

### WOODWORKER'S SUPPLY

**1108 North Glenn Road**
**Casper, WY 82601**
**800–645–9292**
You'll find a good selection of power tools, hand tools, and accessories, including hardware for shelves, doors and drawers, along with vises, bench dogs, and levelers.

# INDEX

# AUGUST HOME
### PUBLISHING COMPANY

President & Publisher: Donald B. Peschke
Executive Editor: Douglas L. Hicks
Creative Director: Ted Kralicek
Senior Graphic Designers: Chris Glowacki, Cheryl Simpson
Assistant Editors: Joseph E. Irwin, Craig L. Ruegsegger
Graphic Designers: Vu Nguyen, April Walker Janning, Stacey L. Krull
Design Intern: Katie VanDalsem

Designer's Notebook Illustrator: Mike Mittermeier
Photographer: Crayola England
Electronic Production: Douglas M. Lidster
Production: Troy Clark, Minniette Johnson
Project Designers: Ken Munkel, Kent Welsh
Project Builders: Steve Curtis, Steve Johnson
Magazine Editors: Terry Strohman, Tim Robertson
Contributing Editors: Vincent S. Ancona, Tom Begnal, Jon Garbison,
Bryan Nelson
Magazine Art Directors: Todd Lambirth, Cary Christensen
Contributing Illustrators: Mark Higdon, David Kreyling, Erich Lage,
Roger Reiland, Kurt Schultz, Cinda Shambaugh, Dirk Ver Steeg

Controller: Robin Hutchinson
Production Director: George Chmielarz
Project Supplies: Bob Baker
New Media Manager: Gordon Gaippe

For subscription information about
*Woodsmith* and *ShopNotes* magazines, please write:
August Home Publishing Co.
2200 Grand Ave.
Des Moines, IA 50312
800-333-5075
www.augusthome.com/customwoodworking

*Woodsmith*® and *ShopNotes*® are registered trademarks of August Home
Publishing Co.

Time-Life Books is a division of Time Life Inc.

TIME LIFE INC.
Chairman and Chief Executive Officer: Jim Nelson
President and Chief Operating Officer: Steven Janas
Senior Executive Vice President and Chief Operations Officer: Mary Davis Holt
Senior Vice President and Chief Financial Officer: Christopher Hearing

TIME-LIFE BOOKS
President: Joseph A. Kuna
Vice President, New Markets: Bridget Boel
Group Director, Home and Hearth Markets: Nicholas M. DiMarco
Vice President and Publisher, Time-Life Trade: Neil S. Levin

CUSTOM WOODWORKING
*Shop Cabinets & Tool Stands*
New Product Development Director: Glen B. Ruh
Project Editor: Barbara M. Sheppard
Design Director: Cynthia T. Richardson
Marketing Director: Nancy L. Gallo
Associate Marketing Manager: Jennifer C. Williams
Production Manager: Ken Sabol

Cover Concept: Phil Unetic/3R1 Studios

TIME-LIFE is a trademark of Time Warner Inc. and affiliated companies.

LIBRARY OF CONGRESS CATALOGING-IN-PUBLICATION DATA
Shop cabinets & tool stands / by the editors of Time-Life Books and Woodsmith
magazine.
    p. cm. – (Custom woodworking)
    ISBN 0-7835-5955-0
    1. Cabinetwork. 2. Furniture making. 3. Workshops –Equipment and
supplies. I. Title: Shop cabinets and tool stands. II. Time-Life Books.
III. Woodsmith magazine. IV. Series.

TT197 .S6425 2000
684.1'6–dc21

                                                                00-037425

10 9 8 7 6 5 4 3 2